SHEER MADNESS

From Federal Prosecutor to Federal Prisoner

A Memoir

Andrew McKenna

For Adrienne,

Best wishes!

[signature]

Table of Contents

Preface

What's made the job of Federal Public Defender interesting over the years are the clients I have represented. Although Andrew McKenna's life experiences are at times alarming, tragic or self-destructive, his story reminds me how close we all are by just simply being human, to stumble and fall. This is what makes taking a look at his life through this book worthwhile.

We met on November 21, 2005, in the United States Marshal's lock up, before his first court appearance. I had just read the charging documents alleging that at 9:30 a.m. he walked into a local bank, handed the teller a note demanding fifties and twenties, and stating he had a gun. He was apprehended 20 minutes later in his AA sponsor's pick-up truck, wearing clothes that matched the teller's description. The affidavit also indicated that Andrew had made a post-Miranda statement admitting to the robbery.

It was immediately apparent that Andrew and I were going to have an interesting attorney-client relationship. Maybe because we shared similar career paths, both serving as Department of Justice Attorneys, we were fairly close in age and lived in the same suburban town. Supporting evidence soon disclosed that he would be charged with multiple bank robberies.

The prosecution described the evidence as "overwhelming," but to me that all seemed to miss the point. What I wanted to understand was why such a fall from grace? A couple of years earlier, he would have been standing at government counsel's table to my right, wearing the white shirt and grey suit, outlining the evidence to the judge and arguing for detention. Instead, he was in the midst of heroin withdrawal, facing multiple felonies, exposed to years in federal prison. I asked, "How are you feeling," knowing he was really starting to go through it. Andrew looked at me, threw-up in his mouth, choked it down, and replied, "Great, how are you?"

And so our relationship began. Andrew has a way of pulling you in. He's smart, engaging, and above all else, he wants to know more about you. He's self-effacing, and considerate to a fault. But Andrew is also a survivor, a fighter, and a touch unpredictable. He wanted to be released from county jail on bail during the pre-trial period of his case, an impossible goal for a bank robber. I had my doubts, but he made me believe it was possible and after five months and two contested hearings, he was released from custody. Andrew had conceived, and put into place, a set of release conditions that the judge could not resist, all from his jail cell.

His book, I believe, will pull the reader in as well. He is funny, sharp-witted, and best of all, willing to laugh at himself. But this story isn't comedy, it's deadly serious. Andrew almost died, at his own hand in a mental hospital, but also at the hands of a violent drug dealer. But perhaps most poignant, Andrew had lost his way, and part of his soul when he wasn't allowed to be a father to his two young sons. His eventual ascent is remarkable. Andrew McKenna is a former attorney, a former client, and a true friend.

-Gene Primomo

Acknowledgements and Gratitude

Above anyone ever, my sister **Carol Winick**—smart, compassionate, and my life-long protector, spent countless hours on the telephone with me combing the manuscript for problems. During our marathon editing sessions, we laughed, cried, and yelled at each other. I had a great time connecting with my Irish twin. She showed me what a demanding boss I can be. Keep track of your hours sis.

Special thanks to **Chad Currin**. Without your publishing and marketing expertise, this work would remain only on my hard-drive. Your energy is infectious, and your know-how has made this project a reality. www.WEBv5.com

Thanks to **Laice Redman**, for turning my hand-written manuscript into digital form. Your professionalism, attention to detail, and dedication in transcribing the manuscript was evident when I first opened the attachment you sent to me. Thrilled by its new form—at a time when I was stalled—it motivated me to finish. For that I am forever grateful.

My great friend, and sometime employer, **Brian P. Barrett, Esq.**, Lake Placid, New York. One of the finest criminal defense attorneys I have known: a fearless gunfighter for those charged with crimes by the most powerful government in modern history. Thank you for your unwavering support, encouragement, friendship, and for buying my paintings. www.bpbarrett.com

Richard Stratton—writer, (*Smuggler's Blues* most recently), director, producer and founder of Big House Productions in Manhattan. Special thanks for reading my work and telling me, every damn time, to make another pass through, to make it better. You were always right.

Special thanks to **Chris Morris**, my copy editor, for finding the little things and explaining and advising on the biggest, most important things. You're a true professional and, in short order, immeasurably improved the work.

To **Pat Barrett**, my friend, and a gracious host in Lake Placid, New York. Pat's sense of the big picture is unmatched. A few assuring words from Pat sets a man at ease—a gift. Thank you for everything.

To **Gene Primomo**, a tireless defense attorney, who put up with my rants from county jail, assuaged my fears, and deftly negotiated and secured a global resolution to my state and federal charges, potentially saving me from an extra 15 years imprisonment. Last winter he told me I was overweight, and gave me a $1500 Cannondale bike.

To **Kelly Hofschneider**, the artist who designed the cover, and advised and gave great guidance on getting to the final version. It was a real pleasure working with a true professional.

And finally to my brother **Brian McKenna**—my rock. If it wasn't for Brian, I might not be alive and happy right now.

For My Love Dawn

You could have left—no one would have judged you.
You could have turned your back, but you embraced me.
You could have accepted it, but you fought it.
You could have folded, but you stood strong,
--and watched me return to this side.
You stayed steady because that is who you are.
You believe in me, and I am grateful,
My love.

Introduction

October 7, 2014

"Chris, you have to meet my friend Andrew."

I was on the front nine of the Whiteface Club when Brian Barrett first spoke those words. It was the summer of 2012, probably June—the exact date doesn't matter. I was still working as a reporter in upstate New York, and Brian was cementing his reputation as one of the region's most unpredictable criminal defense attorneys. Earlier that winter, Brian was fired by one of his clients—now a convicted rapist—after calling him "creepy" during opening remarks. Seriously. My former employer, the *Adirondack Daily Enterprise*, summed it up this way:

It may have been Barrett's opening remarks that got him in trouble. He delivered a rambling, 50-minute address filled with pop culture references and analogies - including to the book and film "To Kill a Mockingbird," the Titanic disaster, football and the 1986 Rodney Dangerfield film "Back to School," in which he quoted lines from a character played by the late comedian Sam Kinison. When he was talking about decades-old allegations of abuse against his client, Barrett crouched down behind the podium and pretended he was in a "magical time machine."

Who quotes "Back to School?" Brian Barrett does. But I digress.

Riding to the next hole, I decided to bite.

"Who is Andrew?" I asked.

Brian began ranting and raving about this federal prosecutor who turned to a life of crime. By the time he finished, I pictured a larger-than-life outlaw—the deranged offspring of John Dillinger, Harvey Dent, and Hunter Thompson. As a writer who loves telling stories about strange, fascinating subjects, I had to meet him right away. But life works in funny ways, and it was nearly two years before I came face-to-face with Andrew McKenna.

9

The 2014 Kentucky Derby fell on a cold, dreary Saturday. Keeping with tradition, my friends and family had gathered for Devito's Derby Dash, a debaucherous annual tradition hosted by Brandon Devito. Brian texted me a warning: "I'm coming. Andrew in tow." So I would get to meet the infamous Andrew McKenna at a Kentucky Derby party. Perfect.

As is so often the case, the man I shook hands with half an hour later did not come close to the image I had crafted in my head. He wasn't physically imposing, nor was he boisterous. He was quiet, polite, and inquisitive. And I learned quickly that Brian introduced us for a reason.

"I'm writing a book—a memoir," Andrew explained. "I need an editor."

Fast forward a few months. After exchanging a few texts and emails, we had come to terms on how to handle the project. Then, on Aug. 22, the manuscript arrived via email.

This memoir is many things. For starters, and please excuse the crass language, it's fucking crazy. It starts with the volume turned up to 11, and it stays there. Some of this stuff is hard to believe—but hey, that's what court records are for.

It's also eye-opening. It's a firsthand account of how our military trains, how our corrections systems operate, what a rehab facility looks like—these are places many will never venture, except for the bold and criminally insane. Andrew might be both.

Here is what this book is not: an endorsement. Hunter S. Thompson once said, "I hate to advocate drugs, alcohol, violence, or insanity to anyone, but they've always worked for me." Fuck that, and fuck him. Hunter Thompson, may he rest in peace, was a great writer and a great thinker. But he was, by all accounts, a terrible human being. Andrew McKenna is not.

This book is a journey. From middle-class roots in upstate New York, to rising star in the Justice Department, to the depths of addiction and depression—Andrew guides us the best he can. Why do we turn to drugs and alcohol? Why, when faced with nine good options, do we choose the 10th and worst among them? Andrew doesn't answer these questions, but he probably doesn't need to. It's the journey that counts.

The point, I think, is that when you peel away the layers, this book has heart, and so does Andrew. And for those of us who have battled demons, Andrew's journey rings true. I, for one, am glad he made it to the other side.

- Chris Morris

Chapter 1

"He graduated from Albany Law School in 1996 and served as a Marine Corps Judge Advocate General. He became a special prosecutor with the Department of Justice in 2000 and in 2003 he was an attorney with an Albany law firm for nine months."

-North Country Gazette

When I woke up this morning, I knew I was about to commit my last bank robbery. Something told me this would be the end of the line. I considered it, but I didn't feel it. I didn't feel anything anymore. I was powerless. I was dead.

I dress in a blue suit that needs pressing, a white shirt that needs starch, and a red tie that one day in the past would have been fashionable, but now merely looks worn. My shoes are black and in desperate need of a shine; the wells of the soles are dusty. I'm tired and my back aches, as it usually does these days. My eyes feel heavy. My breathing is shallow. A brilliant white light surrounds me. My depression is raging—at its strongest—as I try to get a handle on my fear, fear that arrives in pangs. Sleep tugs at me, but I know that the clock is ticking. If I don't do this now, if I don't move on this right now, I'll be trapped in a world of indescribable pain. Maybe I'll die.

I do not shave or shower because water spraying on my body would feel like little needles piercing my skin. Thousands of little stab wounds, over and over. It takes every ounce of my energy to get clothes on my body; the fabric feels like sandpaper on my skin. I take breaks as I go.

Outside. Get into my ugly little green truck, given to me by my former AA sponsor—a symbol, a reminder of how far I've fallen. Forming thought fragments, tiny fragments, about what is soon going to occur; thinking about the very real possibility that someone is going to get hurt this time. Thinking about what it would be like if I got caught: an arrest, a trial, and prison. In spite of these thoughts, the potential consequences don't feel real, just a fantasy, a set of circumstances that don't apply to me.

I approach the bank as I have the others: straight on, with no disguise. A paradoxical blend of confidence, indifference, and defeat protects me from my fear as I move my legs, one foot in front of the other, towards the door. The scene appears familiar, but something feels different, something is wrong. I can feel it in my gut and in my breathing. Something just under the surface tells me this is not going to go well.

The bank is a small, single-story white building, located out of the way on the corner of two rural roads. The entrance faces the busier of the two roads. No tree or other structure is around it—it looks as if it has just fallen from the sky into its place. This is clearly not a good bank to rob, it just happens to be the first one I came to in my urgency. A drive-thru teller window looks out over a small, nearly empty parking lot. Surely the people in the bank saw me get out of my truck.

I disregard this thought. It's not real. None of my thoughts are real anymore. Moving, but not feeling. Bright and sunny. Cool and serene. My legs continue to propel me toward the door. As I enter, I notice the smell of new carpet and coffee. Looking to my right, my eyes meet those of a lady who must be the bank manager. Does she know what I'm about to do? She looks at me as if I don't belong in a bank. She knows why I'm here. The look I see in her eyes stings, feels so wrong because people never used to look at me this way. I always used to dress nicely; I'm a good looking guy. But not today. Today I have bags under my eyes, messy, greasy hair, and a look of profound sadness. Today I look strung-out. I am strung out. I am sick from Heroin, and I need money to buy

13

more. Today I am a Heroin-addicted-bank robber. But it's more than that. I am angry.

Hearing voices now, but can't make out what they are saying. I'm second in line behind an older gentleman with short cropped crew-cut hair. A tall slender well-dressed man—maybe retired military or state police? Can I take him if I need to? Will I have to? I stare at the back of his head and shoulders. Sadly, he looks like one of my old bosses from the Justice Department. The memory causes my chest to tighten with grief. This is unbelievable.

"Next," the young teller says. I try to take a deep breath but hardly any air comes in; just enough to keep my heart beating. Here we go. My baseball cap is pulled down low on my forehead and the brim is tightly curled, the way a frat kid might wear it. This is not a disguise— it's a baseball cap. The teller is a pretty girl, youngish, maybe 23 or 24 and I'm about to scare the living shit out of her. I'm not a terrible person. But I feel no guilt at the moment. I haven't *felt* in a long time. I show her the note. It says the same thing all of the others have said:

Stay calm.

Give me 100s 50s and 20s.

I have a Gun.

Stay Calm.

No Alarms.

Who is watching me? Are there others behind me? Did she push the alarm? I saw her push something. This one doesn't feel right. My heart is now pounding. I can hear it beating in my ears. Adrenaline turns to panic. Our eyes meet and I perceive a certain understanding from her, a mutual understanding. There is no 'why' in her eyes. No "don't do this Andrew McKenna" in her eyes. She sees my sadness. She understands that this must happen just the way it is happening. She sees me for who I am. And for this I am truly sorry.

I'm out the front door now and walking the 50 or so feet to my truck. Holding my head down, chin tucked to my chest. This is no disguise. Release the parking break. Of course I left the truck idling because I've had many visions of the "get-away" car not starting. I try to put the shifter in reverse but it won't go ... the engine revs and I try again, grinding the hell out of my transmission. Still it won't shift. SHIT it won't go! SHIT! FUCK! Finally, almost breaking the metal shifter with my bare hands, I slam it into reverse and tear ass out of the parking lot. Yes! It felt like an absolute eternity. I'm sure the folks in the bank are watching me with wonderment because I can feel dozens of eyes on me and it sends shivers up my back and shoulders. I shudder an uncontrollable shudder that lasts for several seconds. My heart is racing—it feels like cresting the highest point of the world's highest roller-coaster. Screaming through the intersection at the corner, I nearly hit a dump truck. Horns are blowing on my left and right as I run the light. My tires are screeching as they attempt to gain traction and the little green truck is bucking and gyrating like a bull, and I'm just barely keeping it on the road.

I make it to the highway and feel a momentary sense of relief. Then I see the convoy of police vehicles coming from the opposite direction flying past, seemingly coming from everywhere like flies swarming on shit. My heart beat is back, pounding in my ears. No eye contact with the cops going by, I just keep driving. This is not going well at all. My stomach flips over and over and over and over.

My past starts to trickle by in black and white images, moving in slow motion. Memories—connected and disconnected—start to flood in faster, rapid fire, like a dream now, my eyes on the road, my hands gripping the wheel ... My days as a lawyer in Washington, D.C. *I was good, wasn't I?* People thought so, and most importantly, I was getting better and people knew it. I knew it. Voices. *A talented prosecutor. He has gravitas and you can't teach that. If you have questions, ask Andrew. A very bright future. We can count on Andrew. A great dad. Hands on dad. Nurturing. Soft touch with his boys. They adore him. They have his eyes. Andrew loves them so much. It's almost more of a maternal love.*

Talking diapers
Pooh Bear
Hugs

Stinky piggies for toes.

I can't see them anymore. She walked out and took my boys. It was my birthday—January 13th. I was at a counseling session with my recovery guy. When I got home the house was dark and the car was gone.

I am on the highway now. It's crowded with morning commuters going into Albany. I can hear my heartbeat thumping, thumping as I stare straight ahead, a tight painful feeling in my head now. I can feel that this is almost over. Suddenly I feel the thunder-clapping of a helicopter straight over my head. Holy shit this can't be for me. The massive engine of the aircraft whines and I can hear each individual whoosh of its rotors—so piercing, so sharp. Passing a pair of troopers waiting on the median, I don't look, but I can feel them on me. Pretending now to change the station and singing along to a song. I am fooling no one. The noise from the helicopter suddenly increases; they have found their target, locked onto their target, and their target is me. My body becomes numb. My hands are on the steering wheel. I can see them, I just can't feel them. This is for me, not for someone else. Coming up in front of me, maybe 200 yards away, is a concrete divider and if I run into it as hard as possible I will no longer be here. This will be over right fucking now. No more pain, no more sadness.

The family court judge let her call all of the shots. She said safety was her paramount concern. It wasn't though. He told me in open court that, at one point, I was a rising star in my field, but that now, now "no one ever believes a junkie." He said that I could see the boys once a month so long as someone would supervise the visits. We'll review it again in six months. He ended the hearing with "Mazeltov" and a smile. Once a month for the next six months.

I slam on the accelerator to reach maximum speed so that I can slam my fucking brain through the windshield into concrete. Then things start to happen fast. On my left is a big black box truck, and it's running me off the road. My rearview mirror is all police lights and sirens, and screaming:

Let me see your hands…
Let me see your hands…
Let me see your hands Andrew!

When Derrick would wake up in the morning he would call out "da-da," "da-da." I would snuggle him with a bottle of warm milk. He was getting too old for bottles. After family court one day Wendi told me he still walks around her house calling for me.

I can't believe I am going out like this. I'm free-falling. I hear the helicopter pull away. I want to pretend that it isn't happening, that this isn't real. That I am invisible, that I am dead.

The trooper is 10 feet to my left with his gun trained on my head. I am inexplicably calm now. Always calm in terrifying situations where I could get my head blown off. I turn to him and make eye-contact, and notice he is shaking a little and based on my time in the Marines I know it doesn't take much pressure from his index finger to move the trigger to the rear. I could have him blow my head off by just dropping my hands from his view and no more pain, no more sadness. Death by cop? In a defeated monotone voice, not caring what the answers were, I mumbled,

Where do you want me to put my hands.
Where do you want me to put them.
What should I do.

Face-down on the ground with a knee on my spine, a hand on my neck and someone is yanking my hands and arms and wrists into handcuffs behind my back.

Any weapons.
Any weapons.
Needle in your pocket.
Any more needles.
No.

A crisp sunny morning in November, my cheek pressed to the road. The ground smells like burned car oil and tire rubber, and there is

17

now a tiny grain of gravel in my eye closest to the ground and everything is multiplied. I see a crowd of police coming at me with guns drawn, lights flashing and I hear a cacophony of screaming and horns blowing and people saying oh my God as they creep by in their cars, windows rolled down. I either saw, or imagined I saw, two little boys in their booster seats in the back of an old Volvo, and they're watching me, and they have dark hair like their dad, and maybe they miss their dad, and the grain of gravel rides out of my eye in a tear of despair.

The helicopter is back. News people are creeping around with cameras, like hyenas after a fresh kill. This is all for me. My thoughts are mutated fragments again. I think of my love Dawn, pregnant with our little boy, and I want to be with Dawn this instant, holding each other and in love. The wave of sadness washes over me. Each thought brings a heavier and heavier blanket of sadness until my chest and head feel so heavy and each breath is a burden.

I think of sunlight, and then clouds, and then the ocean, and then Heroin. I feel a brief sense of escape, the satisfaction of shutting it all off and escaping this life. But no, that's not going to happen. There is no escaping this.

I'm placed in an unmarked car by a uniformed policeman. He attaches my handcuffs, which are behind my back, to a metal loop connected to the seat. Almost immediately the circulation in my shoulders cuts off. The cop was wearing cologne. I thought how it was weird for a man in uniform to wear cologne. Why, he should join the Village People if he wants some flair with his uniform. He reminded me of a Major I knew when I was in the Marines—a real dandy this one. The Major doused himself in pungent Armani knock-off and carried his lunch in— get this—a small pink Victoria's Secret bag. The cologne and uniform combination seems incongruous to me—it angered me.

The cop's head was shaved like a skin-head and he had the high black boots, and he wore cologne and since my body needed Heroin, my senses, particularly my olfactory sense, was on high alert and I was starting to get cagey. I told him that his smell was going to make me throw-up.

"My smell?" He asked.

"Yes, your goddamn cologne or whatever. Perfume probably." I was frustrated.

"That might just get you an ass-beating," he said.

With that he reached behind my back and crunched the cuffs tighter into my wrists. I shrieked with pain. But the pain felt good in a way. It felt real at a time when nothing seemed real. The pain jolted me back to reality for an instant, a fleeting instant. For a moment I was extremely aware of my existence and aware that I was fucked.

A burly detective pulled me out of the car so I could be photographed. Why I wondered, would they want to photograph me there at that moment, in the middle of the highway during morning rush-hour. It was a trophy photo—the FBI Agent on my left arm and the detective on my right arm, smiling for the camera held by a junior police officer— they got their man. Six banks and two grocery stores later, and here I am.

After a few photos, I turned to the detective and asked him, "Can I leave now?" He liked that. The cop asks me about who I am and where I live but really this was an academic exercise. Judging from the police turnout, I've been a potential target for weeks now. For all I know, they could have followed me this morning as I left the house. Anything is possible. I had already robbed five banks and the bank this morning was my sixth and last.

I complain that the handcuffs are too tight, that they are cutting into my skin. They ignore me. Then I explain that there is no more feeling in my shoulders. They ignore me some more. This is truly unbelievable and frustrating to an extreme. Then I feel an itch in my private area—I require an adjustment—it's pretty clear they would ignore this complaint as well. Hey chief, how about adjusting my privates for me. Come on, be a trooper. It's funny because I have obsessed about the risk of someday being in a coma and not being able to scratch an itch. I've lost sleep thinking about this, so much so that I have actually instructed one of my brothers to shoot me dead if I ever were incapacitated to such a degree.

19

Death seems like a good option right now. I should have made the cop shoot me—the one with the cologne. Of course he might jump at the chance to adjust me. That might be his title down at the station: Cop-in-Charge-of-Privates-Adjustment.

Sweat is pouring down my face now because my body needs Heroin. Camera crews have doubled. Is Dawn watching this at home? The detective and the agent prop me up for another photograph, again, an on-the-scene photograph taken by a junior uniformed officer. In a moment of ease, after he snaps the photo, I casually turn to the detective and ask again, "Can I go now?" He doesn't laugh this time. He says, "You're a lawyer, right?" And I say, "Sort of."

Now they've handcuffed me to the wall at the State Troopers Barracks, the metal has broken the skin. Overhead florescent lights beat down on me and the smell of Pine Sol totally engulfs the room, reminding me of the Marine barracks in Quantico. I should be throwing up soon; it's getting close to that time. The interrogation begins; Detective on one side, FBI Agent on the other side.

"You are Andrew McKenna?"

"Yes, that's right."

"Andrew, what the hell happened? I mean, how did this happen?" The detective seems beside himself. He appears sympathetic, genuinely so.

I wish I knew. I don't answer. I don't have an answer for him.

"You had the world by the tail." He continues.

I know.

"You look sick." He says, almost as a question.

"I am sick. I'm withdrawing from ... from … Heroin."

The FBI Agent, white collar guy, young, handsome, buttoned-up, asks,

"Do you need medical attention?"

"No, I need Heroin." And with this, the salty detective laughs.

"Are you too sick to continue with this interview, this meeting?"

"Not yet, I'll be alright for a little while," I managed to say. "But can I have a cup of coffee? It helps stave off the sickness sometimes."

The detective looks at me like I am full of shit, and I am full of shit. Coffee does not ease Heroin withdrawals, Heroin does. But, I am a coffee drinker, and after the morning I had, I really could use a fucking cup of coffee. I'm being manipulative. But he thinks, as all cops do, that if he does me this big favor—the coffee—that I'll feel like I owe him. And this is very important for his interrogation. Even though they have me dead to rights on all of the robberies, they still feel they need a signed confession. It's an ego thing, number one, and number two, it seals a defendant's legal fate. It's as good as a defendant's voice on a wiretap. The cop comes back with a cup of coffee. The agent starts asking me questions, and shows me surveillance pictures from past robberies. I'm thinking two things: I look fat as hell in these photos, *and* they have me dead to rights.

I'm not saying much, not sure why. I am sick as a dog and every passing minute, it gets worse. But I think it has more to do with the fact that I've sat through interrogations and witness interviews so many times that I expect a little more from these guys. And so they start with the good cop, bad cop routine, which we all know too well from television, and this method is so overdone, so overused, and so ineffective with anyone who has an intelligence quotient of more than sixty. I think about the interviews I sat through with Colombian drug traffickers, guys that actually killed people for the fun of it by stuffing their live bodies into 50 gallon drums and walking away. I'd watch as skilled agents with the FBI and DEA masterfully work them over with questions and combinations of questions, interspersed with data, utilizing feeling and emotion, and how I would look at my watch during the session and realize that four or five hours had already passed since our last break. Through their methods, we had enough new credible information to add several new defendants to the indictment.

So maybe I was feeling a little insulted, and maybe I was playing a little game—my last-stand so to speak. My crimes were minor compared to what I had seen. I was a small fish, clearly. But they needed something from me to close this string of cases in upstate New York and Vermont, and wherever else I had been. And I'll be damned if I didn't need something from them. I need a cigarette, and I need one right fucking now.

"God help me," I mutter.

"What's up? Are you OK?" The detective asks.

"No, I'm really sick. This is going to be very bad."

"Well you made your bed," the FBI agent says. A real boob this one.

"Well hold on a minute, the detective interjects, is there anything that would help you to feel better?" Bingo. He really wanted my confession.

"Sometimes cigarettes relieve the symptoms a little, you know, the throwing up part." No one wants to be in a small room with a guy handcuffed to a wall who is throwing up.

"Whoa McKenna, this isn't a convenience store ... you should have thought about this...."

"It's a non-smoking building Andrew," the detective interrupts the agent again, "and it's definitely against our rules." At this point I know I'm going to get that cigarette. He's letting me know that for him to do it, it would be a big deal—his leverage. And then I would owe him a signed confession to all of the robberies.

"I understand," I say with the proper balance of disappointment and despair. It's a game for me, and a gamble for him.

"I'll see what I can do." Check-mate.

As sick as I feel, I still have enough energy to play little games with them, to outsmart them. Not to be a dick, just to feel some semblance of control, some feeling of equality. I wanted to be a peer again as opposed to a criminal. I wanted to be relevant, not a Heroin addicted scumbag.

At some point—it could have been twenty minutes or two hours, I had lost the concept of time—the detective comes through the door with a pack of Marlboro Reds, my brand, in one hand with a book of matches in the other. The fact that he had cigarettes was amazing, but the fact that they were Marlboro Reds was nothing short of divine intervention.

"Ready for that smoke?" the detective asks.

After un-cuffing me from the wall, and re-cuffing me with my hands in front, he asks me if there is going to be any funny business. We exit the room and proceed out the back door of the trooper barracks where they light a cigarette for me. A feeling of dread came over me because I felt a sense of accomplishment for getting a smoke out of them. What had I become?

There was this Colombian. A cooperating witness, on loan from the Federal Bureau of Prisons so that he could testify for us in Washington, D.C. I used to bring candy bars to him at the local jail where he was being held. He talked me into it. He was a dangerous man who happened to love chocolate, but I needed him to be extra cooperative. He seemed to remember more details after eating some chocolate. He'd sit there and eat the chocolate and smile at me the whole time. He was my witness, meaning I was responsible for debriefing him, checking his story, preparing him to testify at trial. The Justice Department had worked hard to get him indicted, and even harder to have him extradited from Colombia. He added a critically important aspect to our case because he was the only one who had met face-to-face with the cartel leaders. We had wiretaps from other countries with their voices and everything, but my witness could actually point to the defendants in the courtroom and identify them as the people who sent him, literally, tons of cocaine.

Not surprising, the cigarette was the best I had ever had, and I desperately wanted another one. The second cigarette made me happy, but no more cooperative than before. Two cigarettes total. Escorted by five or six cops, none of whom smoke, they just stare while I bring my cuffed hands up to my mouth and take enormous pulls from the cigarette, each time tightly closing my eyes and laying on the couch with Dawn, and wanting to live.

"Andrew, finish up there, we need to get you downtown for arraignment. Here is a copy, a written copy, of what we talked about here today." He hands me a confession to all of the robberies and a pen. I read it. I don't sign it.

"Thank you," I say looking him in the eyes.

"Well I need you to sign it Andrew," he answered sternly.

"I know that you believe you need me to sign this," I continue, "but you don't. And I can't sign it, and I won't." I tell him.

"That's some real bullshit Andrew. We've been very reasonable here today: polite, patient, the whole nine yards. Coffee, cigarettes. Let's go, I need your signature." The man is angry, red-faced now, with eyebrows and mouth all contorted. He looks and sounds insane.

"I'm sorry, but I can't," I say calmly. "And do you know why? Your reputation is not on the line, you don't need this to convict me. You don't need me to sign anything."

"Don't you see? The Constitution says I don't have to say or sign anything. The fucking Constitution! You gave me coffee and cigarettes? Thanks for being a decent guy. But make me feel like I owe you, and that I should give up my rights because of it? Don't you see how twisted that is?"

God this is crazy.

We're on the highway now, in the back of a big black FBI Suburban. We are flying down the road at 100 miles per hour. My head nods and sways as we weave through mid-morning traffic. I'm wearing a fleece pull-over given to me by an agent because my shivering disgusted him, and the fleece smells overwhelmingly of old people and fart. I dry heave once, and then a second time. The bugs are on my back and neck and arms.

I stare up at the judge. The bright lights of the courtroom sting my eyes and the smell of carpet cleaning solution burns my nose. I am about to throw-up, and worried that I won't be able to choke down and swallow the vomit; that it will come spewing out of my mouth onto the defense table in front of me.

A federal public defender—Gene Primomo—approaches me, stops and just stares. I begin, between dry heaves, to assess his credentials. Where did you go to law school? How long have you been defending? What did you do before? Former prosecutor, private practice, and now this. He looks a little put-off by my questions, but I don't care. I don't care about anything. He knows about me from the local news reports, and what the pretrial services officer told him. He asks if I'm going to be alright, and just at that moment the vomit comes up. Placing my index finger to my lips as if to say, "Just a moment please, sir," I choke down the bile in two swallows.

"I'll be fine."

He looks at me in amazement, mouth gaping open. He can't believe what he sees. I explain to him, that under the bail rules, I don't have a chance of going home. He concurs with a nod, averting eye contact with me because it's obvious that I'm trying to show him that I'm smart, and know the law, but this really just makes me look like a pathetic loser. I know all of the arguments that the prosecutor will make—danger to the community, risk of flight, crimes of violence—I've made the same arguments a dozen times. And, ultimately, the prosecutor would be right. I was a danger, and would flee if given the opportunity. The judge knows this too. Gene and I decide to waive the bail hearing. I am also entitled to a probable cause hearing. The government has the burden—on a criminal complaint—to establish that probable cause exists to support the charge that I committed the offenses. Well, let me tell you, when the FBI brings you to court in handcuffs, you can pretty much count on the court finding that probable cause existed to arrest you. Judges love the FBI. They trust the FBI. There was no point in a probable cause hearing. The judge looks down at me with disbelief. He knows that I am gone, and he remands me into custody. I'm going to the Albany County Jail. I've never been to jail before.

Chapter 2

Sitting in a holding cell at the federal courthouse, waiting for transport to the county lock-up, I puke my guts onto the cement grey floor. The spatter from the vomit hits my dress pants, and dress shoes— the costume that I wore to my final robbery. On the floor in front of me between my feet is rancid green and yellow bile. Every few minutes my body goes through the involuntary process of throwing up, and my stomach muscles contract, and I can't breathe, and I feel panic and fear because I can't breathe. And then everything relaxes for a minute, and I feel relief, and then it comes again, and I know it's coming again, and I panic, and feel fear, because it hurts and it's scary and the guard walking by chuckles and shakes his head, and then it stops for a minute, and then it comes again. And this happens three times a minute. My body needs the Heroin, and it is letting me know this fact with its own sick exclamation point.

After several hours, the Marshals bring me to the jail where I will remain for the foreseeable future. During yet another long booking process, I dry heave constantly as the Corrections Officer (CO) in Receiving and Discharge fingerprints and photographs me. He too has seen the news reports and cannot believe that I am there. At the same time they are booking in a medical doctor from the VA who falsified medical records in order to make certain cancer patients eligible for some special trial treatment. Well apparently, he signed-up people who shouldn't have been given the treatment and they died. The CO was asking him for medical advice, something about reflux or a rash, I couldn't really make it out. The doctor practically treated him right there on the spot, feeling his glands, rubbing his temple, saying *ahhhh*. And I thought to myself, "Hey I'm a lawyer, ask me a legal question. I used to do divorces." But of course the CO doesn't ask me.

In the medical ward, now throwing up. They, of course, will not give me anything for the extreme cramping which causes me to involuntarily flail my body around like a hooked fish. I vomit and sweat, and every now and then a couple of CO's, probably on their coffee break, come up to the window of my secured cell, and look in. I hear them say, "That's one crazy motherfucker." "Yeah, twelve banks. Dope sick, too. That shit's crazy." And they'd walk away. I'm the new baby panda at the zoo. *And it was only six banks asshole.*

I can't sleep. I only slip away into semi-consciousness for a few minutes where I see my boys, their faces, and little Dylan asks me, "Why are you crying daddy?" And I see Derrick crying and asking when I'm coming home, he wants to snuggle. Each time I hope I don't regain consciousness, that I just keep slipping away further and further, but no, I come to and throw up and shiver uncontrollably yet again. The shivering turns to twitching, the absolute involuntary jerking of my body parts. It feels like I need to stretch my legs and toes … the need is so intense, but when I do I don't get the satisfied feeling, but my mind is sending signals that I need to stretch to get the feeling of relief, but the relief never comes. No eating, no sleeping, no stillness, no warmth, no coolness. I beg God to let me die, to end it. But He ignores me. Then I slip away again and repeat this process over and over again, no-ending, no beginning, just a constant loop of full-blown torturous Heroin withdrawals.

All week I went through these thoughts of wanting to die. Unless you've ever felt so bad that you wanted it to be over, you simply cannot fully understand it. I thought of my mom. I saw her face as clear as day and it was right up against mine. I could hear a song that she used to sing to me when I was a child—*Lara's Theme* from *Doctor Schivago*.

I saw myself pedaling down the driveway on Belmont Avenue on my Big Wheel without noise-makers because the repetitive sound drove my father nuts. And I saw myself on my dad's shoulders walking down

27

the street to the store to get groceries. All of the images that should have felt good and wholesome and real, were somehow dark and painful and I wanted it to end. Each memory came to me like on an old 8mm reel, each frame went across my mind's eye. When the frames went by, I feared that they would be lost forever, that I'd never have the memory again, and I tried to keep a focus on it, because I didn't want to let it go. I was afraid the thoughts were running out of my body like blood, gone for good.

Day eight or so. The judge won't let me out. Apparently Gene, even though I had no recollection, had come to see me at some point in the past few days and said he'd ask for bail so I could go into a treatment program. Thinking of the judge's initial order detaining me was all a blur. Demonic addiction and menace to others? Menace? Is this what he wrote in his detention order? The robberies are my last chapter? Did he write that the robberies were my last chapter? I would ponder tortured thoughts like these for hours. Awake, pacing around my cell, muttering to myself, I dropped 15 pounds in six days. I drank low grade grape juice from Central America that came to me frozen and I would suck at the frozen solution like a fiend. It was nothing but sugar, and the sugar must have gone to work on my dopamine receptors because I felt for an instant some kind of pleasure; the first time I felt anything remotely good in days. I would knock on my thick plexi-glass window and hold up the empty container, grape stain around my mouth, and ask the COs for more. "Are there any extras? They are really delicious." And they'd yell things through the plexi-glass like, "Shut your fucking cake hole, McKenna!" At that, I would laugh and cry at the same time, and then they would laugh really hard; real sadistic bastards here.

The total recall moments would still come, but not deep childhood stuff. More recent memories of being out on a run for days, either dope-sick trying to get Heroin, or being high and not caring, and the whole time Dawn is home pregnant with our boy, and she is going crazy with fear and worry. These frames are as bad, if not worse than the childhood shit, except now I am fully conscious and can't get away from them.

It finally occurred to me that I don't have tuberculosis. When I first came in, they pricked me with a TB test on my forearm. A few days passed before they checked the site on my forearm to determine if I had it. Because my brain was in such rough shape, and my body in such pain from no Heroin, my mind played tricks on me. Over the few days, I gradually convinced myself that I had TB. I would stare at my arm for hours, thinking the color and shape of the redness had changed. I thought I overheard guards talking about it with the medical staff. Pressing my ear to the edge of the cell door straining to listen; I was experiencing mild auditory and visual hallucinations. Hearing things—I swear—like:

"He only has a few months to live, or Did you see his arm? or Have you smelled him lately?" I would say things to this one particular guard like; "I know you know I have TB." "What the fuck are you talking about McKenna?" I'd say it like I knew the jig was up, letting him know that I knew he knew I had TB. "What the fuck are you talking about, dumbass?" This particular CO called all of the inmates dumbass.

"I can hear everything through this door," I'd say, putting him on notice.

"Oh yeah? Well hear this: Shut the fuck up, and enjoy your few good days left on this earth dumbass!"

"I heard that!"

Finally I am cleared by the jail medical people, and transferred to general population. I didn't want to move—I was getting attached to my cell.

"But I have tuberculosis."

"Goddamn it McKenna, you don't have fucking TB, now pack your shit and let's go!" It was night time when I got to my new block. All the lights were off, and the 80 other inmates were locked in their cells. The next morning I came to and looked out of the bars of my little cell. Literally dozens of tall black people were staring at me. Or so I thought. They were actually watching Bernie Mac and laughing right along in unison with the laugh track. The T.V. is mounted directly above my cell, so naturally they were staring in the direction of my cell, just not at me. Thank God, because I thought they were getting ready to deliver some perverted jail initiation. When that feeling of terror went away, the next thing I know, my gate cracks open and I walk out barefoot in a bright orange jail jumpsuit. "Man, someone get that nigga some shower shoes." Did he just call me a nigger? I sat down and watched Bernie Mac, half in a daze, half out. I couldn't believe how bad the stereotypes were on this show. Every time I looked away from the screen, I made eye-contact with people looking at me like they hated me. So I decided to really try to focus on the screen. What was this great Bernie Mac infatuation? Let me try to focus my Heroin shit brain on this show and understand what they see, because they clearly see something. And I'm still getting the shivers and the sweats pretty regularly, so why not try to get with it; shake off some of this funk, man!

So I stare at the screen like a mental patient. Apparently, Bernie's son Jordan is being bullied again by the neighborhood kids, which isn't a surprise to me because he's 11 years old and weighs only 40 pounds, with lots of change in his pockets. I think he was a crack baby, which always makes me a little sad. The bullying intensifies. I mean they're really giving this kid the business. You'd never see this on a white show. Anyhow, I'm sitting there staring at the look of fear on Bernie's son's face and I'm really feeling it.

Unbelievably, my fucking eyes start to tear up. What the hell is this, I thought. My eyes are getting wetter by the second, I clench my fists, fingers interlocked and pressed to my mouth, elbows on table, and I'm biting my right index finger, because man I am about to let it out. What am I doing? Where are these Goddamn tears coming from for Christ's sake? Maybe this would be a good time to introduce myself to these folks: "Hi, I'm Nancy, and I don't belong here." I'm holding my breath, trying to keep it together, but I can't. They won't leave Bernie's kid alone. Suddenly, angst and grief explode out of my nose and mouth, in a terrible sound, a thumping, gurgling, weepy sound of emotional release. Now eyes are on me and no one is laughing. I bite down on my finger until I break

30

skin, as a tear rolls down my cheek. But I hold my stare on the screen. My face is contorted, my body tense, I'm sweating, and every second or so my whole body shudders. This is the stupidest fucking thing I've ever been associated with.

This is all happening, of course, because my brain hasn't had to produce any of its own feel-good chemicals, because of the whale-size portions of Heroin I have been feeding it. I'd cry watching a fucking shampoo commercial right now. Dandruff! Flakes! This just isn't fucking fair! This is crazy! Can't his fucking doctor prescribe something? It looks like he's been through a fucking snow storm!

The "good" news according to the recovery people and confirmed by the jail shrink is that it will only take a year or two for my body to adjust and start producing these needed chemicals again on its own. No wonder people relapse. Who can wait two years to feel good when a $20 bag of dope and a $1 needle are only a phone call away?

It's bedtime. I smell ass. I sleep with my face 12 inches from my stainless steel toilet-sink combination. It's one piece of molded steel and I can't help but think it has weird artistic sculpture-type value. The thought makes me feel like a loser and I wish it away. Someone is crying. It sounds like he might be trying to muffle his whimpers in a jumpsuit or something. Other than the crying, the tier is silent; consumed with the silence of trapped men, caged and left alone with their thoughts, a daunting place. Who talks like this? I sound like Frazier Crane in my head and it makes me sick. Can't I just be normal and sleep like the rest of these lost souls? Lost souls? Jesus, I can't shut it off. Hearing the echoed cries of a faceless man is haunting. Help me stop Jesus! A corrections officer making his rounds stops at my cell and peers in. I have my tattered blanket pulled up to my neck and I am squinting, pretending to be asleep. Nonetheless, I think we make eye contact, although with the light behind him, he appears more as a silhouette. So I'm straining my eyes trying to see if he's looking at me, and I think he's doing the same thing to me. I lay motionless. Is this where the guards take my dignity down in the depths of the old stone jail? *Thanks a lot, Jesus, really?* He just stands there and stares at me. Is he going to relieve himself right in front of me? He looks agitated. To my relief he pivots and walks away. I can hear the click-clack of his steel-tipped guard shoes on the concrete catwalk as he goes. The crying resumes.

Light comes on. It's morning. My toilet just made a loud burping sound. The plumbing in this place is notorious. I've witnessed crazy white men flush clothing down their toilets just for laughs. The toilet just sucked stuff down with incredible force, and without fail, it burps in satisfaction. Like a fat person. It's really pretty cool seeing it the first three or four times. One minute part of a sheet is there, and the next minute it's gone. Whoosh. During one particular flushing frenzy, where inmates were running around like mental patients looking for test objects to flush, I saw a guy stuff the better part of a dictionary, a full-size Webster's Third Edition minus the hard covers, down the fucking hole while his partner continuously pushed the steel flush button. The hole is no larger than the one in your mother's house by the way. Another lunatic came behind him and crammed half a Scrabble board into the hole. The toilet had no problem with it either, although the board had to be folded. Each item it was fed just disappeared. It was almost like the toilet came alive. And each time the crazed crowd would wait for the payoff, and sure enough without fail, the toilet would burp. That was the finale, the point when the crowd could rejoice, because collectively they knew they had satisfied the great toilet.

One night I had a really detailed dream about Derrick. I woke up sobbing, and the folded up second-hand boxer-shorts, a pair that had probably 10 previous inmate owners that I used as a pillow, were soaked. When Derrick was about a year or so old, before Dylan was born, I used to take him on weekends to the National Gallery of Art. We lived about 10 minutes away. Derrick was too young to understand the magnitude of the place, its significance. I could barely grasp it myself, but I know he liked it. He liked the old masters, the Dutch painters, and Picasso. He was partial to Picasso, I'm sure of it. He also liked Chuck Close.

As soon as we went too modern, he would crap in his diaper and laugh while I changed him. The gallery would reek of baby shit, and he would wrestle and kick me while I tried to put on his diaper. Several old snobs in their corduroys and sweaters would gasp or stare, and being as over protective as a dad could be, I'd inevitably ask, "What the hell are you looking at?" Or say, "Mind your fucking business." Here I was, a prosecutor for the Justice Department, and I was levying threats against old ladies in front of Rembrandts, but God was I furiously protective of Derrick's feelings. My love for him was deeper than any emotion I had ever known. He had the deepest laugh you've ever heard from a human without teeth. He was "chief-without-teeth," as my brother-in-law Kent used to say. After the galleries, with time spent getting really close to the paintings, so close that the security guards would become agitated, we would go to the café and he would gum a grilled cheese sandwich and I would drink coffee, half thinking about my current cases at Justice, and half focusing on this little guy with the big brown eyes.

I lie on my one-inch thick county jail mattress that probably at one time was 5 inches thick. But now it was 1 inch thick and smelled like piss, cocoa butter, and hair grease. The pain in my back was excruciating. My balls hurt too. I started to think I had testicular cancer. I was so depressed I didn't want to think about anything or feel anything, so I just stared at the impressive toilet, my friend. I thought if I did a handstand and stuffed my head deep into the bowl, really cram it in there as far as I could, and then let my body fall to the side, I could break my own neck. Just then it burped, and I'm not sure if it had just read my mind and was saying "go ahead and try it Andrew," or "don't do it because it won't work." But I do know for sure that it wasn't saying, "DON'T DO IT: YOU HAVE SO MUCH TO LIVE FOR."

My whole body was stiff from the mattress. I've been through some pretty demanding training in my day, and survived sleeping in some strange positions, but a few days in Albany County jail, and I'm practically paraplegic. I was obsessed about getting out of there now. I went to the law library, shivering and with muscle spasms from continuing withdrawals, to research how I could get bail. I was convinced that Gene was missing something. When I would return to the tier from the library I would call Gene collect from the filthy payphone, and tell him which cases to look at. He was gracious.

"Hell no, I'm not wasting my time on that. You know it doesn't matter Andrew."

He was telling me what I already knew, and that is, no matter what case you find to support your argument for bail, the judge wasn't letting out a guy with a Heroin problem, a mental condition, and a bunch of robberies to boot.

Lying down staring up, I noticed human shit stuck to the ceiling. I dry heave. I turned my body to the left and faced the wall. My body shifting causes air to poof from the perforated mattress and the smell of piss emanates up into my bloated face. There is a bugger on the wall in front of me. I close my eyes because they're too heavy to hold open, and I lay there and smell piss until I doze off into a tormented afternoon sleep. My dreams were horrible—lots of loss and fear, and rejection. Derrick and Dylan, in one dream, had a new father. Half-awake I think about escaping from jail—an absolutely absurd thought. To escape, I would have to get through two reinforced steel gates and an enormous steel electronic door, just to get into the hallway. I could try to jump over the fence outside in the recreation area. The fence must be 50 feet high, and not your typical chain-link fence, either; it's one with the little holes. No way could I even get the toe of my flimsy orange jail slipper into one of those holes. I'd have to rely on pure finger and big toe strength the entire 50-foot traverse, lugging my 200-pound frame just with my fingers and toes. Then, once at the top, assuming I wasn't unconscious from the finger pain and hadn't been shot by the guard who watches the recreation yard, I'd have to get over triple-strand razor wire, jump down 50 feet, and run the distance of 10 football fields to the road, where I'd have to car-jack someone who was traveling 45 miles per hour. God, I need bail.

One day I asked the CO for some toilet paper. They're supposed to hand it out twice a week. You have to turn in the empty cardboard cylinder from the center of the used-up roll, and in exchange, they throw a new roll at your head. Everyone is out of toilet paper, except for the long-termers, guys who have been in the county jail for 6 months or more awaiting trial, who have been hoarding rolls over past months. The long-termers will sell you a roll for a bag of instant coffee, two bags of chips, or four Honeybuns. I have none of these items in stock, so I've been wiping my ass with an old t-shirt, and washing it out in the sink. My ass is completely raw. My frustration level is through the roof.

"I need toilet paper," I say to the CO on duty.
"So don't I," the CO says, not looking up from his newspaper.
"But I have to go to the bathroom."
"So don't I," he responds, being a complete dick.
"I use my t-shirt to wipe my ass."
"So don't I."
"You use *my* t-shirt to wipe *your* ass?"
"Yup."
"Can I speak to a lieutenant, please?"
"No."
"OK, thank you."
"You're welcome."
I walked back to my cell and used the t-shirt again and wept.

An older black man with two teeth keeps handing me little slips of paper on which Bible verses are written. He slips them into my hand right before we are locked into our cells for lunch. We have to eat lunch locked in our cells so no weak people have their lunch taken by an extra-hungry inmate. I sit on my steel stool, which is cold and feels great on my raw ass. I open the slip of paper, and this particular time, I read:

"For He so loved the world...." and I didn't read on. The man has a major crack problem and he comes to jail and turns into the deacon. Then he gets out of jail, and turns back into the guy with the major crack problem, only to be locked-up again, where he again turns back into the deacon and gives people little slips of paper, because he's the deacon.

I break out my mini-bible which is missing several pages (inmates use the thin bible pages to roll cigarettes with tobacco which has been smuggled into the jail during visitation day), and I search around for an appropriate passage. When the cell gates are opened, I go up to the deacon and very piously with a bow of my head, hand him the slip of paper. On it was written, "If a man lay with a beast…." Leviticus.

The deacon did not find this funny—at all. He charged at me, gangly, unstable on his feet, brain twisted from decades of crack.

"Hey! Hey!" He screams. I spin around feeling vulnerable.

"What?"

He gets right up in my face, lint caught in the hair on his head and face. Breath like he just ate a shit sandwich, mangled index finger from holding a pipe day-in and day-out for half of his life, wagging it in my concerned face.

"HEY! NEVAH MESS WIT DA LORD!"

"Whoa chief, take it easy." I'm ready to crush the old loon if he persists. My eyes are crazy now.

"NEVAH MESS WIT DA LORD!"

"OK, OK, fine … never mess with the Lord."

And with that he walked away.

The next day I get in a fight with a basketball player. I was sitting in a seat that is bolted to the floor. My back aches from all of the standing I've been doing, and I don't "own" a seat because they're very limited in number and I'm way too new to have acquired ownership of one. Seats are like property was in the 1800s. People will defend to the death their ownership.

"My seat."

"What?"

"My seat."

"What?"

"That's my muthafuckin seat."

"Stop your bullshit. It was free, so I sat down."

"This seat is nevah frees."

"The seat is nevah frees? What the hell does that mean?"

"It mean, get the fuck out my seat, white boy."

I snapped. Everything that had built up over the past few days, weeks, months, I don't know, rose up so quickly and I was past the point of return. In one fluid motion I jerked myself to my feet and punched him in the throat as hard as I could. I could have hit it more squarely, but it was still a hell of a shot. He grabbed his throat in a panic, and started making a choking sound. He had no wind, no oxygen. He was like 6'3" and spinning around, eyes as big as olives, panicking, and making this terrible noise. He sounded like a seal, choking and barking at the same time. The inmates love this shit. Immediately a circle formed around us; everyone was fired-up. For the most part, blacks were on one side, and whites and Hispanics on the other. Hispanics almost always side with the whites if things get crazy. Blacks outnumber us at least 30 to 1, but they can't seem to organize as a single group. But that doesn't apply when it's even remotely about race; they will unite and kick the living shit out of all the white people.

I hear the sirens blasting from the ceilings and CO's yelling. I punch him one more time in the throat, but his hands are in the way and he's still doing the spinning around thing, so he doesn't get the full brunt. Immediately everyone disperses to their cells and we're locked in while the CO's secure the tier. From my cell I can see the CO who I had asked for toilet paper, talking quietly with the Lieutenant who had just arrived on the scene. I couldn't make out what he was saying, but it looked, from his facial expressions and body language, like he was advocating a point. I thought for sure I was going to the hole because I acknowledged that he had wiped his ass with my t-shirt.

We're locked in all day and night. They need to give the races a cooling down period. No riots here. A little while later I'm woken by a rap on my cell gate. I had fallen asleep on my cold stool leaning against the wall, dreaming I was a little brown person farming a poppy field in Afghanistan. It's the toilet paper CO, and he's pushing a roll through the bars.

"McKenna, here's your shit paper. Good job on that nigger."

Wow, I thought, I don't need this right now. He said it really loudly, and I don't want to be associated with white supremacy. But, I did need the shit paper.

And then I used the toilet.

After a few weeks, I tried to get the jail medical staff to prescribe me medicine. It became my project. First, I was still fully convinced that I had testicular cancer. I spent numerous hours doing ball examinations. I felt something, I was sure of it. Second, I needed a project, and trying to outwit, outmaneuver, out-manipulate these folks fit the bill. It started with the jail shrink.

"How about an Ambien?"

"No."

"How about a tranquilizer?"

"No."

"A Xanax."

"No."

"A Valium."

"No."

"Motrin?"

"Maybe."

"Maybe Motrin? It's an NSAID!"

"I'll have to talk with the regular physician first."

"Seroquel."

"No."

"Paxil."

"No."

"Trazadone."

"Yes."

"Trazadone. Yes to Trazadone?"

The first night of Trazadone—they gave it to me at 7:30 when the pill cart came around—it seemed like I was asleep within four minutes. I barely made it back to my cell. I slept for two and a half days. I woke with a painful erection. The next time I took Trazadone, it made me hungry. Not garden variety hungry mind you; I was fucking ravenous, the sickest case of munchies ever. I searched everywhere for snacks. My two friends had nothing. I went to the "store-man," the inmate who has a whole bin of commissary goods under his bunk. He charges 2 for 1. That means if you get a Snickers bar, you owe him two the next time you go to the commissary. If you don't pay him back, he and his thugs will beat you to a pulp. He thought I was a wealthy guy. Little did he know, I couldn't afford a loaf of bread. But he believed my credit would be good. He was quite the enthusiastic store-man, too. He sounded like Chris Rock.

"Man, what else you need here, some Kool-Aid? You drink Kool-Aid? I got grape Kool-Aid, go ahead and get yourself some grape Kool-Aid."

When I woke up the next afternoon, a CO was yelling at me to "Clean up this fucking mess McKenna!" On the floor were well over six candy bar wrappers, an empty bag of sour cream and onion chips, an empty thing of grape Kool-Aid, several cheese stick wrappers, at least five super-sized Slim Jims, Pop-Tart crumbs, and more. It amounted to almost $30 in commissary, which meant I owed the store-guy $60. That was the second night on Trazadone. Every night seemed to bring a different experience. One night I couldn't stop laughing. I laughed for three hours straight. The next morning my stomach muscles hurt from laughing so hard. People were asking me where I got the weed, and if they could get some. This made me laugh even harder. One night after my Trazadone dose kicked-in, I became very emotional, and wanted to talk about my feelings with strangers. People would say things like, "Get the fuck away from me." I would answer with, "Just because we're in jail doesn't mean we can't be human!" My voice would be shaky with emotion. I heard someone call me a faggot, as he walked away.

The erections were a bit of a problem. I didn't have any underwear—I had traded all but one torn pair for food. I couldn't get the store-man, despite my ardent protestations and high pressure sales technique, to accept the torn ones in exchange for a honey bun. It was a really awkward conversation, too.

"Homey, I'm not giving you two honey buns and a grape Kool-Aid for a pair of torn draws! Do I even look like I would wear torn draws?" It was a valid question because by jail standards he always seemed very put together—always new jumpsuits, new slippers, fresh doo-rags. On the street, I bet his car was always very clean and well fragranced.

So without underwear, I would just be free-balling in my jumpsuit, commando. It looked like a bright orange tent when I had an erection. Not a huge tent, a moderately sized, slightly above average, respectable Irish tent. When the gates would crack in the morning, I would wake up and walk my erection downstairs to get my tray of food and then retreat back to my cell. I was so tired and groggy from the Trazadone that I didn't care. I heard one CO say, "Oh come on, no one wants to see that." He was absolutely repulsed by my boner.

I stayed on the Trazadone until one day at pill-line the nurse told me that the doctor had stopped the prescription.

"But aren't they supposed to wean a person off a psych-med?"

"Did you say wean?" And then she burst out laughing.

"Never mind," I was so frustrated and defeated by this.

For the next several days I was convinced I was going through Trazadone withdrawals. The crying fits returned, and when I wasn't crying, I was insanely angry—always on the verge of snapping.

"McKenna! McKenna!" The CO was screaming my name while I stared out the three inch wide window planning my escape.

"What!"

"Watch your tone asshole! Go see the Lieutenant."

Oh shit this can't be good. When any inmate gets called off the tier to see a staff member, everyone notices. People become very suspicious. Everyone is so goddamn bored in jail that they key in on any movement

40

out of the ordinary. The problem, of course, is that I start to feel self-conscious, like people are staring at me, wondering what I'm doing. Do they think I'm a snitch? The jail is full of snitches—guys that tell the CO's everything that goes on in exchange for a peanut butter and jelly sandwich on the down-low. I believe they don't only always do it for material gain such as food and tobacco—they do it to feel important. It's sad. A snitch who is outed will get his head beaten in. That's not sad. And once they're outed, the CO's throw them away like an old prostitute—they have no use for them anymore. So, I'm not a snitch, but again, my brain chemicals aren't firing correctly, so I become paranoid. I literally start to act suspiciously—like initiating conversations with inmates I wouldn't normally talk to and explaining why I had to leave the tier and go to the doctor two days in a row.

"I have testicular cancer." I explained to Beatdown. That's what everyone called him. Beatdown.

"You have testicular cancer," Beatdown repeats back to me. Beatdown has done 14 years of federal prison time, seven years of state prison time and now he is back again awaiting trial. Beatdown has killed people. Beatdown doesn't believe I have testicular cancer.

"Yes. Testicular cancer. I did the exam. In the shower."

"You did the exam."

"Yes. And I felt something. A tumor. Perhaps. I think." Beatdown made me nervous. I was afraid of him.

"So the doctor needs to keep seeing you, examining your balls, to ensure that the tumor hasn't grown, day-to-day?" Mike's staring at me like a detective.

"Yes. No. I don't know. That's a weird statement, Mike. I don't know."

I haven't been terrified of many people in my life, but I was terrified of Mike. I believed Beatdown thought I was leaving the housing unit to tell on people.

Andrew McKenna

Two weeks had passed since I sent the last letter to Derrick and Dylan. I did little drawings and tried to write funny things to make them laugh. I told them that I loved them and missed them, and on the backs of the letters I drew three stick figures holding hands representing me, Derrick and Dylan. I didn't know their address so I sent the letters to their grandmother's house. I hadn't heard back from them. The lieutenant was a short fat guy with hairy forearms and a big Skoal in his lip. He was spitting into an empty Diet Coke can.

"Do you know a Wendi Spelling?"

"Yes, she's my wife, or well, we're broken up."

"She called the jail and said she had a protective order against you. She doesn't want you to contact the kids."

"Protective order?"

"Yup, no more writing to them."

"But how will they... they'll think I forgot about them."

"No contact at all. Do it again, and you'll catch another charge."

"But lieutenant...."

Chapter 3

Dear Andrew,

I hope you are doing well and that you are a happy boy. I've been thinking a lot about you lately and it occurred to me that you are wondering about the meaning of things. It is in your nature to do so, and sometimes the thoughts can seem a little overwhelming. Maybe you're feeling a little alone or isolated, and maybe a little scared. Because you're so young, it is hard for you to know what exactly you are feeling or why you are feeling it. Here is my request of you. When you are feeling sad or worried, or feel like you're thinking too much, talk to mom and dad and tell them that something doesn't seem right. You're a good boy and I love you.

Your friend.

When I was six or seven years old, a hillbilly and her children moved in next door. She had a two-inch space between her big toe and the next toe, and candy apple red, chipped polish on all of her nails, fingers and toes. The family hailed from Ohio by way of West Virginia, and they called soda "pop." Why, I wondered, didn't they just call it soda? The younger boy was my age, and he was terrified of his mother, but also very much a momma's boy. I was always getting into mischief, and this made him nervous—he was afraid of his mother's reaction. One day I suggested that we go into the woods behind our houses and light things on fire. I had stolen a lighter from the corner store and finally figured out that I had to spin the tumbler, and then press the red button to get the flame. I told Les to drag a wagon-load of newspapers into the woods. I was fascinated by fire.

"Is this OK? I mean, that we're doing this?" He asked, nervous as hell.

"Just drag it, we're almost there."

The fire was not huge, but a neighbor had to respond with a garden hose and buckets. It was quite an ordeal. I ran like hell and Les followed me, whimpering that his mom was going to "get on the switch," which was an Ohio term. I had no idea what that meant. I thought of a light switch.

"She's going to make me pick my own," he said as we ran through the woods.

"Your own what?"

"My own switch."

After a series of intra-neighbor phone calls between parents, it turned out that I was the prime suspect. My brother Brian, three years my senior, caught onto this and felt that it was his moment to get involved, to shine, to influence events.

"You need to tell mom that it was you."

"What?"

"You need to tell mom that it was you who started the fire, or I'm going to."

"What?"

"You heard me. Tell her."

My mother spanked my ass until it was beet red. First, she commanded me to go upstairs to my bedroom and take my pants down. The walk up the 12 stairs was, in retrospect, like going to my execution. Each step was a labor just to keep my legs moving. My mother was not a large or violent woman, but I'm pretty sure her New England puritan upbringing would not allow her to raise an arsonist for a son. That's the only explanation for the sort of beating she put on me. Mom climbed the stairs five minutes later, bounded in fact. She literally beat the arsonist right out of me. Later that evening I sat in the bathtub staring at the wall, thinking that huge flames really weren't all they were cracked up to be. My ass cheeks were burning in the hot bath water. Mom poked her head in the bathroom to tell me that she was going to choir practice.

We grew up in a middle class neighborhood, went to middle class schools, had middle class friends, and did not take vacations. We belonged to a public pool, and I was in love with a 12 year old girl with a great tan and a bubble butt. I would follow her to the snack bar and watch her devour a Popsicle. I had no idea what it meant, but I couldn't take my eyes off of her. She gave me a boner.

Our house was a bungalow at 1390 Belmont Avenue, in Schenectady, New York, formally known as the "electric city" because GE had a big factory there where they made turbines. They were the economic anchor of Schenectady. When GE left for cheaper wages and lower taxes, the city fell apart. People from New York City moved up and started selling drugs and forming gangs. Fortunately, they were quarantined to a place called Hamilton Hill by the Schenectady Police. We lived nowhere near Hamilton Hill.

My neighbors were strange. The one next door was a well-dressed gay guy named Art who lived with his elderly mother. He died of AIDS before people knew what AIDS was. Art was cool. At Easter, he'd always bring us a butter sculpted lamb, and at Christmas, he'd bring an album like the BeeGees or Barry Manilow's Greatest Hits. Art hung out in a Speedo and watered his flowers in a Speedo, and sunbathed in a Speedo, and made eye contact with me in a Speedo. He was an usher in our church and he wore cream colored suits and shoes with tassels, and he would bring the collection plate down the aisle, and whenever he walked by he would wink. Nice guy, I thought.

The neighbor across the street may have molested his son. I was eight or nine when one time I answered the phone at our house and an FBI Agent was on the other end. The Agent asked me questions about the neighbor, about his political leanings.

"His what?"

"What kind of person is he?"

"I don't know, he has really hairy legs and he wears tight shorts and runs up and down the street." The guy happened to be a marathon runner.

"What?"

"What?"

"Is he funny with his son?"

"What?"

There was something going around that the guy was inappropriate with his son, but I was so young it didn't make any sense to me. When my father got home and I told him about the call from the FBI, he became very agitated. But again, it wasn't clear to me why. We never discussed adult situations in my house.

I shared the upstairs bedroom with my two older brothers. Never a good sleeper, I used to stare at the ceiling when cars would go by and the light from the cars at night would dart across the ceiling. I used to pretend that they were movies. We lived close to a hospital, and sometimes an ambulance would go screaming by, and the movie would be in color.

Occasionally the Italians that lived down the street would add some drama. Late one night, I think his name was Tony, short for Giovanni, kicked his girlfriend's ass up and down the street. They were drunk, and Tony thought she was cheating on him. I watched from the window as they took turns slapping and kicking each other and pulling each other's long hair. Tony was winning, but only barely. It went on forever, it seemed. No one intervened, which was amazing because they were so loud about it; everyone must have realized that this epic battle was taking place.

A single black family lived around the corner from us, and someone painted "Niger" on the front of their lime green house. They must have used some seriously adhesive paint, because no matter how hard the family tried to get it off, the shadow of the misspelled word remained. I would walk by on my way to the corner store, Normanskill's, and try not to stare at it, but this was difficult. It was such an ugly thing to do to someone; I never heard anyone talking about it though. It would have been a good opportunity to discuss racism. Later in life I became sort of friends with a member of the family, named Marcus. He was one of the nicest guys I had ever met—just easy to talk to, and friendly. Years later he was charged with burglary. Apparently Marcus called a taxicab to pick him up at his house, and then he had the taxicab take him to a house around the corner to rob. He apparently had the cab wait outside while he went in and robbed the place. He came out of the house with a television and VCR, got in the cab, and went home. He was arrested within the hour. But he had a big heart, that guy. His heart was just bigger than his brain.

One day when I seven or so I was riding my bike up and down the sidewalk about a block away from home when this guy comes up to me. He was well dressed with khakis and a dress shirt. Neatly cut short blond hair. He was younger than my father, but older than my oldest brother.

"Hey kid," he waves me over, "Hey how ya doing?"

"Good."

"Good, good, what's your name?"

"My name is Andrew. I live over there." I pointed towards my house.

"Andrew, okay, Andrew." He smirked when he talked, and rolled a toothpick around in his mouth.

"Well Andrew, do you know Ronnie?" Ronnie was an older teenager that lived about 20 houses away. He had issues; a drug problem. I remember overhearing my father say that Ronnie's parents had tried everything to get him "cleaned-up." The word Heroin was associated with Ronnie. The thought of him, to my young mind, made me uneasy, nervous. He represented something sad, something bad.

"Yeah, I know Ronnie." I pointed in the direction of his house. "He lives across from the school."

"Well do you want to make a quarter Anthony?"

"It's Andrew. Yeah sure, how?"

"I want you to ride your bike up to his house and tell him something for me. Tell him Confidence is waiting at the corner."

"Confidence is waiting at the corner?"

"Yeah, that's right." He had serious eyes, blue and eerie, and he stared right into mine. He held out the quarter, and then pressed it into the palm of my hand with his thumb. His hands were ice cold.

"Thanks, kid."

"You're welcome, Confidence."

My heart raced as I pedaled my bike down our street, passing our house on the right, keeping my head down. I knew I was doing something wrong, but just wasn't sure what. Any family member, if they saw me, would suspect something was going on, or at least that's what I thought. I passed house after house. Princess, an enormous old arthritic German Shepherd, tried to attack me. She leapt off of her front porch with teeth bared, really catching me off guard. I was so focused on getting to Ronnie, I forgot that she would be lying in wait, as usual. Princess scared the living shit out of me. I screamed like a girl and swerved away at the last second, avoiding her gnashing teeth. The dog was vicious, and should have been put down long ago. Pumping my pedals extra hard now, Princess slowed her pursuit from fatigue and medical problems, and I got away. My heart was beating like crazy when I arrived at Ronnie's house. I looked back and demented Princess was still there staring at me, maybe 200 feet away. Why was this dog so bent on mauling me? I never did anything to that damn dog.

Ronnie's father answered the door in a wife-beater, or a Ginny-t is what they called them in the neighborhood. A smell of garlic and marinara sauce whooshed into my face. The man had enormous, hairy forearms. I couldn't help but stare. They were disgusting. The hairs looked like thick, black cables and they were sweaty. His belly was enormous. He looked troubled.

"Who sent you?"

"Confidence sent me. He's at the corner. For Ronnie."

"You tell that son of a bitch to leave my Ronnie alone or I'll call the cops!"

"Okay but will you give Ronnie the message?"

With that he slammed the door in my face. I stared at the door, and considered knocking again. The guy looked pretty upset. He must not like Confidence. Riding back I was sure to stay on the far side of the street from Princess. Usually, when I was paying attention, I could see Princess on her porch from a few houses away, and sometimes I would turn back and go all the way around the block just to avoid an attack. But now she wasn't there. Maybe she was inside. Maybe her owners realized that she had attacked me again.

Suddenly from the right, not the usual left, Princess attacked. She came bounding, crooked back legs, bent spine, angry as hell. She got the drop on me while I was looking the other way for her. The dog hated me. I screamed again. She had the element of surprise. She knew she had the advantage; my foot slipped and the pedal slammed my shin. I screamed again, praying the chain hadn't come off. If the chain came off I would be chewed to bits, torn to shreds. I regained my composure and the Lord was with me. The chain stayed attached. I kept pumping my legs, whimpering, while grunting like a bear. I was terrified and courageous at the same time. I was a mess, but that damn dog was not going to get me.

Confidence was no longer at the corner when I arrived. There was no sign of him. I felt disappointment that I hadn't completed the mission, but somewhat relieved too because there was a danger element to Confidence. I knew one thing for sure: Ronnie was in trouble. I enjoyed the adrenaline rush of being attacked by Princess and briefly employed by Confidence.

I used to walk down to the elementary school and lie down in the middle of the field and stare up at the clouds and blue sky. Why was I here? Why was my mom my mom, why was my dad my dad, what the hell was I doing lying in the middle of the field staring at a sky that was infinite in scope and distance. I was alone. My conclusion was that I was alone in this world. No matter the amount of good family feeling, and snuggles and cuddles with my mom, I was alone. I was a child, and I knew no matter what that I was alone.

Chapter 4

Mick's mom abandoned him so that she could follow bands around the country. Mick was left with his grandparents, who lived right between Princess's house and Tony's house. His grandmother was one of the sweetest people in the world, and she doted over Mick. The grandfather loved Mick but was irritable towards everyone else. Mick and I had a kinship. I was involved in all types of activities, like little league, and I had friends that lived in other areas of town. I would go to their homes for sleepovers or parties, or just to play for the day. Mick had only me, and he was a little different, and found it difficult to make friends I guess. Anyhow, I would come back from my games or friends' houses and Mick would be really happy to see me. He was a little down because he didn't fit in, and he knew that I had probably had a lot of fun. I would downplay it though, and say, "Well, it was o.k. I guess, but I'd rather be home here with my friends." Mick probably didn't believe me, but he knew I was protecting him from bad feelings, and I think he appreciated it.

One day I had come home to find that Benny, from down the street, and his half-retarded brother Eugene, had dragged Mick feet first through an enormous pile of dog shit. There was so much shit, apparently, that someone had commented that a cow had crapped, or maybe a circus was in town. I looked in the trash can at his pants and shirt that his grandmother had to throw out. The sheer volume of shit was unbelievable. It had to be a cow. Mick was lying on the couch in the parlor recovering from the trauma. I sat next to him and found out what had happened, how Benny and Eugene had basically lured him into a shit ambush, tackling him and each grabbing a leg and spending the next several minutes dragging him back and forth through the pile.

I knew that Benny and company would be playing in the woods behind the houses. I told Mick to get ready, and to follow me. Out we went to the edge of the woods, crouching down like Indians listening for the white man. Eventually we heard kids laughing and running and shouting in the woods. It was Benny. As soon as he came into focus, I told Mick to stay put. I took off in a full sprint towards Benny, weaving through branches, feet silent, still, stealthily crouched low like a linebacker going after an unsuspecting running back. I sprang at him, shoulder first and knocked his big ass to the ground. Benny was bigger and stronger than I was, but not angrier. Few kids I knew had my rage. His friends were shocked. I was so amped that tears were streaming down my face. Benny fell to his back, shocked and surprised, the wind knocked out of him. I kicked him up side his head, yelling through clenched teeth that this was for Mick.

"Don't you ever go near him again!"

"Leave him alone."

"That's my friend!"

Each command brought another kick to Benny's torso. All I heard was a voice saying, "Andrew! Please stop. That's enough." It was one of Benny's friends pleading with me to end the attack. His words snapped me out of my psychosis. I turned around and looked at his friends and said something unintelligible about revenge. They looked at me with amazement, fear, admiration, and like I was just plain nuts. I started to walk away, then turned back to Benny one more time, swung my leg back, and gave him a savage kick to his balls. This was because I *was* just plain nuts. Benny let out a shriek and grabbed his privates in pain. With that I walked through the woods back to where Mick was. He tried to hide his smile of pride and friendship and gratitude. His eyes were a little misty. He turned as I came up, and we walked back to his house in silence. His grandmother always had good food in the house, and since being dragged through shit the day before Mick hadn't been able to eat. But now we ate.

We talked about other things. *Star Wars* maybe? After lunch, I was getting ready to leave, almost to the side door, and I heard Mick quietly say, probably so his grandparents wouldn't hear, "Thanks, Andrew."

Little league was a huge amount of fun for me. I was pretty good. When I played with the neighborhood kids, I played with friends that were a year or two older than me. That's a huge age difference when you're young; they were more developed, faster, stronger, and had been playing a lot longer. So when I got to little league with kids my own age, I was a little better than many of them. Speed was my greatest strength. Oddly, during the first phone call with my mom from jail she reminded me how good I was at stealing bases.

When it was time to sign up for my second season, my father asked me if I was sure I wanted to do this. His words stopped me in my tracks. It seemed like a no-brainer. Why would he even ask me? Wasn't I pretty good? Wasn't it fun for him to come and watch me play? Wasn't he proud of me? Years went by before I figured out why he asked. It had nothing to do with me. It had to do with the other parents. My dad was smart. Little league parents were, generally, ignorant bullies. Coaches and parents would show up wearing wife-beaters stained with spaghetti sauce; the men reeked of booze. People screamed at the umpires, parents screamed at the coaches. My dad hated watching parents scream at their own children for missing a ball, a throw or a strike. He worked all week, and to show up to the little league circus on a Saturday was a sacrifice—I understand that now. And my dad, true to form, made the sacrifice; he never complained, other than the occasional eye roll. He was there for me, and only mingled with the other fathers and my coaches. He took his turn working the concession stand with the snow cones and fried dough, and took his turn treating our team after the game. He cheered me on when I did well. I can hear his south Bronx Irish accent now yelling from the stands, "Okay Andrew! That a boy!" Clear as day. Those words made me melt with pride as I reached second base on a double, or cleanly fielded a hard ground ball.

That year, I made the all-star team, but I wasn't getting the playing time I wanted and believed I deserved. The all-star team coach favored his kids from his regular season team. Someone screwed up the uniform order; they were all extra-large. We looked emaciated, dwarfed, under-sized. In a later inning, I'm standing out there in left field, staring up at the sky, angry I hadn't started the game and that I wasn't in my usual position, in center field. It was the fall classic, so it was a cool sunny day, with a blue sky and enormous cumulus clouds. I was pissed off.

Why didn't I start the game? This is embarrassing being put in the game in the fourth damn inning. This is humiliating. Look at this clown, he just walked another batter? Good Lord.

"Look alive out there McKenna!" the coach yells from the dugout.

Shut the hell up. You look alive fatass. Smoke another Camel why don't you? How about this coach: Look less dead!

"Get on your toes outfield, be ready!" Another command from our leader.

Get on my toes? What the hell is he talking about? Our pitcher can't throw a strike to save his life. Besides, you can't even see your toes with that enormous gut of yours coach. Look at yourself in the mirror for Pete's sake. You get on your toes! Just try without them breaking under your fat body.

Man that is one huge bird. I'm pretending to watch our pitcher walk in another run, by keeping my head level, but I'm really straining my eyes to look up at the sky. *Coach can't see me staring at the sky, because if he could he'd say something stupid like, Get your head out of the clouds McKenna! Man that is a huge bird, what is that an eagle or something? A hawk? Look at that thing soar in the air current. Beautiful bird. I love nature.*

"Keep your heads in the game boys!" He's staring right at me as he gives this "general command" to the whole team. He wants to say, "Quit staring at the fucking pigeon McKenna."

Keep my head in the game? Where the hell else would I keep it? In a box? In a freezer? On a dashboard? CRACK!! Our pitcher had finally found the strike zone. Dead center, and slow—the batter crushed the ball. The sound of aluminum on a faux leather little league ball echoes against the stands like a symphony, out to me in the outfield. I take my eyes off of the eagle and try to locate the ball. I am out of position, not on my toes, and my head was not in the game. With a horrible jump on the ball, I move to my right towards the left field foul line. I am sprinting now, arm fully extended, glove open. I am covering a lot of ground now, the white ball is screaming through the air, line drive fashion, arcs at the top of its flight path, and appears to pick up speed. Pumping my legs, every fiber of my body is going after this damned baseball, my body feels limp, like running in a dream.

The ball flew over my glove and rolled all the way to the fence. The bases were cleared except for the hitter who ended up on third base with a triple. People were screaming, not just cheering, although there was some of that too, but we were playing at our home field, and this last occurrence seemed to send the home team fans into a frenzy of anger and resentment. Big men were pointing fingers at each other, screaming at the coach. The coach yelled: Goddamn it McKenna! Women were arguing in the stands. Someone was pushed down the bleachers head first. It was absolute mayhem. The kids on the field started in on each other. The dugouts cleared, the crowd spilled over onto the field. I stood still. My hands on my hips, head sunk down, feigning contrition, while secretly hoping the father of the child that I replaced in left field in the fourth inning would kill the coach. I looked up and saw that my dad had left the bleachers for a safer spot along the fence, closer to the parking lot. He was looking right at me. I put up my hands as if to say, "God Dad, how did I miss that?" He did the same back to me, as if to say, "Hey, it happens. Don't worry."

On the ride home my dad was acting a little funny, fidgeting in his seat, like he wanted to say something. I initiated with, "I can't believe I missed that ball." My dad, not one to beat around the bush, said, "I hope it wasn't because you were angry. That would be a terrible thing to do to your teammates. I know you weren't happy about not starting, but that's no excuse not play your hardest. Always give it your best Andrew. We don't always get everything we want out of life. You could have made that catch."

I almost protested and said that I didn't throw the game or it had nothing to do with me being angry, but I realized that my dad had paid attention to what was happening with me. He knew! And for a guy that wasn't the most hands-on father in the world, at least when I was younger, that meant a lot to me. My dad knew me better than I could have ever imagined.

"You're right," I said.

"Next time," He said, not wanting me to wallow or feel too bad about it.

That was my dad.

Chapter 5

As I grew older, I became increasingly drawn to taking risks. At the same time, I was afraid of it because it was scary, dangerous. My thoughts about my existence and existence in general were almost constant now. My grades were decent, not great. I had trouble focusing my attention on tasks. Whenever I had an assignment it was like torture trying to stay attentive. I could physically feel the stress of not being able to focus: blood pressure rise, perspiration and nervous farts. I hid these feelings from everyone, and I became good at making the outer me look okay. I was always told that I was good looking, and some of my teachers paid a little extra attention to me. My parents instilled in all of us the importance of good manners, so that helped me get along, too. But inside something wasn't right. My thoughts weren't regular kid thoughts. I was active socially, but never comfortable. I couldn't wait to get away. I didn't mind being alone; it was easier. Charming the pretty girls was never a problem, because I always got them to talk about themselves. As insecure as we all were in middle school, to help someone feel confident and interesting, especially a girl, was something I could do, almost as second nature.

My first date was with Lizzy, who offered to help me with math. She couldn't believe how much I didn't know.

"How are you even passing?" she asked.

"I sit next to Jim O'Neil during tests."

Instead of math work, I had other plans for Lizzy on this particular Saturday afternoon. She lived around the corner from me. Her parents were together and her father looked like a freaking lumberjack, except he was clean-shaven and had a good haircut. I think he was an eye doctor, or maybe in sales. Anyhow, I show up to her house to pick her up. The plan is to take her to the high school park and kiss her and touch her boobs through her shirt. Instead of Lizzy answering the door, Paul Bunyon does.

"What?" he says.

"Oh," I say, "I was wondering if Lizzy was home."

"Who's asking?" He says, maintaining eye-contact with me with furrowed brow.

"Andrew … McKenna," and with that, I shot out my hand for a good firm handshake. Bunyon accepted, although he held the shake a little too long, and I tried to release mine a little too early, and it felt like he was trying to hold my hand or something sloppy. It was a terrible handshake ending. We both felt it. Her mother appears behind the big guy, and introduces herself with a big warm smile. Her mom was hot. Big smile back to her. Then the Irish Setters came to the door, and one smacked my balls with his snout. The dog was shameless, I mean really going in, like I had hamburger down there or something. I tried to pry its face away from my privates. But he would not relent. Lizzy's parents got a kick out of it. I was literally doing a dance to keep the dog away, almost jogging in place, moving my hips, short swatting, like shooing a fly. Lizzy shows up next and yells at her dog. The other Setter must have thought it was her turn, because she came right at me. I did the dance again, wanting, though, to punch the dog in the mouth. *Come on Bunyon, call off the hounds! This is madness.*

I kneed the dog in the throat. I couldn't take it anymore. At this point I was sweating and angry. Angry at Bunyon. Bunyon relented and almost apologetically said, "We think Lizzy is too young to go on a date." I could see what he was trying to do here. Play the age card. Time for action.

"Well, sir, the truth is that I don't have a lot of friends. I'm kind of shy, and I consider Lizzy one of my few friends. I don't think of this as a date. My parents say we're too young, too. Maybe it's just a couple of friends going to get ice cream, or going for a walk."

Mom was thinking, *what can we do to adopt this young man right now? He's perfect.* Bunyon looked at me like I was full of shit. He knew that I wanted to fondle his daughter's breasts, and he was either going to go against his wife and his daughter and his Irish Setters and send me on my way, or he was going to weigh the pros and cons, and take a chance on me. Bunyon hated to be the bad guy at home. I could tell. As Lizzy and I walked away, I turned and gave Bunyon a smile.

After the date, I was walking back home, and instead of feeling great because I had just kissed the prettiest girl in the school, I felt down. I felt like I didn't belong; almost a feeling of shame. It had nothing to do with the date. We had fun and laughed and kissed. But this morose mindset kicked in, as it often did. Why was I feeling this way? I was 12.

When I got my first real girlfriend a couple years later, my mom came home early from work and found clouds of marijuana smoke in the basement laundry area. As she peered through the cloud, she saw my girlfriend and me, both naked as jaybirds. My mom screamed, Tina screamed, and all I could say was, "Oh fuck." Tina threw her clothes on about as fast as I had taken them off her, and ran out of the house. My mom, white as a ghost, was ranting at us both, screeching and shouting and moralizing. Because I was a volatile young man, I stormed past her, threw front porch furniture into the street, and went after Tina, fuming and embarrassed and utterly stoned out of my mind. I had discovered pot not too long before. I smoked with some older kids in the woods at this big park nearby, and smoked practically every day thereafter until I was 17. Pot had a way of shutting down my brain.

My mom sat me down over Christmas break and confronted me with several salient facts.

"You've smoked enough pot since September to kill a horse."

"I don't think that's necessarily true mom."

"I can see it in your face, in your eyes."

"No mom, one of my eyes droops naturally. People tell me that all the time."

"I can smell it, Andrew."

"I can smell it, too, mom."

My girlfriend and I spent a lot of time together. I used to sneak into her house in the middle of the night and fornicate with her. Often times, I would be pretty buzzed and fall asleep. I would have to sneak out in the morning, after everyone else was awake. I would sneak—at times low crawling, or crab walking—around furniture and down hallways to avoid her three older sisters, all of whom were hot, and their mom, who wasn't bad either, and her step-father, who I had no interest in. I would sneak out, go to the front door and ring the doorbell and sit down with the family and eat bacon and eggs.

At night we would get together with our core group of maybe five friends, pool our resources and buy weed, beer, and sometimes acid. The night would almost always end in some type of violence. We were all a little jealous—well the guys were anyhow—and fights would break-out wherever we went because we all had hot girlfriends and they received a lot of attention. Our underdeveloped brains couldn't handle the stress. It was easier just to kick off some old fashioned violence by attacking another guy for saying hello. When we weren't fighting other guys, we were fighting each other or with our girlfriends. We were either fighting or fucking.

School was a distraction. I used to leave school early and party, or not go at all, or wait for the bell to ring and sit in my friend Harry's Fiat and smoke gram after gram of hashish. One time we smoked for four hours with the windows up in the winter. In a tiny Fiat mind you. We couldn't see each other the smoke was so thick. My ears were ringing I was so stoned. Harry couldn't feel his feet.

Chapter 6

My parents sat us down and told us they were getting a divorce.
"You're what?"
"We tried marriage counseling and…"
"You're what?"

I had no idea they were having any problems. When did they fight? Where the hell was I? Did they go into some secret sound proof room off the basement and beat the hell out of each other? Who cheated? This is madness. I was devastated. I left the house and stayed away for about three days. I looked at my brothers and sister as I left. They looked like wax figures that had been put into these melancholy poses. *What the fuck is wrong with these people.* No motion, just staring, heads cocked to the right or left, looking forlorn. They're getting divorced? I yelled at them. My dad's eyes were watery. My mother looked like a rubber doll. This was fucking madness. It felt like I had been punched in the stomach. Why were they together in the first place?

Eventually my siblings and I went to family counseling with my mother. The therapist was the wife of an insurance guy, who years later would get indicted for fraud. Her name was Mona and she was pretty put together. She would smoke fancy cigarettes during our counseling sessions, the whole time flashing a little leg at me. Mona intrigued me.

"I'll meet her halfway," I told Mona, "but she has to relax some of these rules." My mom realized that we were all smarter than Mona, and we intuitively knew how to play the counseling game. Mona sat there dragging on her cigarette.

"Go on," she said.

"Well, looking at basic freedoms for example, and feeling comfortable in my own space."

"Go on Andrew." Mona liked this kind of talk. Talk with feeling. She was riveted.

"I would like to be able to smoke cigarettes in the privacy of my own room."

"Absolutely not!" My mom's head was about to explode. I stayed calm. The idea of smoking in our house, with our family, was about the most absurd idea ever. Children in my family didn't get to do things like that. We were traditional. I had picked the hardest issue of all to start the session.

"Well, let's explore that," Mona said.

The next day we began our agreed upon trial period—I closed my bedroom door, put a towel under the door crack, and lit a cigarette. I smoked it down to the filter, exhaling naturally, not out the window, not sneaking it, not worried about being caught. I could hear my mother's footsteps down stairs getting louder and angrier. She knew exactly what I was doing and it must have taken all of her energy and concentration not to lose her shit. When I was done I left my room and walked into the hallway to check the air quality. I was surprised to find that the entire second floor of the house reeked of smoke. Later that night, I smoked a little joint of killer weed, and had a cigarette going at the same time to mask the weed smell. It didn't work. The entire house smelled like an old head shop from the 60s. I had pushed the envelope too far. The trial period ended immediately that night. My mom had exercised her executive authority.

Next session, Mona wanted to know what made me think that it was okay to smoke pot, when we had only agreed on cigarettes, not illegal substances.

"I don't know."

My reaction to the divorce, and my tormented, overactive thought process, resulted in my decision not to attend school and just run wild. I changed my set of friends—from good kids mainly, who listened to their parents, went to school, did well and played sports—to kids that lived on the edge: police involvement, group homes, no curfews, risky behaviors, and with them I found a mentality that wasn't conformist. My frequent temper tantrums, and anger, and wildness did not seem out of the ordinary with these folks. It was just accepted. I could stop thinking just by smoking weed, or drinking, or dropping acid, or whatever else came along. I could stop thinking by robbing houses of televisions and stereos with my friends. Everything was a potential diversion from my thoughts, and I explored them all.

I failed a class in 10th grade—I think it was science, and I had to attend summer school. No one in my family ever failed a class before—so once again, I was breaking new ground. My father, who I now lived with, offered me a deal. Pass summer school, and he would send me out to Los Angeles to see my aunt for a week. This caught my attention, and science became my focus for the next few weeks.

The flight out to California was my first time on a plane. I had some cash in my pocket, and some hash in my sock, and I was ready to tear-up some California girls. I had broken up with my girlfriend a couple months earlier. She caught me cheating on her with a girl from Brooklyn. I couldn't resist the accent. But within three days of the break-up, she went on birth control and her breasts had tripled in size—sweet revenge. I was devastated. So I was rebounding from a bad break-up and ready to get back in the saddle.

I sat next to a business man. Nice suit, nice shiny Rolex, well-spoken and drunk on scotch. I was assertive for my age, with a good build. And I looked into the flight attendant's eyes with dominance. "I'll take a scotch too." We really hit it off. He bummed a cigarette from me and we smoked and drank at 35,000 feet. He told me about his wife and kids, and his girlfriends, and showed me pictures of his boat. I decided that hashish was in order. I went into the lavatory, broke off a little chunk of blond hash, and stuffed it into the end of a Marlboro. I walked back to my seat, sat down next to my new friend and lit the hash cigarette. I passed it to my friend who took a healthy pull, and started into a laughing, coughing fit. We both started laughing uncontrollably. At this altitude, the hash was stronger, as was the scotch, and I was wasted within minutes. Other passengers were turning around and staring at us in amazement. The entire cabin smelled of hash, a sweet pungent odor. A stewardess made a bee-line for us, with a look of disbelief.

"You need to put that out," she said sternly.

"The cigarette?" I asked. My partner was laughing and coughing.

"Put it out. This is a federal offense. Put it out this instant."

My aunt and cousin—really wholesome people—knew that I was a bit off kilter. I'm sure they had a contingency plan with my dad, in case something got tricky. I really wanted to just stay out of trouble, respect my aunt, and enjoy the West Coast. I wanted to get laid.

My cousin and his friend brought me skeet shooting. It was awesome. For three hours I fired a 12-guage at clay plates flying through the air. It was just like throwing a football to a sprinting receiver—all I had to do was lead them a little. I got the hang of it immediately, and I was as good as my cousin and his friend, or even better, and they had been shooting skeet for years. It was a great time.

I decided the second night in Norwalk, because I was already out of hash, that I should find a watering hole to set-up shop and get involved. Mingle among the people.

"I'm in town for a skeet shooting competition, I'm a National Champion." I lowered my voice a bit in case the real National Champion was sitting in this particular bar.

"Wow," said the slightly worn, bottle-blond with piercing blue eyes.

Bingo.

"Aren't you kinda young for that, son?" says the drunk Burt Reynolds clone, perhaps the blonde's keeper. He's clearly trying to undermine me.

"I'm here in LA to defend my title," I say, ignoring Burt Reynolds.

"Hmm." Burt moans dismissively. He doesn't know who he's fucking with.

"Does food get caught in your mustache?" I ask, sounding sincere and concerned.

"No," he says, clearly uptight.

"Because I used to have a gerbil and sometimes food would get caught in its fur," I say, staring intently at his bushy mustache. "It was really fucked up when that would happen." The girl laughs at this.

"Want to smoke a joint?" Blondie asks me.

"Sure," I say, still staring at Burt Reynolds' mustache. He's fuming. We travel through what seems like a dirty labyrinth of back rooms, finally arriving in an alley behind the bar. It was something of a scene out there. Like a set from a Tennessee Williams play. The light seemed filtered.

"I'm divorced," she says, firing-up an enormously fat joint of stank weed. "Well actually, I'm trying to get an emullient."

"A what?" I asked, perplexed.

"An emullient, you know, where the church says the marriage was unvalid," she clarifies.

"Oh right, the Pope, the Holy See, does it," I say, thinking that it isn't even fair how easy it's going to be to get laid.

"So, do you think the emullient will go through?" I ask.

"I would hope so," holding in the smoke, "I caught my man humpin' his own brother."

"Jesus!" I say, shocked and disturbed, coughing out a cloud. The sheer freak-show factor here was too good to be true.

"Jesus had nothing to do with it. That motherfucker went sick with it!" she says.

"Gosh! I guess so." I sympathized with her. "That's just horrible."

The whole time Burt is just standing there bogarting the joint, taking enormous drags and letting out massive clouds of smoke, admiring them as he exhales.

"The worst part is when I walked in on that motherfucker, he just kept going, just kept humpin' away on his brother while looking at me."

"Jesus! Did his brother look at you, too?" I asked, just completely stoned and intrigued. The question just hung in the air. I don't know why I asked it.

"Now how could he?" she asks, "He was blindfolded."

"Good God!" I say with a shudder. The scene was deviant and perfect.

"Bubby, you smoked that whole motherfucker yourself? That's glutononymous behavior!" Blondie says.

"Glutononymous," I mumbled to myself. In the light of the alley she looks like a dead person, maybe in part because I was so high. I felt like I was in a play or something. They don't get weed this good on the East Coast, I thought to myself. Bobby kept shifting from one foot to the other, each time he looked like he might topple over.

"Just take the motherfucker off," she says to Bobby. "It ain't no good." I looked at him trying to figure out what it could be that he should take off. Is it the gerbil mustache? The filthy Dodger's cap?

"Bubby only has one point five legs," she says with a smirk. "He wears a prostosis."

"A prostosis?" I ask.

"A false leg," she explains.

Bobby pulls up his pant leg to show me. I was beginning to wonder if the weed was laced with hallucinogens. The whole scene was, well ... the living dead, the brother humping, the prostosis. I started to feel nauseous. It looked like he must have gotten the prostosis from a yard sale. It was old and wooden, and had crusty leather straps that just dangled there.

"The buckle broke," Bobby says with a grin. The angle of the light hits his face; he now appears to be the product of incest, and he, too, looks dead. Bobby only had a few teeth.

"The buckle broke a year ago! The motherfucker is too lazy to get a new leg," Blondie says as she draws one last drag out of the roach and holds it in. She starts to pass me an ember.

"No, no," I say, dizzy now, wondering if they drugged me. "I need something to drink, it would be best if I could have something to drink."

"Pretty boy has cotton mouth," Blondie says. The pot was so goddamn strong … I was so utterly stoned, I just stared at her. We enter the back door through the kitchen, which is merely a deep fryer and a slop sink. A bucket of something sits on the floor next to the deep fryer. A live cat sits off to my right on its haunches. It stares back at me and meows. I keep it moving.

Bobby stops to talk to the cat.

"Come on motherfucker, I'm thirsty." Blondie is thirsty and what I earlier detected as an Oklahoma accent has gotten steadily stronger. *What's with "motherfucker" all the time?*

"Just wanted to say hello to Pussy," Bobby explains. The cat's name is Pussy and because I've just smoked nuclear treated pot, this makes me crack-up; finally something to break me out of the creepy mental head case zone.

"Oh, Bubby don't like no pussy!" Blondie says with a shrieking laugh. Bobby looks at me, cocks his head to the side, and smiles.

What the fuck was that look for? The creepy fearful feeling came back instantly. I feel like I need to be in a public area all of a sudden. Call it a sixth sense, but a vision of me strapped to the deep fryer with a ball-gag secured in my mouth just passed through my chemically affected mind.

"I saw that Bubby!" Blondie says angrily.

"Saw what?" I ask. Internal alarms on high. "Look, let's just get something to drink." Bobby gives Blondie a dirty look as if she exposed him.

The bartender, who only has a right eye, puts a pitcher of beer in front of us, and for just an instant gives me the once over—probably because I'm 16 and look 17.

"He's with me," Blondie says, "and we need some shots." Tequila, especially without salt or lime, scares me. A huge possibility exists that it'll come back up as fast as I get it down. The lime and salt seem to constrict my throat after the booze goes down, and keeps it down. Without these accessories, tequila is rough. I see my reflection in the mirror behind the bar and for a second it didn't look like me. I looked dead. Just like my new friends. Dead. Blondie puts her hand on my leg and starts to move it toward my penis, which interests me and I can't figure out why because she looks dead, but my penis hasn't figured this out yet.

"How's that cowboy?" she asks sexily.

"That's good, cowgirl?" I answer, which sounds so fucking stupid but I've never been so stoned and frankly I've always wanted to be a cowboy since I was a kid. One Christmas my parents bought me a hat, chaps, and toy twin six shooters with holsters. I wished I had those at that moment because I would have donned them.

"I'm unzipping your pants," Blondie informs with a giggle, and sure enough she is.

"Yes you are." She slowly, discreetly unzips my pants. I'm trying to act inconspicuous and trying not to look at the reflections of dead people in the mirror. Her hand is ice cold, like a dead person's hand would have to be.

"Jesus! What's wrong with your hand?" I say as my penis recoils.

"Bad circlamation," she explains.

"Bad circlamation, indeed," I agree.

I lean over to kiss the dead girl. People are watching us, two dead people, kiss. Her frozen hand is on my penis which barely wants to cooperate now. My tongue hits a huge gap in her mouth which, I assume, once housed at least two teeth. I open my eyes, still locked in a tongue punching match, and she stares back at me. It's something out of a fucking horror film. I had hit my breaking point for darkness and death. I jumped off the barstool and literally ran for the door. Blondie laughed a maniacal laugh. Bobby just smiled at me and yelled, "Will I see you again?"

"Fuck you Bubby!"

Chapter 7

I had already run out of weed and I still had almost four days left in California with my aunt and cousin. One guy, an old grave-digger dude, was probably my only hope of getting more. I met him at the same bar as Bubby and Blondie. I decided to call him up and ask if he could get me anything. I think his name was Tex, or Rex, or Dex.

"Not on the phone! Meet me at the basketball courts in ten minutes." And he hangs up. He pulls up in his gold Pontiac Firebird, with some Steely Dan playing, some Mexican Indian turquoise necklace swaying from the rear view mirror. His mirror aviator glasses looked ridiculous but he thought he was cool, and I think he wanted to have sex with me. In fact, I'm pretty certain.

"So what are we talking about here?" he says, reeking of Stetson cologne.

"What's that Goddamned smell?" I ask, overpowered with disgust, as I stare at my reflection in his eyewear.

"What can you get?"

"Everything—weed, coke, H, microdot—you name it, I can get it."

"Weed is a must, I can't afford coke, and micro-dot ... hmm, tripping balls in my aunt's house probably isn't a good idea ... what was the other one?"

"H"

"H?"

"Horse."

"You can get a horse?"

"Heroin!"

"Whoa, what? No. What's that like?" My 16-year-old brain was intrigued. I thought of Confidence at the corner.

"Never mind."

"Why?"

"Because if you've never done it, you don't need to, shouldn't, and won't ever get it from me. Not on my watch." This guy was serious. His whole demeanor changed. It really got my attention. Whatever he was thinking about was having a physical effect on him. He became more animated, less cool, more fidgety, more loopy.

"Sounds serious dude," I said as I watched his bizarre hand movements.

"Way fucking serious dude." I stared at him, wanting him to elaborate. Finally he relented.

"Here's the deal. All of the other stuff is in one category, right? The pot, the cocaine, acid, drinking—all of that stuff you can do as much you want, but H is different—it will change you. You will never be the same. It's different from all of the other stuff. You must never touch it, or you will die. That's all I'm going to say. You will die."

I thought he was being a bit too dramatic. I ended up with some incredible buds, bright leafy green, almost Christmas tree green, with interesting yellow and purple hairs. He said it was real Purple Indica from some exotic land. We rolled a joint, lit it and smoked it. The whole thing, right down to our finger tips. Toke after toke, just passing it back and forth. I lost my hearing for a moment and, at times, it appeared that the joint was getting bigger instead of smaller.

"Dude, where are we?" I was so stoned just sitting there staring at the half-moons of dirt on his windshield. The evening sun was down low, shining in at me. Through my half opened eyes I watched the sun sink lower. Resting my head back I took a deep, deep breath and just enjoyed it.

My body was detached from my head. Gonzo.

Returning to New York represented returning to reality. The same problems existed: divorce, truancy, ex-girlfriend with newly developed breasts who had found a new boyfriend. My friend Harry had just gone through a similar break-up with his girl, so we would pool our money, get a bottle of Southern Comfort, sit in two broken down Salvation Army recliners, and watch reruns of Johnny Carson, MASH and Columbo all night long. I would stay away from my house for days, not wanting to deal with my family. When I would go home—because Harry and I were getting on each others' nerves—I would end up just staring at family members without their knowing as they performed regular tasks: mom emptying the dishwasher, Brian combing his hair in the mirror, Carol talking on the phone. I would stare at them and wonder what they thought about everything that was happening in our lives, in my life. That sucked, so I spent my days and nights with Harry.

Harry and I would eventually get the munchies and drive his Fiat to the local Price Chopper and steal food. The store was barely manned at that late hour and the way we looked—long hair, leather jackets, big ass steel toe boots—no one paid any attention as we loaded up on Ritz crackers and cream cheese. One time Harry literally reached over the back of the night manager, who was loading up the shelf with cartons of cigarettes, and said, "Excuse me," as he grabbed a carton of Old Golds. We would walk out of the store with armfuls of free stuff. I imagine the store employees just thought it was easier to ignore us than confront us.

Andrew McKenna

We were burnt and wild and severely on the fringes of our respective realities. Mine was that my family was falling apart, his was that his mother was progressively losing her mind, and we just didn't care to follow rules and regulations.

Harry was an enormously strong individual for a high school kid. He was the brawn of the operation, and all the weed dealers in school knew this. When they saw us coming, they became visibly uncomfortable.

"Front me a bag, I'll get you on Friday," Harry would say.

"Andrew, come on dude, say something to him."

"Hey chief, I would interject, Harry's good for it. Don't insult the guy."

"I know, but I barely have any left, and what I have is my profit." The guy was pleading.

"Well then, just break him off a couple joints, and I'll see that you get paid on Friday."

In many cases, I would see that the guy got paid. Other times, things just didn't work out.

All Harry knew about his father was that he lived in California and had a 4 handicap. Friendships meant everything to Harry. He was fiercely loyal, and understood that I was going through it, just as he was. We could sit in a room together, and without talking, know what the other guy was thinking. He was one of my closest friends ever.

"I have an announcement to make," his mom said one day at 1 a.m. Her hands were red as hell because she had been vigorously rubbing them for weeks.

"Aw, come on ma, not more announcements!" Harry could not handle the announcements. I on the other hand thought that they were interesting, and could tell that the poor woman, losing her mind, needed to talk. I was just about to recommend Mona, when she said:

"I'm going to start painting again. Jelly beans, lots and lots of jelly beans."

"Oh fuck, not the jelly beans again ma! Come on, give it a rest."

His mom ignored this, and proceeded to name probably 25 colors—artist colors—that she would use to paint a variety of jelly beans. Harry handed me the bottle and I took a major pull.

"That sounds awesome, Ms. G. I'd really like to see them when you're done."

"You won't because she burns them after she paints them so no one sees them," Harry explained. With that, Ms. G, frustrated and embarrassed by Harry's comments, stated that she was going for a walk. Harry yelled, "Have fun ma!" and just shook his head.

The walk, which normally started in the middle of the night, would sometimes last three or four days, and end with a psychiatric stay, or at the very least, an emergency room visit.

My dad was a dean at a college around this time, so he would often get home later in the evenings because of meetings and administration stuff. We often, instead of cooking dinner—and my dad was an excellent cook—would go to a great restaurant called the Lobster Pound. It was perfect for me because after a day of baking, I would get vicious munchies, and who can beat surf and turf for the munchies. The waitresses were pretty smoking hot, too, with biggish breasts and I would watch them flirt with my dad, a good looking guy. He would sip Chivas or Old Grouse, and I would always notice that things were a little nicer after he had his first. A little less official, but also a little less predictable, which could be dangerous ground with my dad. My dad had largely hung in there with me, even though he knew I was a little nuts, but every now and then we would have come-to-Jesus talks about my conduct.

"So, you never told me what the fight was about," my dad says.

I had recently finished a three-day suspension for fighting in school—well it was after school, but the conflict started right after lunch. The bell had rung and everyone was walking to their classes. I was walking with this girl that I was trying to bone. I'm pretty sure she had smoked a joint for lunch. Anyhow, I go to hold the door for her into the school, and this heavy-set weird dude was coming out as we were going in. He placed his hand on the door, and at our eye-level. He was being polite, except he was staring at her body. At the same time, we both noticed on his thumb, a dry caked, smear of mustard.

"You got a little mustard there chief?" Well the girl thought that was the funniest thing she had ever heard. She broke into loud, roaring and rolling laughter. It was truly infectious. Students around us started laughing, too. The poor guy was mortified. His ears turned beet red.

"That's pretty funny douche bag."

"Who the fuck are you calling douche bag?"

"Behind the bleachers after school. Your ass is mine McKenna."

All afternoon, kids were running up to me, asking if I was really going to fight Bruce.

"Who's Bruce?" I would ask.

"The kid with the mustard on his thumb. He's livid, says he wants to kill you."

"Kill me? That's a little extreme."

"No, he's fucking pissed, for real."

"Good Lord."

I didn't want to fight this big bastard. I had plans to be with this new girl after school. My rebound.

"I'll just come to the fight, and then we can hang-out after," was her solution to our scheduling conflict. Now I *had* to fight this big angry bastard, in front of my rebound, and hope that he didn't kick my ass all over town.

"He's really pissed. He says he wants to kill you," she added. "See you at the big fight." And she gave me a quick peck on the cheek. Sweet girl.

This is just fucking great.

There were a good 25 people attending the match. I got there last, hoping it would thin-out a bit, maybe my rebound would decide to hook-up with someone else and leave the scene.

"There he is!" shouted my rebound. Very alert girl.

I walked up, somewhat indifferent, somewhat confident, somewhat calm. The big bastard was about eight feet away, seething, blowing snot and spittle from his nose and mouth. His ears, once again, were beet red. He was amped. With that, he suddenly charged at me, covering eight feet in two huge bounds. As his foot hit the ground following the second bound, he slipped and fell, tearing the t-shirt from my torso, as he unsuccessfully tried to maintain his footing. He ended up on all fours with a thud, his head basically knee-high. A fatal mistake for big angry Bruce. Not one to pass up an opportunity, I immediately hauled back and kneed him in his face. My calm turned to rage in a millisecond. It was almost like a switch had flipped in my brain. I couldn't hear a thing, except for the kinds of sounds one hears when they are submerged in water. My vision narrowed to a small point on the back of his head, as I delivered blow after blow to the sides of his head and ears. He collapsed onto his stomach and tried to cover his head as I continued to blast away. Finally one of his friends pushes me off of him and gets between us. "Enough," he keeps saying. "Enough Andrew!" "Enough!"

People were silent and just staring. I had gone completely savage on this kid, releasing my anger, my angst, and my frustration.

The assistant principal, Mr. Incitti, hauled me away, shirtless, swearing like a madman, pumped beyond belief. He held tightly to my arm, and the look on his face was of pure concern. Not anger, not disappointment. He knew what was going on in my life, skipping school, smoking pot, getting into trouble, but he also knew I was a smart kid from a "good family" and that this shouldn't be happening. Mr. Incitti and I really got along well. He cared about his students and wasn't on a power trip. We would always greet each other in the hallways. Now he had to apprehend me, and he knew I wasn't right. He looked at my hands which were red and busted up and swollen from beating Bruce's head in.

"This is not good Andrew."

"Mr. Incitti said that you kept hitting the kid, even though he was down," my dad said to me. "Is that true?"

"Yeah, it's true," I said, not looking up from my plate. I felt ashamed; blood rushed to my face.

My dad was on his second, and starting to get his emotional sea legs. My hat was totally off to him. Going through a break-up of his 23-year marriage, after trying marriage counseling with a therapist, who by most accounts, simultaneously channeled Gloria Steinem and Sylvia Plath, maintaining his post at the college, and dealing with my stuff, was much more than I would be able to handle, even as a grown man.

"So, what gives?" He asks.

"Smoking pot helps me unwind."

"What, you mean after your busy day?" My dad says sarcastically, but gently too, with a smile as he sips.

This is somewhat of a dangerous time to navigate a conversation like this with my dad. He was hard to read; Irish to the core. *I can't let this conversation turn too serious. I must keep it light. He doesn't need anything heavy right now. He needs to relax and unwind. I've caused enough trouble.*

"You just have to graduate Andrew. That's all. You're bright. You can turn this around. What choice do we have here?" This last part was rhetorical. Rhetorical signaled safety to me. We were winding this down.

"You are capable of doing anything you want in life."

Chapter 8

My old girlfriend and I got back together for a time. One weekend, about 15 of us decided to head north into the Adirondacks to someone's camp. They were throwing a huge party. Everyone decided to drop acid before we left, convoy-style. Our thinking was that by the time we reached our destination, we would be good and fucked-up. Midway through the travel, a bunch of cars stopped at a country gas station to get beer and other provisions. We all got out and many of us ended up jumping into other vehicles, a sort of acid-induced, frenzied musical vehicles. When we took off again, the car I was in with about six other teenagers, was behind a guy named Paulie, who drove a two-seater Toyota truck. Francis, driving a motorcycle, came up from the rear of the convoy and passed each car one by one. He ended up between my car and Paulie's truck. Francis was a pretty safe rider on his incredibly powerful, incredibly explosive crotch-rocket. He started to gun it and crossed the center-line on the left, to pass Paulie. Just as he did, Paulie suddenly jerked his truck into a u-turn. He thought he had accidentally left Wyatt behind at the gas station, and he was going back to retrieve him. But Wyatt was in our car. Francis, just as quickly as he gunned the power on his bike and went to pass Paulie, smashed into the side of Paulie's truck and flew in the air like he had been shot out of a cannon. I saw it happen right before my eyes, and I had to blink and blink, because I didn't believe it. People in the car with me were screaming bloody murder.

The next thing I remember is Wyatt, Norma Jean and I, crouched over Francis's limp body. Others were milling around, holding each other in disbelief. Francis's helmet had turned around halfway on his head, so his ear was visible through the visor now. He was moaning, but his body was broken and unmoving. Wyatt, a natural leader, was telling Francis that he was going to be alright, that he was going to be ok. Norma Jean was really upset, and in shock. I was tripping, so my stupid drugged brain couldn't grasp it. If there was anything to be done, and there really wasn't, I would have been useless. The sun had just gone down, and the sky, a gray orange mess, gave off an eerie light. Francis lay at the bottom of a hill on a country road, mangled close to death, with a bunch of friends around him. Suddenly a car crested the top of the hill, and came roaring down the hill towards Francis. The car was flying. Wyatt and Norma Jean jumped in front of Francis, waving their hands at the car, trying to let the driver know to stop because our good friend was lying in the road barely alive. Wyatt and Norma Jean jumped out of the way just in time and rolled onto the shoulder. I stood watching the entire event unfold. It was like my feet were nailed to the ground. As I looked away from Wyatt and Norma Jean and back to Francis, I watched the car's tire roll over Francis's helmet, and heard a crunching sound. Then his body disappeared under the car and was taken out of my field of vision. When I turned my head to the right, his body reappeared in my focus, only to see Francis's body get rejected by the undercarriage, coughed up, and spit out onto the shoulder. I'm standing over Francis again. The car came to a screeching halt 50 feet away. A man gets out and yells, "Should I stay?" And Wyatt answers, "Yeah! You just ran over our friend!" The guy got in his car and sped away.

We're in the waiting room of a rural hospital. I was standing around with about eight other people, and by now the LSD had fully taken effect. It was not good. I stared at a plant in the corner that was moving, swaying. I turned and saw Francis's mom running into the emergency room, frantic, in crisis. Someone, Mark maybe, asked me what Francis's mom was doing at the party. I just stared down and said that I didn't know what his mom was doing at the party. Someone else, maybe Vince, said, "It's Francis. We're here because Francis is dead."

Francis was brain-dead and he wasn't coming back despite years of expert medical care in Boston and despite a family, despite a mother, that wouldn't give up.

That was the last time I took LSD.

I stole my father's car in the middle of the night and crashed it into the Hospice of Schenectady. I was speeding on a wet road, when the car veered out of control, up an embankment, and into the foundation of Hospice. No one was wearing seatbelts and we all emerged disoriented and concussed. My friends and I took off running into an enormous wooded cemetery. Running through the pitch black cemetery added to our pain. Falling down over and over, face-planting down hills, bashing groins into headstones, scared out of our asses, and convinced that trained trackers, with dogs, were on our tails.

I lay low for a few days, while everyone tried to get in touch with me. I had gone into seclusion. When I emerged everyone was relieved that I was alright, but I was suspect number one, and I had to do some creative lying. I told my father that I had nothing to do with the car theft, that I was out of town when it happened; a wholly unbelievable concept. Five days later, under intense pressure and scrutiny I confessed that it was I who had snuck into the apartment and taken the keys. My dad punched me in the face.

"Maybe you should join the Air Force. Ralph did and he's doing great."

My brother Brian, an incredibly smart and talented guy, and one of my few best friends, knew that I had to get out of town. I needed to change my surroundings, get a fresh start. His best friend had gone into the Air Force, another very smart kid like my brother whom I respected, and he was doing things that kids in Schenectady never get to do. But I couldn't see myself doing it. It seemed too huge or something so I made a joke out of it.

"Would they teach me to be an assassin? I always thought that would be cool, but I could never figure out how you get customers. You can't advertise in the Gazette."

Brian allowed me to finish, and then quietly said, "If you ever want to have a serious conversation about it I'm here. Ralph really likes it." The worry in his voice, but even more than worry, almost despair, that I could hear was becoming more and more common when I spoke with people close to me.

The walls are closing in on me. My world doesn't make sense. They're looking at me like I'm different. Like I'm fucked up. I don't belong here. Why does my head feel like it's about to explode? Why does my chest feel so tight all of the time? Why do I feel so lost?

"I want to join up, ship out, you know, get the hell out of here." The recruiter looked at my long hair and red eyes with suspicion.

"McKeena."

"No sir, no sir, it's McKenna. One e, two n's, sir." I called him sir, and I sat up straight in my seat, at the position of attention. This was official business. He had a Hitler mustache, because in the military the edges of the mustache cannot, by regulation, extend past the corners of the mouth. The man had an unusually small mouth, so his mustache— well, you get the picture. He was the spitting image of Adolf Hitler.

"It says here, that you've had truancy problems, run-ins with the police, and you admit here to "recreational" drug use. You wrote the word "recreational" on your application."

"That's true," I said.

"Do you want to explain any of these issues? Defend yourself? Your actions?"

"Well I could, but what's the point? To convince you to take me as an enlisted man into the Air Force?" Hitler stared at me as if I had insulted his institution, his occupational specialty, his sense of integrity. Frustrated, all he could come up with was, "You're going to have to cut your hair McKeena."

"Yes, sir."

So I arrived at Lackland Air Force Base in Texas. I left behind my girlfriend, who was starting college in the fall, my family, my friends, and Schenectady. It was a proud moment. I was alone, but I was always "alone" anyhow, and I was turning the page. No pot or other stuff. Just me and the bright blue yonder.

The drill instructor picked a guy named Dickson to be our flight leader. He initially picked a big intimidating black dude named Jackson to lead us, presumably thinking we would be afraid of big Jackson, and fall into line. The drill sergeant wanted us in line, no matter what. It was all about staying in line or standing on a line, or not crossing the line. Problem was that Jackson wasn't very bright, and he quickly became overwhelmed by the responsibility of leading airmen. Jackson had a nervous breakdown, started violently swinging at people one evening when he was unusually stressed out. Jackson was taken away, crying his eyes out, and we never heard from him again.

I believe the drill sergeant picked Dickson, a crazy white dude from Tennessee, because Dickson had the biggest penis out of everyone. Dickson's trunk hung clear to his knee. The drill sergeant felt this would instill fear and respect, the two critical attributes of any leadership relationship. The power went to Dickson's head. He became distant, paranoid, and controlling. He had his southern-type boys, his "lieutenants," who would encourage people to rat on each other, to finger people who might try to undermine Dickson's authority. They ran the place like the Gestapo. At night, after lights-out, Dickson and his boys would walk up and down the squad bay calling people out on their infractions or demerits for the day. They'd stop at the offending airman's bunk, with clip board in hand.

"Smith, John R., got a chit for dirty boots today. Made us look bad in front of staff."

Dickson would then ceremoniously pull out his enormous penis, well over a foot long, and slap it against Smith's forehead. The thwacking sound could be heard throughout the squad-bay. Depending on the severity of the infraction, there could be several whacks from Dickson's penis. Typically, this would go on for an hour. Up and down the squad bay, Dickson would beat a select few with his penis.

One night the drill instructor had come through, probably around 2 or 3 in the morning. He kicked my bunk.

"McKeena! McKeena! Why are these fucking socks hanging over your fucking bed and not on your fucking feet! What are you a fucking Puerto Rican or something?"

The man had obviously been drinking. "Puerto Rican, sir? No, no I just can't sleep in wool socks in 100 degree heat." *Puerto Ricans don't sleep with socks on? This is weird.*

79

"Well put your fucking socks on, and quit being Puerto Rican!" *Good Lord. He must hate Puerto Ricans.* The next morning he came in and yelled at us for three hours. He was hung-over and miserable.

"And that fucking Puerto Rican McKeena! Hanging his socks over his bed! Things are going to change around here God damn it! Brooks sleeps naked! Did you all know that? Fucking Brooks!" *Why isn't he calling Brooks a Puerto Rican?* "You people are just fucking terrible, just fucking terrible! If I could beat the shit out of you I would. I'd crack your fucking heads with a baseball bat. I'd saw off your fucking limbs! You make me fucking sick!" With that he walked out. My body was aching from standing still for three hours and being yelled at by an insane person. Man he really hated us. I looked over and Dickson was staring at me, fuming.

"Motherfucker, bring it. Bring it Dickson! I'll tear that shit right from your fucking body you fucking queer!" The place went silent. I was irate. Zero to sixty anger, a real problem for me.

"Whoa, take it easy McKeena, I didn't say anything."

"I would love to castrate your fucking redneck ass. Nothing but a little bitch!" And then I pointed my finger around the room at the others and I yelled, "I'm not a fucking Puerto Rican! I just can't wear socks when I sleep! I'm fucking Irish!" Everyone was extremely confused. It just wasn't a good day for the platoon. As I stormed out of the room, I heard someone ask, "What's wrong with McKeena?"

Later, Dickson came up to me. "Look McKeena, I don't want any trouble with you. You and me have always gotten along."

"Dude, just keep that fucking thing away from me and we won't have any problems."

My head was starting to clear quite a bit without the marijuana and other stuff. My performance was solid, but I was still depressed. I couldn't figure out why. I had learned that after boot camp I'd be sent to Hurlburt Field, Florida, for training. I was going to be a Forward Air

Controller. Infantry. Bombs on Target. Death from Above. Napalm sticks to kids.

It was Spring Break time in Florida—Pensacola, southern girls. I went on an absolute tear. I was having sex with a girl from Alabama in a hotel elevator, covered in sand, suntan lotion, sweat and I had a belly full of Mad Dog 20/20. The doors opened on the 10th floor and we were just going to town. A family was on their way to the beach: cooler, chairs, floaties. I yelled for them to close the door! "Dude it's an elevator. Kids, look away."

"Please, please close the door!" I implored, quickly covering our bodies with a beach towel.

"Come on, let's take the stairs. This is crazy." How did I expect *them* to close the elevator door? Raving lunatic.

One morning I woke up in a hotel room. I threw back the covers in a panic, disoriented, not knowing how I'd gotten there. Everything about the night before was a blur. The girl next to me had this beautiful leg showing, muscular, tanned, shapely, very strong calf muscle. At the top of this leg was a beautiful ass. I pulled the covers back a little more. Next to her leg was nothing. She only had one leg. I looked around the room for crutches or a wheel-chair, or a leg. Nothing. She was passed out cold. My head was killing me. I stared at the ceiling debating the merits. Oh what the hell.

Training consisted of running around the woods in Florida, lots of push-ups, lots of yelling back and forth like kids playing cowboys and Indians, and confusing classes where we would simulate talking to pilots who weren't really flying overhead, and who weren't really dropping bombs where we told them to. We just pretended that was happening. The guy on the other end of the radio wasn't a pilot; it was Bob, one of our instructors. In class we had to call him Sgt. Smith, but at the bars downtown, we could call him Bob. Bob always wanted to be a fighter pilot, but he was too stupid. So they let Bob play the pilot on the radio with the trainees, and we had to pretend to take Bob seriously even as he made fighter plane noises as he was "banking in" on the target that only existed in our imaginations. It was sheer insanity, but because of budget cuts to defense spending, we had to listen to Bob "hit the after-burners" when the mission was done.

"Why are we doing this?" I asked another instructor. "That's Bob on there, pointing to the radio handset."

"No that's an F-15E pilot, on there. Give him the respect he deserves, McKeena."

"No, that's Bob. He threw up in the bathroom at the Blue Lagoon last night. You were there."

One day in class I had an acid flashback. I was sitting there listening to an instructor drone on about honor and commitment and reaching higher. He had terrible teeth. People would say he had the teeth of a dinosaur. Anyhow, I was staring at his grill trying to conceive of how he came up with the nonsense he was spewing. My classmates were riveted, listening intently. Some appeared to be taking notes as this buffoon spoke. All of a sudden, my hands started to grow. Not cartoonish, but significantly. Then my fingers began to turn green and orange like Mike and Ikes.

"McKeena! Are you listening?"

"What?" I stared at my hands in disbelief.

"Airman McKeena! Are you listening? The fingernails started to grow out past the tips of my fingers, a half-inch then a full-inch, then two inches. My mouth hung open as I stared, terrified.

"McKeena!"

"What! What the fuck do you want?" I yelled as I stared in terror at my hands. I sprinted out of the classroom, hands out in front of me, eye level. I ran, full sprint back to the barracks, and sat on my bunk in my room. I watched as the nails started to slowly recede, the color changed back to normal skin tone and my fingers returned to normal length.

I had to meet with the base psychologist the next day. An old crusty lifer, former infantry type from Vietnam.

"What the hell happened out there McKeena?"

"Out where, sir?"

"In the bush. Sarge said you went haywire."

"The bush, sir? No sir, it happened in a classroom, here on base."

"Things a bit too stressful out there, McKeena? Too much responsibility putting bombs on target? Worried about danger close and friendly fire?" The man was a lunatic.

"It's not really stressful at all sir. Really it's—"

"Talkin' to the jet jockeys, guiding them into the target area, knowing you got friendlies in the AO? That ain't stressful McKeena?"

"Well sir, we've only talked to Bob so far, you know with budget cuts and the price of jet fuel and stuff…and—"

"Sarge says you were yellin' that your hands were growin'! Were your hands growin' McKeena?"

"What? No. Who said that? Sarge? Sarge doesn't know his ass from his elbow."

The incident was chalked up to a miscommunication. This conclusion is always the way in the military. They just check boxes by sending you to the psychologist and then quickly back to your unit.

The next week during night land navigation, I was attacked by an armadillo. I was alone, it was pitch dark, and the noises of the forest had me a little spooked. As I walked along checking my compass heading and knocking branches out of my face, I kicked something hard, but not stationary. It started to hiss, scampered away a few steps, got a running start, and charged me, biting me in the lower leg. I screamed bloody murder and took off running. I guess I was running west, but it might have been east—I have a horrible sense of direction. In any event, the Armadillo was in full chase, I was certain. Clothes-lined by numerous branches and outcroppings, my face was cut and bleeding, I pressed on. I saw a set of jeep headlights peering into the forest, changed my direction slightly and went straight for them. As I emerged from the woods, onto the dirt trail, I stepped into a ditch and hyper-extended my knee, bending my body down forward, knee locked in the out position. I screamed in pain as the sheer torque of the unnatural movement shot me into the air.

I landed face down in front of the instructor's camp. They were grilling steaks and drinking beer and waiting for trainees to finish their navigation.

"What the fuck?"

"I've just been attacked!"

"What the fuck? Is that McKeena?"

"It's McKenna, sir!" *It's fucking McKenna.*

"Hey! At ease airman," he said defensively, putting me in my place.

I told the drunken instructors the story and when they finally stopped laughing and making fun of me—maybe 10 minutes later—one had an idea. He slammed the beer in his hands, pulled out his machete, and handed it to me. "Now get your fucking city boy ass out there, and complete the mission McKeena!"

"Can I use my flashlight?"

"Hell no! Do you want the VC to see you?"

"VC! Oh for Christ sakes, everyone knows it's Bob!"

"Aren't you concerned with the VC smelling your corn-on-the-cob?"

After training, I received orders to Monterrey, California, to an Army infantry unit. I was to provide expertise in the area of close air support. One of my classmates in Florida received orders to Hawaii. He was a nice simple man from Kentucky.

"I just thank it's tew far. Tew far from my fam-il-y."

"Well California is way closer than Hawaii. Because of the ocean. There's no ocean between California and Kentucky."

"Really?"

"Yup, really. Your people could drive to see you. They wouldn't have to … take a boat. I could talk to the sergeant; maybe they would let us do an Orders Swap."

"Do you have any idea what I'm talking about David?" I asked.

"Sure. Not really."

Chapter 9

After training in Florida, and before leaving for my first official duty assignment in Hawaii, I took a few weeks of leave and went back to Schenectady. I gained some muscle and maturity in the 20 weeks I was away. I attended a party a night because everyone who had left for college was returning to the Schenectady area. I ended up reuniting with a lot of the friends I had abandoned when things went south for me after the divorce. Guys I used to play sports with, and other activities unrelated to drugs, were happy to see me, and I them. I noticed that since their first semester of college, their capacity for alcohol had gone bananas. These were bookworms and athletes who morphed into some serious drinkers. One guy, with like a 4.0 average in high school, and no chance of seeing a vagina up close, much less touching one, was snorting shots of vodka up his nostril.

At other parties, I would see my burnout friends, who had stayed pretty much the same. Some had nicer cars than when I left, some had lost their cars. Some had lawsuits pending for slip and falls, and one guy, I was told, was doing 4-7 upstate for robbing a convenience store with a handgun.

Another guy—who had issues—challenged me out of the blue, with a "Who's Dick is Bigger Contest." That was very strange. He and I didn't even really associate in high school, and we hadn't talked at the party or since I had been home on leave, but he called me out in a very aggressive fashion at this crowded, noisy party.

"Hey Andrew!" he yells across 20 loud people. "You think your dick is bigger than mine?" Like a game-show host.

I couldn't really hear him other than the words dick, bigger, and mine. I turned to my friend next to me and yelled, "What did he just say?"

"I don't know, something about his dick or your dick. I didn't catch it."

"Because it isn't and I can prove it!"

I turn again to my friend, "Did he just say something about our dicks again?"

"Yeah," my friend yells back to me. "He said he can prove that your dick is bigger than his or something? I didn't catch it."

"What the fuck is he going on about? Look at him would you, he's going crazy." Rick was puffed-up, gyrating like an orangutan.

At this point, Rick was screaming across the room at me, pointing, wildly gesturing, grabbing his privates. Some perverted form of charades. This must be for the other guests, but I could see the other party guests didn't want to play. People were becoming increasingly uncomfortable.

With that, Rick unzipped his fly to reveal his two-inch penis. The roof came off the place with laughter. Rick was seething with anger, staring at me like he wanted to sword fight. Eventually the laughter subsided—naturally, because it was my turn. I looked at Rick's two-inch penis, I looked around the room, making eye contact with friends and girls I had been with—most were nodding as if to say, "You got this Andrew, you got this!"

"Nah, I can't beat that." I raised my Solo cup of shitty beer and just said "Cheers" and winked at Rick. The place fell-out again in a state of madness. People were drunk, and they enjoyed a good show. I quickly made my exit so Rick wouldn't beat me up. I wasn't there to offend.

Things were starting to shape up for me. My head was getting clearer as the days went on, and my mind, which was always considered strong by most standards, was starting to really fire. People started to view me with some esteem—nothing mind blowing but, respect. They believed I was smart, and I became the go-to guy on things that required a brain.

I started to worry that my brain wouldn't develop because I wasn't in college, I was running around the woods yelling. My girlfriend was a freshman in college. I took her freshman reading list for literature and went to Barnes and Noble and bought every book on the list. Within two weeks I had read everything. So I went back and bought commentaries on the works and read those. I took her freshman accelerated math book, loaded up on coffee, and sat down with the intention of completing the entire text. I couldn't figure out the first chapter, and wanted to blow my brains out. I was never good in math. So onto art history, religions of the world, and world history. Those things I could grasp and retain. I started to read her statistics text and almost threw-up, biology same thing, chemistry same thing. I decided to stick with the humanities.

When I arrived in Hawaii from leave, I found paradise. If you've never been to Hawaii, go. My reputation as a bit of a hothead followed me from Florida, and right off the rip I realized I needed to tone things down and make a good first impression. When the story about the killer Armadillo came up I didn't get defensive, or at least show it. One thing I hate is being picked on by men. Girls, women, children, I can joke around with all day and it doesn't phase me—in fact I enjoy it. But something about men intentionally pushing my buttons drives me nuts. *Who the fuck do they think they're dealing with?*

"That's it, fucking armadillo! fucking armadillo!" I had the guy in a choke hold. One for the ages, too.

"Release him McKeena, release him airman, that's an order!"

"I was only fucking around with him," I said with a laugh, "we were just playing." The guy's face was purple.

But as time went on, I replaced the reputation as a hothead, with one of a brainy hothead. I started taking college courses at night, working as a grunt during the day, and going absolutely ape-shit crazy with the beach life on the North Shore, and the night-life on Waikiki. Every weekend was a trip to the beach. On any given Saturday or Sunday, we would load up and drive from the center of the island, to the North Shore and land at Waimea Bay. We would grill, drink beer, swim, fall asleep in the sun, play football, volleyball, you name it. We would mingle and party with the tourists, the locals, members of the other branches of the service. Rarely were there any fights because everyone was always in such a good mood—it was paradise, after all.

I was picking up as many course credits as I could. The classes were interesting, and I was growing along intellectual lines. Devouring material, getting into good study habits, working with friends on class assignments and projects, I was transforming from a wayward 17 year old to a strong-minded, centered adult. In addition, I was voted Airman of the Month, then Airman of the Quarter, and I was a finalist for Airman of the Year. I was the shortstop for our unit's softball team, and the second season I played with them, we won the Base Championship.

My girlfriend back in New York decided that she wanted to transfer to the University of Hawaii for school. I had mixed feelings about this. Obviously it would be great to have someone close to me in Hawaii, but I was also enjoying the true fruit of paradise. My girlfriend back in New York was enjoying something for herself, I'm certain. We kicked the idea around, and decided that the only way to pull it off was to elope in Hawaii when she came out, and that way I would be eligible for a married person's housing allowance, and eventually base housing. This was the only way to swing it. And we did it.

Unfortunately, while she was finishing out her semester before transferring and moving to Hawaii, I got involved in an altercation with a girl on base and had to do 13 days in a lockdown facility. I slapped the girl in the face, pimp style, after she hit me with an iron. She thought I slept with her best friend and she had a really bad temper. When I walked through the door to her room, she clocked me with an iron. The part about the iron never made it into the official reports, even though I had a gash on my head and a concussion. Well, close to a concussion. Her friend was hiding in the bathroom, and when I denied sleeping with her, she walked out and called me a liar. It was all a big set-up, you see. Debs came at me again with the iron but I slapped her so hard, she couldn't get off a good whack. Her face blew up like a balloon, and I knew at that point that I was fucked. I don't advocate hitting women; in fact I'm against it. I remember reading in the paper when I was younger, when I was a paperboy, that a man beat his wife to death because she overcooked the pasta. I felt terrible about this. But it was an iron!

The fact remains that Debs's vagina smelled horrible and I have to suspect it was from over-use. Her hunger for sex was insatiable. When we were "together" she showed up at my job with lunch. That morning I fornicated with her best friend twice but didn't have time to shower, and so when Debs serviced me on my lunch break it was a very awkward moment. She complained that something didn't seem right, something was out of order. A real prize this one. It was all about her. A real dirty dog, but then again, I too was a dirty dog because I hadn't showered after I climbed up on her friend. I saw Debs's nose scrunch more than once. As I said, it was awkward. My need for physical gratification was greater than my good sense of decorum.

We had to travel to the Philippines for a "mission," a "training mission," and it entailed heavy drinking, and prostitutes that were dangerously close to being illegal. The beer was San Miguel, which was brewed with formaldehyde. I had this idea that the formaldehyde is what kept my penis erect as I had sex with a bed full of brown people. I was like a stallion. Eighteen years old with formaldehyde in my penis. I blacked out.

At breakfast the next morning I sat at a table in the Blake Hotel's restaurant. I ordered bacon and eggs and toast and a San Miguel. There was little chance that I could hold anything down given the night I had. The fact that the guys were watching a woman getting it on with a mule on the television made it even more difficult. Outside the hotel armed guards—Philippinos with AK-47s—patrolled. Apparently there had been a major coup attempt against Corazon Aquino, the Philippine President. Because there were Americans at the hotel, they decided to post guards. Things became very stressful. A lot of shouting and communicating in

Tagalog—a strange sounding language, and the small brown folk were really wound-up.

Back in my room, packing to leave for the safety of the base, I stuck several Blake Hotel towels in my dufflebag. There was a girl in my bed asleep, so I woke her up and asked for her phone number. She didn't have a phone, she told me, no one in her village did, but she offered to do my laundry and shine my boots. Spit shine my boots. I declined, telling her that there had been a coup attempt and her country was in upheaval. She yawned, and fell back asleep.

Down in the lobby, as we were getting ready to board the truck back to base, a hotel worker—a manager—came rushing at us screaming in Tagalog.

"She says they're missing towels." Our translator told us. Here we go. There's a fucking takeover of the country by crazy generals, and these people are worried about their towels?

"McKenna, do you have the towels? Please give her the towels Andrew, we need to get the hell out of here."

"I do not have the woman's towels, Sergeant."

"Who has her fucking towels then?" Sergeant asked. He looked like his head was going to explode. The woman reached for my dufflebag. I mean these weren't plush Ralph Lauren Body Blanket towels or anything. I mean Christ, we were in the Philippines. I had just spent the night in a sex pile with four girls, with food breaks, and all told, it only cost me just shy of 10 dollars. The towels at the hotel were like something you'd get at an American gym to wipe down the elliptical after some circuits.

"Don't touch my shit lady!"

"You have towel fuckie! You have towel fuckie! You have towel fuckie! You have towel fuckie! You have towel fuckie!"

"Shut the fuck up!" Sarge couldn't take the sound of her voice. The repetitive, frantic, hysterical sound spitting out of her hole was unbearable.

"We'll pay for the ratty-ass towels!" Sarge told her. He threw like 30 dollars in pesos, or whatever they're called, at the woman. She stomped away in a fury. We quickly turned to leave, and as I looked back I saw her slapping a small brown man in his face as she ferociously screamed at him.

"McKenna, I know you have those fucking towels."

When Tori moved out to Hawaii, all hell broke loose for three weeks. We would be out somewhere and I'd run into a girl I had known and they might call me a fucking bastard. I'd get some seriously angry looks, or surprised looks, or angry surprised looks. Apparently a girl named Donna had given me crabs at some point, and I had shared them with others. I didn't know.

"Andrew, you gave me crabs!" Some girl yelled into the other end of the phone.

"That's impossible."

In a grossed-out panic, I shaved my entire body, including eyebrows, and bathed in Kwell Shampoo—kind of an extreme reaction given the circumstances. I was prone to extreme reactions. But the crab problem became epidemic, growing like wildfire as everyone gave them to everyone else. Married people were coming down with cases of crabs, and it was used as proof of infidelity in divorce proceedings. Everyone was suspect. Any amount of itching or scratching would send a ripple of rumors through the community. It became a witch hunt. I believed, rightly or wrongly, that some people thought I was responsible. My completely shaved body didn't help.

"But he shaved his eyebrows." I heard someone whisper as I went by.

Tori was wise to such things.

"You were with some of these girls that keep staring at us, weren't you?" she asked.

"Not really."

Tori treated me like she did when we were seeing each other in high school, even though I had since grown-up a bit, and matured. Either way, I wasn't going to be controlled by anyone. Control is just an illusion, anyhow. But her efforts wore on me. I found myself having to lie or shade the truth or omit things to avoid her irrational reactions. Of course my actions often caused her to be suspicious. Granted, I was a little wild. But a lot of it came from her upbringing, and some instability that she experienced as a child.

One night I was late getting home from the club, so I took an enormous potted plant from the lobby of the officer's club next door which was next to our club, the enlisted club. It was a tree really, and I ran with it through backyards, as a short-cut through the neighborhoods, to get to our little cement military home. Dogs were barking, lights going on, car alarms going off. When I arrived at our front door, I was a sweaty mess, with Hawaii red clay and dirt all over my legs.

"I brought you this," I said to Tori, as if I had done something good. Something to mitigate being so late and shitfaced.

"What the hell is this Andrew?"

"It's a flower," I explained.

"A flower? This isn't a damn flower, it's a tree, a potted tree! You stole this? You stole this tree! What the hell is wrong with you?" I was in tears at this point. Tears of frustration and despair.

"Nothing makes you happy anymore!" I was hysterical at this point. "I try and try and try!"

"What the hell are you talking about Andrew? You're drooling, crying like a crazy person, and you stole a fucking tree from the Enlisted Club!"

"This is not an enlisted tree Tori! I stole this from the Officer's Club! It's an officer's tree! For you! All for you!" My hands are out in front of me, palms turned up in a pleading manner. I needed validation that I had done something worthy of her appreciation.

"Sleep on the couch. Don't come near me."

"You fucking bitch! How could you!"

I passed out in the neighbor's yard that night. I woke up with early stage hypothermia. When I walked to my place, the potted tree was still on the stoop. I lugged it around to the back to hide it in case the military police started sweeping the neighborhood. The thing weighed at least 90 lbs. How the hell did I run with this thing in my arms? I made it to work, barely on time. The Sergeant was doing morning announcements, reading from a clip board.

"There's a car wash being put on by the base Cub Scout troop this Saturday. The general's dog ran away again, so we might be tasked with putting a detail together, a search detail, stand by for further notice. And finally, it appears a potted tree was misappropriated last night from the Officer's Club sometime between 0100 and 0300 this morning. Apparently it was enormous." The sergeant looked straight at me. Three other guys turned my way, too.

"Did you say a potted tree, Sarge?" I asked. A bunch of guys laughed.

"McKenna, did you take the fucking tree? Just answer the damn question. Did you take the fucking tree McKenna?" Sarge was frustrated.

Before I could answer, the Captain walked into the meeting. "Listen up folks, a tree was stolen from the O-Club last night. Spread the word among the enlisted that no one is going to fry, they just want the tree back. Just the tree, no questions asked."

On my lunch break I went back to the house, grabbed the hatchet and started whacking at the big boy. No way was I getting sucked into some false immunity amnesty trick with these bastards. For the next 90 minutes I cut that thing into toothpicks because the military eats their young. You get in trouble for not making your bed, stealing a tree from the officers' club would make the front page, and Tori wouldn't like that.

I couldn't take what was to me, the structured and stifling nature of the airman's existence. I was too smart to follow all the time. It drove me nuts to have to take direction from morons. Definitely some guys were really sharp and efficient, and had good ideas, and could lead.

Others were idiots; they were only in charge because they had been in longer. It had little to do with merit or ability. I couldn't take it. I decided that I wanted to go to law school. When I sat Tori down and told her I wanted out of the Air Force, she went insane screaming at me and slept for two days. The girl loved Hawaii and did not want to leave. That's all there was to it. She was so opposed to returning to upstate New York that we went almost a week without talking after I suggested it. She viewed it as a defeat.

As a compromise we agreed to move to Florida where she had a pot-smoking lesbian aunt in Tampa. I enrolled at the University of South Florida, where out of the 40,000 students, 20,000 were blondes. I worked in the pre-med advising office on campus for peanuts. My job was to operate the copier. I would often smoke a little weed in the morning after Tori went to work, and then ride my bike to the office. I have no recollection of how I got the job, and the fact is, I was not qualified to run a copier. It was a big copier. It was the size of a boat. My boss, a hot thirty-something assumed that everyone knew how to operate a machine such as this. I am not mechanically inclined, and well, felt somewhat intimidated by the goliath.

"It has pictures on the buttons Andrew—they tell you what the buttons signify."

"Signify?"

For my first job, I needed to make 50 copies of an information booklet: collated and stapled in the upper left corner. I made 500 copies that were not collated, and stapled in the lower left corner.

"But the button, the graphic shows you where the staple will go, all you had to do was push the right button. Do you smell marijuana?"

"No Darlene, I do not. I do not smell marijuana. No."

Darlene decided that she should give me several small jobs to "build up my confidence."

"Andrew, I need two copies of this." She handed me a two page letter.

"No problem. Collated?"

"Collated Andrew? Really? Okay, sure collated."

I was pretty baked, and very relaxed.

"Good job," she said, as I handed her the copies.

A few days later, she gave me the big job. The big test.

"I know you can do this Andrew. I need fifty copies, collated and stapled in the upper left corner. Remember the picture on the buttons. I'll be back in about an hour or so, so no rush."

I stared at the buttons, methodically going through the various screens, selecting from the little drawings what I wanted. I was baked and relaxed.

I hit start.

I watched as the feeder sucked in the pages of the original one by one. So far, so good. Then the machine made a strange noise and started beeping. The display window said "paper jam," and seemed to indicate the area within the machine where the jam had occurred. I stared at the window for several minutes. The picture, indicating the location of the jam, did not resemble any part of the machine that I was familiar with. I saw a bend in the molded plastic front that appeared to be a door of some sort. I opened it and stared some more. There were levers that were green in color. I looked back at the display window to see if I could identify a match. No luck. I closed the door. I opened another door. The relaxed feeling was being replaced by anxiety. *I can't fuck this up. I'm smart. Darlene will think I'm retarded.* I loosened my collar a bit and actually rolled up my sleeves like Rosie Rivet. I took a deep Zen breath. I had to stay calm to solve this problem. Behind door number two were more green levers and machine guts. Again I checked the display window. Nothing matched. *You gotta be fucking kidding me.* In a moment of irrational fear, I started pushing buttons on the control module. Nothing happened. I opened door number three, and saw a green lever that matched one on the display window. I pushed and pulled and twisted it until it came loose, exposing a trapped piece of paper. My confidence started to come back. I ripped the paper out in maybe 47 pieces. I stared at the green lever and sort of worked it back into place. Door number three wouldn't close though.

95

The green lever needed to really be jammed, punched, and slapped back into place. I rose from my knees and looked at the start button. A big green lighted square button. Before it was a red lighted button, when it was jammed. Now it was green. Green for go. I placed my index finger over the button, and stopped for a second. I was nervous. I was pretty baked and nervous. Thoughts of Darlene ran through my head. She would be back soon.

"How did it go stud?" She was forever calling me stud. Her husband was a dork and obviously not taking care of business. She walked the fine line between meaningless politeness and sexual harassment. I was used to this from women and totally unaffected by it.

"Good, I made 5,000 copies and I'm about a third of the way through stapling them. I have about 3,000 more to staple. I have to staple manually because the machine didn't do it right, and even though I unplugged the goddamn thing when it continued to regurgitate paper after paper after paper, and I was swearing at it and punching it to stop, it must have had a battery back-up, because it seemed to speed up, or at least didn't slow down."

"5,000?"

"5,000."

"You know what? I don't need these until Monday, and you have at least several more hours of stapling, so you wanna go get a drink?"

"No Darlene. I just want to go home."

Tori hated her job. Her aunt had gotten her a job at an insurance company and she had to commute through Tampa traffic every day. One Saturday her aunt and her boyfriend Theresa came over to our apartment. They brought lettuce to make a salad. Her aunt spent 45 minutes washing the lettuce, as we stood around pretending to enjoy each other's company. Her aunt and boyfriend would suddenly break into laughing fits.

"I think the lettuce is ready," I told her aunt.

"Almost." Her hands were wrinkled from the washing session.

"You've practically washed the green out of it," I said.

I played on a University of South Florida intramural basketball team. Most of the team members would share a joint before the game, and our win-loss ratio reflected this. I was a good basketball player, just not when I was baked. We played night games on these huge outside courts on campus that were really poorly lighted. Some people had no problem with it, especially really good players. But I smoked weed and I learned in the military that smokers have impaired night vision. I can't be sure, but I think I picked up the nickname "air-ball" along the way. At times I would take a long jump shot and miss, just short, or really short of the hoop. But because of the lighting, and my impaired night vision, I would think it went in. The opposing player would grab the rebound and head back up court.

"Hey, you need to take that ball out dude!" I'd yell at him as he flew by me in the other direction.

"What? You didn't make that!"

From the bleachers, someone would say, "That was an air-ball dumbass! What are you stoned or something!"

"Yes I did make it!"

"What did he say?" I'd hear someone ask.

"He thinks his shot went in."

Our team captain, if you could call him this, was an engineering major dork that didn't know we smoked pot before the games. He was extremely competitive, too, and so when we would start screwing up, he would become very angry. One of my teammates, Bob, couldn't handle weed, so whenever he smoked, he would burst out into laughing fits. He would run up and down the court, totally lost, and just laughing his stoned ass off.

"What the hell's so funny, Kurt?" the captain would yell from the sidelines. "Play some goddamn defense! And don't pass it to Andrew, he's off tonight!"

One night we were playing a really good team, and we didn't score a single point in the first half. The score was like 41-0. The captain was irate. Someone forgot to bring the orange water cooler, and it was an incredibly hot and humid night, and after chasing the Harlem Globe Trotters up and down the court for 30 minutes, we were drenched. Because of the weed, and the cottonmouth factor, most of us had white dried saliva cakes in the corners of our mouths. One guy, Rod I think was his name, looked terrible. He was dry-coughing so bad it sounded like a cat trying to free a hairball. The captain had singled him out for not picking up the double team, or something absurd like that.

"Rod, what's your fucking problem?" The captain was shouting at him. Rod couldn't speak because his tongue was stuck in his throat. Bob—the laugher—was bent over, belly laughing at the whole situation, and I was just staring at the dim court lights, watching big bugs crash into them.

Florida wasn't working for me. I tried to make a go of it for Tori because she was terrified of moving back to New York; the whole failure thing. But I was bored—I didn't want to spend my time smoking pot and losing basketball games. Not to mention the oppressive fucking heat. I hated Florida.

"We need to move. I can't take this anymore," I told Tori.
"Where are we going to move?"
"New York."
"No we're not Andrew!" She went into seclusion for two days.

The trip to New York was arduous; 25 hours straight with no pharmaceuticals except for over-the-counter *No Doze*. I popped a few before we left and they didn't seem to do anything. I started thinking maybe I had a bad batch, maybe they were the placebos from the drug trials or something. I popped a few more and by the time we reached Georgia—19 *No Doze* later—I was seeing little bugs running across the windshield. Tori was in REM sleep next to me, as I gripped the wheel and tried to focus. I heard a sound of little pebbles banging against each other in rapid succession. I looked all over the cab of the U-Haul, and imagined that the wheels were coming off of the truck. I noticed that every time I bit down on my lip, the pebble sound would stop, and I'd hold my breath and listen for it. When I released my breath and breathed in again, the sound would start up.

My mind played tricks on me. At about hour 15, I convinced myself that I was going the wrong way, against traffic, on the highway.

"Tori! Wake up!" She was totally out. I imagined that maybe she had passed away and I didn't know it.

"Tori! Tori! Wake the fuck up!"

She shot awake in a panic.

"What? What!"

"Are we going the right way?" I tried to stay calm, but my voice was shaky.

"Just stay on 95 Andrew."

"No, I know, I mean are we in on-coming traffic?"

"What! What the fuck!" Tori was terrified.

I pulled over to the shoulder of the highway. We both just stared straight ahead. The pebble sound was louder than ever. We heard the roaring of a truck as it came from behind us. Catastrophe averted, thank god.

"Are your teeth chattering?"

"What?"

"You can't hear that? Your teeth are chattering Andrew! What the hell are you doing?"

"Coffee pills."

"Coffee pills Andrew? Really? This is crazy." Tori didn't sleep another wink the entire ride home. Somewhere near New Jersey, the *No Doze* started to fail me. The crash came hard. But somehow I couldn't give up the wheel. I had to keep pushing myself to the outer limits.

We moved into my mother's house and lived there for about six months. Tori, being a total clean freak, used to run around my mom's house complaining under her breath how dusty everything was. But it really wasn't that bad at all. The slightest sign of dust would send Tori into obsessive compulsive disorder mania.

"What the hell are you doing?"

"I'm cleaning." Tori's body was contorted around the toilet bowl. She had bleach and a scrub pad and was washing the back of the toilet.

"The back of the toilet, dude? For real?"

"I can't take it anymore," Tori grunted.

"If my mom sees you doing this in her house, the roof will come off this place." Tori was now on her back, like a mechanic. She had removed a bolt from below the bowl and was polishing it with a cloth.

"You need to tell Tori to stop Andrew. She scrubbed all of the cabinets and organized the garage, and now she's in the attic. Can you hear her up there?" My mom was offended. I could hear Tori up there making quite a ruckus. It sounded like she was hurling boxes around and swearing. Then I heard a vacuum cleaner.

"Tori, I don't need the attic vacuumed!" My mom yelled up the stairs.

"Yes you do, you do. I don't mind," Tori yelled back.

We moved. I started at the State University of New York at Albany, and Tori started work with an older female lawyer. They seemed to bicker a lot. I was able to land a job at a bagel store. I was the bagel guy. I would take frozen bagels and submerge them in a boiler until they became plump, and then transfer them to a pizza oven. My day began at 4 a.m. I wasn't partying really, so the hours didn't bother me. Occasionally I would smoke a little weed with a co-worker in the morning, just to take the edge off the boredom of life. But sometimes the weed would cause me to have overly emotional responses. A co-worker arrived at 7 a.m. with a black eye. Her husband had punched her. I went in the bathroom and cried for her.

I was bored. School was the same as it was in Hawaii and Florida. I loaded-up on 18 credit hour semesters, sometimes 21 credits, because I wanted to just get the damn degree. Political Science. I planned to go to law school because I couldn't figure out what else to do, and law school would delay thinking about things for at least three years. But first, I had to nail the bachelor's degree.

In one of my undergrad courses, a classmate and I teamed-up for a major project. We had trouble getting started, and actually didn't start until the night before it was due. The subject was, of course, the decriminalization of marijuana. A topic beaten to death by millions of stoned undergraduates nationwide, every year. We decided to beat it some more with a 15-page paper complete with interviews of drug dealers. We attacked the economics of failed drug policy. We made up interviews and used street talk and slogans in the question and answer sections. No way was the professor going to buy that we went out to the hood—two white college kids in khakis and Polos—and did interviews. But we made it all up anyhow because we thought the professor would get a kick out of it. While we were writing the damn thing, plagiarizing sections from scholarly studies and texts, dropping convoluted footnotes left and right, his roommate sat in the living room and did bong hit after bong hit. Our goal was not to smoke until we had the thing completed. Concentration was necessary, and time was running short. The paper had to be turned in at 8 a.m., without exception. A late paper was a full letter grade lower.

Sample question and answer from the interview of Darneek Williams:

Q: Mr. Williams, what would happen to your profit margins if the government legalized marijuana, and made it legal to grow and dispense.

A: Sheeeeeit! My ass would go outta bidness. You see it's all about supply and demands, son. If the streets is flooded with the shit, then the price go down. If a nigga can just go to CVS to get some reefer, then it mean it cheaper there then what I can sell it fo'. I ain't competin' with CVS nigga!

Q: I see.

A: Don't even get me started on da tax implications, dey even mo' real...

Darneek was starting to pontificate, so we ended the interview prematurely.

And on and on. The entire paper was structured with these interviews, and with footnotes of studies that supported the "dealer's" conclusions. The street was meeting academia, and their respective findings and data jived.

The next morning we woke up just in time. We grabbed our paper off of the coffee table, shook off the excess marijuana and seeds and stems (we had used the paper to "clean" our pot before we smoked). My partner and I jumped in my old $150 Subaru, lit a joint and raced to campus. As I came up on the left-hand turn onto campus, the light turned yellow, so I floored it and went into the turn. The rusted rear left axle split in two and we did two complete three sixties in the middle of morning traffic. My partner yelled holy shit and started laughing hysterically. He jumped out of the car and ran across campus with the paper in his hand. It was just a few minutes before the deadline. Some guy pulled up next to me and said that his friend owned the same car and the same thing happened to him and that it was under recall. The car was 14 years old. Sure enough, the dealership replaced the entire rear end of that rusted out turd. When I asked the service manager if I could get a loaner, he laughed.

"A loaner? Fuck no."

My partner got the paper turned-in on time and we ended up getting an A. The professor wrote on the top of page one, the words, "Unbelievably Good" and a smiley face below it.

At least twice a week I would blow off classes and go to see my best childhood friend Charlie. He worked labor at UPS and usually didn't get home until 3 or 4 in the morning. I would get to his place around 9:30, usually with bagels and coffee, left over from work. Charlie would always say not to come over until at least noon because he needed sleep. UPS was putting a beating on his body.

He lived on the second floor, and usually would forget to lock the window by the fire-escape. Bugsie, his dog, knew me and loved me, but would sometimes attack people he knew and loved. When I came through the window, I had to be very careful to not spook Bugsie. I'd use baby talk as I slowly lifted open the window from the outside.

"Hi. Bugsie, Bugsie, what a pretty Bugsie." Usually I would hand a bagel with cream cheese through the curtains and wait for him to snatch it from my shaking hand.

"How did Bugsie sleep? Is Bugsie happy to see Uncle Andrew?" As soon as he took the bait, I would crawl the rest of the way through the window. Always on the table was a bong and a little shake weed. To calm my nerves, I would usually take a big pull, and sit and wait for Charlie to wake up. *Good weed, Always good weed here.* Always, there was something good to read, something a little alternative, that I would become engrossed in.

"What the hell is that?" Charlie was looking over my shoulder into Bugsie's food bowl. I had dropped half of a day-old pumpernickel bagel into Bugsie's bowl, thinking that he would be happy. The big husky dog looked at me, as if to say, "Fuck you, would you eat that?"

Charlie was pissed because I had gotten there too early, and he had a girl in the bedroom. She walked out after him, wearing a hockey jersey. The girl was hot, which was par for the course for Charlie.

"Wow, who is this?" I stared at the girl.

"I'm Monica."

"I'm Andrew."

"Oh, right, Andrew, I've heard so much about you!" She was genuinely excited to meet me. Monica wasn't wearing a bra and I was stoned from the bong-hit.

"Dude, stop staring," Charlie said.

"Huh?"

Monica thought this was funny and she smiled at me. But Charlie and I had a steadfast agreement not to bang each other's girlfriends, and with only a handful of exceptions over the years, we honored this agreement.

"Wow, you are smokin' hot!" I said and started laughing.

"Okay, thank you Drew, that'll be all." And with that Charlie tugged me by the arm towards the door. Monica was laughing, and I looked at her over my shoulder.

"How about breakfast guys? It's on me."

Chapter 10

The University was full of girls from the city and Long Island. A lot of big-breasted Jewish girls, who for some reason thought I was smart. I think it's because I was a couple years older than our peers and because I had travelled a little in the military and lived a little outside of my hometown. I was somewhat confident. Not cocky at all. Cocky people offend me. They're weaklings at their core. Anyhow, I loved to participate in class.

"How do you know so much?" Sarah was my favorite girl in the world. She "got" it, unlike so many other young undergrads. Sarah understood what made the world go around. She had a certain maturity, a certain irony. But I was determined not to have sex with her. My fidelity record was not perfect, I understood this. However, I was a pretty good guy to Tori, and worked very hard, well at least diligently, at staying faithful.

"How is it that you know so little?" I deadpanned back to Sarah with a tinge of disapproval in my voice. Sarah gasped when I said it and punched me really hard in the chest.

"How can you say that?"

I was grimacing in pain from the punch, trying to hide my discomfort. The pain made me angry, like when I stub my toe.

"Don't ever punch me again you little shit!" I said staring into her eyes. She bit her upper lip to keep herself from laughing. She was clearly enjoying this. People were walking by in the hallway, as we stared at each other. The energy between us was palpable. As I looked at her with anger, she suddenly appeared very vulnerable and beautiful. This was by far the most intimate interaction we had ever allowed ourselves to have.

"Why, what are you going to do about it?" She said very quietly, not quite sure of herself, not sure if these were the right words to say.

"I'll slap your face."

"Oh my God," she said under her breath. She moved closer within inches of me, as I stared her down.

"And I'll pull your fucking hair."

"Oh my God," she said again, looking away from me. It looked like she was going to come undone right there in the hallway. My penis was like a telephone pole. Ten feet away was the girl's bathroom.

"Get your fucking ass in there." And I grabbed her by the arm and pushed her through the door. Eyes were on us, but time just kept flowing towards the stall. Thank heavens it was empty, because even if it wasn't I would have kept going. I spun her around, bent her over, reached up, tore her underwear off, worked myself free, and took it. I mean I took it. Rhythmically pounding into her, listening to her erotic discomfort, I didn't stop. Grabbing her hair and yanking back I let go one last punishing thrust, and came in her, pushing her head forward as I let go of her hair.

"That's what I'm going to do about it." I walked out of the stall and towards the door. As I did so, I heard her say, in a sensually "defeated," and yet still defiant voice, "Fuck you."

That was a Friday. Monday in class, Sarah's seat was empty. Sarah didn't show up to class on Wednesday either and I became nervous. After class I went to the library, and found my little corner where I would often read and nap. I dozed off into a deep sleep and dreamt that Sarah had just walked in on me and one of her friends having sex. She charged at me in anger. Startled by her charge, I quickly sat up in bed to defend myself. Just as I did, I woke-up, and low and behold I head-butted Sarah in the nose. Not dreaming now, but in the library. She was going to sneak-up on me as I slept, and coincidentally, she was in the same position—in front of my forehead—as she was in the dream.

"What the fuck?" Sarah held her nose as a little blood started to trickle.

"What the…?" Was all we could say back and forth. She was dazed from the blow. I was completely freaked out and disoriented because of the parallels between the dream and reality.

"What are you doing?" I implored.

"What am I doing? What the fuck Andrew?" She stood up, stated how crazy this was. I finally got a grasp of what was real. The bloody nose was real.

"Where have you been?" I asked.

"In the city for a funeral," Sarah said muffled through her hand. "Walk me to the infirmary, what the fuck!"

"Wow this is crazy." As we walked it occurred to me that we better get our stories straight.

"We have to tell them that you were mugged, and that I saved you."

"You're such a fucking narcissist Andrew."

"Enough with the name calling."

"Why, what are you going to do about it?"

One day Tori, who was really having a tough time re-assimilating to life in upstate New York, decided that she was going to meet with a U.S. Marine Corps Officer recruiter for an "informational session." I wasn't really paying attention when she told me. It was more like, a "Yes dear, that's nice dear," type of reaction. I had taken the Law School Admissions Test and did okay. I applied to Harvard and didn't even get the rejection postcard from them. In fact, Harvard didn't even acknowledge that I had sent in the application with the $50 fee. Albany Law School was on my list because it's a solid school, regionally recognized as a good education, and it was close to home, and I could get in. When the acceptance came from Albany Law, I breathed a sigh of relief.

"I met with the Marine Officer recruiter today," Tori said as she planted herself in front of me.

"Oh? That's nice." I was reading the paper and drinking coffee.

"It seems like a huge challenge."

"I bet. Jeez, it's the Marines after all." I was flipping through the arts section of the Times.

"They have a great program for lawyers."

"Oh? That's nice ... Oh hell no, I am not joining the fucking Marines. If you want to, that's fine! But I am not joining the fucking Marine Corps!"

Tori had to get out of Dodge, there was no question. But we didn't have children so I had no problem with being separated from her. Follow your dreams, I would say. I was going to start law school in the fall with or without her.

"Tori, listen to me. I am not joining the fucking Marines. I would rather drag my scrotum over a mile of rusty nails! Final word. End of story. Fuck no!"

The flight down to Marine Corps training in Quantico was rocky. Everyone had these exceptionally foolish haircuts, except me. I was not gung-ho about this. Others were gung-ho, sitting up straight during the flight. I sipped a beer, and later napped in the back row.

"You're not supposed to drink on the flight to Officer Candidate School." This was the high-and-tight wearing moron sitting next to me.

"Mind your fucking business chief."

Tori won this round. It was the summer before I was to start law school and the Marines had a program where law students could go to 10 weeks of Officer Candidate School, receive their commission as second lieutenants, and then go into inactive status while they attended school. The Marines are the only branch of the service that do not contribute to tuition, but they do pay you to work during semester breaks and during the summer, in uniform, in the south, as a Marine Student Lawyer. *How did I get roped into this madness?*

The first three days at Quantico were all about standing in huge lines in 100 degree humidity. Unlike the Air Force enlisted boot-camp, where they yelled at you the minute you landed in San Antonio, the Marines tricked you by lulling you into a false sense of safety. There would be time for yelling later. Right now I had to fill out forms and answer questions from 18 year old Private First Class Marines.

"If you die while here at Quantico, who do you want to get the Service Members Group Life Insurance policy insurance money?"

"If I die while in training?"

"Sure, every Company that comes through, seems like someone dies."

"Really?" When does training begin?"

"I can't answer that."

"Because you don't know?"

"Next!"

On day four, everything changed. People were not as polite. I couldn't put my finger on it. Even my fellow candidates were acting edgy, and they couldn't explain why either. Day four was also hotter than any of the other previous days. When we lined up to march to breakfast, the sun wasn't up yet, but the damn heat was stifling. Guys were questioning how it could be so hot without the sun. By noon, after sitting in yet another class (or block of instruction as it's called in the Corps), concerning rank structures of all branches of the service world-wide, we lined up to march to lunch (or noon chow). I couldn't breathe it was so hot. A strange haze encircled our formation, as the sun beat us down. The admin guy who had been marching us to chow for the past several days seemed very angry at us. Something was afoot.

That afternoon, we did a field-day. A field day is not a barbecue with tug of war and three legged races like I thought when I first heard the term. It is a full dismantling and cleaning of every centimeter of U.S. Marine Corps property. Bunks are taken apart and cleaned, rocks are painted, grass is clipped, literally with scissors. Floors are stripped and buffed sometimes two and three times. Walls are washed and rewashed and rewashed, light fixtures are removed and cleaned, coats of paint may be indicated, uniforms are cleaned and pressed, boots are shined, stripped of polish and re-shined. But the biggest part of a field day is cleaning the head. The head is the bathroom. When I first heard the term, I couldn't stop laughing. The head. Drill instructors always were ranting about their heads being filthy.

"Why isn't my head clean? I want my goddamn head to shine. Get in my head with your goddamn toothbrushes and scrub it. If I find even one pubic hair anywhere near my head, heads will roll!" The heads in the Marine Corps were generally spotless anywhere you went. It was a badge of honor for a Marine to keep his head clean, free of urine and excrement. The head had to shine and smell like pine sol. Many of these heads were old, and constructed with the best materials, and by-God, as a tribute to those who had gone before us, those who had fought to give us our freedom, we were honor bound to keep our heads in the highest state of police.

"Okay, listen up candidates. Tonight we're marching over forthwith to Classroom 6." They always added things like forthwith, and post-haste, without delay, etc., even when it didn't make sense.

"From there we will march, without unnecessary delay, over to Classroom 10, and from there, post-haste, onto Classroom 12—right next door. There you will meet the Colonel, the Commanding Officer of U.S. Marine Corps Officer Candidate School, Marine Corps Base, Quantico,

109

Andrew McKenna

Virginia." They also had to include full mailing addresses with everything to make it sound impressive.

"Be advised, that the Colonel is a war hero. He did three tours in the Republic of Vietnam, and killed hundreds of Viet Cong. If and when he makes eye contact with you, and he most certainly will, I here forth command that you look away. Under no circumstances are you to look into the Colonels eyes. Thereupon, you've been henceforth warned." I was totally confused at this point.

"Now pack up your trash (uniforms underwear, socks, hats a/k/a 'covers' boots, hygiene products, canteens, web belts, linens, poncho and poncho liners, ruck-sacks, weapon cleaning materials, etc.) and stand-fast. Don't forget your knowledge (written materials such as manuals, Marine Corps history and traditions books, anything that contained any type of knowledge). Pack your knowledge the same way you would your shit paper—use the waterproof bag. Keep your knowledge dry at all times. You need your knowledge. If anything is left in my squad bay, I'll find out who it belongs to and kill that person. That is all. Godspeed U.S. Marine Corps Officer Candidates."

All of my trash must have weighed a little over 120 pounds.

"McKenna, where are we going where we would need to pack our shit paper in a waterproof bag?" A fellow candidate asked nervously.

"I don't know man, these people are obviously insane." The trash was now on my back and we were marching, well actually the guy marching us, said we were a huge gaggle-fuck walking down the street, not candidates marching. Marching was out of the question—the staying in step, the cadence, the cover and alignment—none of these were possible with our trash on our backs.

When we arrived at Classroom 12, we were all sweaty and exhausted from hauling the trash. A strong looking sort instructed us henceforthly:

"You have 3 minutes to use my head! Leave piss in my head and you'll spend the rest of the night cleaning my head! The use of my head is compulsory!" Try not laughing at this. Class was about to begin, and 75

110

candidates had to use his head; it was compulsory. We lined up at the wall urinals and tried to go, even if we didn't have to. The guy next to me was very nervous because he didn't have to go. He was frantically flushing the toilet, hoping that the running water would make him have to go. He was causing quite a ruckus. Other candidates who were waiting to go, were getting antsy.

"Come on Jones, just fucking piss and get out of the way!"

"I'm trying!" Jones was pleading with them. FLUSH, FLUSH, FLUSH.

"Who is repeatedly flushing my fucking head!" The strong looking sort demanded.

"Jones, just walk away from the urinal dude. Pretend you went. No one's going to know," I told him, as I shook and flushed. Jones was overwhelmed. He looked really stressed out.

"Is that fucking Jones flushing my head!" Someone gave Jones up.

"Yes Sergeant Instructor! It is Jones who is incapable of urinating forthwith and it is Jones who continues to flush in the hopes—

"Shut your fucking mouth!" Jones yells, starting to unravel. The man was in tears. *Oh my God this is crazy.*

"Exit my head Jones! Immediately!" The strong looking sort commanded.

We were now in our seats. Sweating bullets from the stress and the heat. I look around the room. Total silence. Gradually filing into the outer isles were men in Smoky Bear hats, pulled down low so their eyes were shaded. The fluorescent lights were so bright, one had to squint to see across the room. Thirty of these guys turned into 40, and then into 50. All I could think about was the fire code requirements. A small faded sign on the wall indicated a maximum capacity of 100. We had four times that many packed-in.

An older man with silver eagles on his collar, bounded up the stairs of the stage. A deep voice roared, "Candidates, Atten hut!" We all snapped to our feet. For the next hour, the Colonel graveled on about the meaning of his Officer Candidate School at Marine Corps Base Quantico Virginia. I was within spitting distance to the Colonel, and very aware that at any point he'd make eye contact with me. I was ready to avert my eyes pronto and forthwith.

"Candidates, the Marine Drill Instructors that are surrounding you now, are the finest. Handpicked by me, they represent what you must become. Watch them, follow them, for over the course of the next ten weeks, they will transform you from mere civilians into Marine Corps Officers. Many of you won't make it because you don't have what it takes. You're weak physically, you're weak mentally, you're spiritually weak, morally weak, and you don't belong here. These fine Marines are trained to find you and to weed you out because you don't belong here." *Nothing like an ice-breaker Colonel.*

Then his eyes rested on mine, and I forgot avert my eyes posthaste. A chill ran up my spine and without unnecessary delay, it ran right back down. I shuddered. He stopped talking and just stared at me. I tried to look away but I couldn't. He had me locked-in. I was hypnotized. This must be why the guy earlier said not to make eye contact with the Colonel. I tried to look away, I tried to close my eyes but they wouldn't shut. Finally he looked away, and the spell was broken. His next words I will never forget.

"Drill Instructors, assume control of your Platoons!"

Chaos. Drill instructors by the dozens start running at us, they're turning over chairs and tables screaming for us to get out of *their* seats, to get out of *their* classroom; these people were so proprietary. It was an absolute stampede. Guys were trying to put their trash on their backs. Some decided to forget the trash, and just try to run for it. They were turned back to get their trash. There were logjams and bottle necks. We were tripping over each other running in different directions trying to find a door. People were screaming like women and children. The guy ahead of me tripped and smashed his head on the table. I've never seen anyone hit their head that hard. I'm sure the weighty trash on his back contributed to the force of the impact. He got up and somehow made it back into the flow of bodies shuffling towards the exit. He was totally disoriented from the blow. No time to think. The guy now directly in front of me pissed his pants. I looked as he turned his eyes to me, and I realized it was Jones. Jones finally had to go. This made me laugh for a split second. Suddenly a Drill Instructor pounced at me. I could feel the warmth of his breath as the wetness of his filthy spittle hit my ear.

"What are you laughing at faggot!" This nearly made me shit my pants, but I was able to regain control over my bowel. He had come from nowhere, and was screaming in my ear. *Who the fuck is he calling faggot?*

"Oh pretty boy didn't like that did he? You fucking hippy! You faggot hippy" *Come on man. Faggot hippy? Pretty boy? Seriously? Why am I doing this?*

I wanted to punch him in the throat. And then he was gone, seemingly into thin air. Did I just imagine that? Someone else called me a bitch.

They chased us out of the classroom, across the enormous parade deck and drill field and into our new barracks. We had to haul our trash up three flights of stairs (called ladder wells in the Corps) with these maniacs yelling at us. Men collapsed with exhaustion and dehydration.

"From this point forward if you fallout from dehydration, you will be left for death!" *Jesus. What happened to leaving no comrade behind?*

"Dehydration is a character flaw! And a failure of self-leadership!" *Is he making this shit up as he goes?*

"Now grab a damn canteen and get on line!" We had to stand next to our bunks on an imaginary line.

"Extend the damn canteen!" This meant to hold it out in front of us.

"Lock out your damn elbows!" We stayed in that position for 15 minutes while we were berated with insults. Once again I was called a faggot and a hippy. Someone else called me a bitch, I just know it. Now a 20 ounce canteen filled doesn't weigh that much right? Try taking, say a hairbrush, and hold it directly in front of you with your damn elbow extended and have a stranger yell at you and call you names for 15 minutes. Man they had this abuse down to a science. Jones pissed himself again. One guy cried and was never seen again. Some douche named Postenskull, or some such nonsense may or may not have died that evening.

"Push!"

Push?

"Get on your Goddamn faces and push!"

What the hell is he talking about?

"Assume the front lean and rest position!" Some type of homosexual cult is what we have here.

Front lean and rest is in reality what the Corps calls the push-up position; it's not sodomy.

We did push-ups for 30 minutes. Doesn't sound that bad right? Try it.

"You shitdicks are going to learn what it means to listen."

Shitdicks. Sweet Jesus.

"But more than that."

More than what? That wasn't a complete sentence. He apparently lost his train of thought when he cued in on Westerfelt or feld or something.

"Westerman, you annoy me! Did your nasty momma send you all the way—where you from Westerman?"

"Texas, sir!"

"Right, now did your nasty momma send you all the way from Texas to annoy me boy? And are you a steer or a queer?"

"Um, a steer sir?"

"Then make a steer noise and prove you're not a damn queer!" Westerfeld made steer noises.

"SHOWERS!" This can't be good.

"I said on your feet!" We came out of the front lean and rest position. My arms and chest muscles were numb. Too much lactic acid in my muscles. Unsteady on my feet. The drill instructors corralled us by means of threats and intimidation and fear, into a line of bodies.

"GET NAKED! YOU'RE NOT GOING IN MY MARINE CORPS SHOWERS LIKE THAT!" Seventy five men hopping an gyrating trying to remove articles of clothing, all while moving towards the showers. Everything was happening so fast. Men were yelling at each other in frustration.

"Get out of my way!"

"I'm going as fast as I can."

"Hey Numbnuts! Take your socks off!" The instructors watched as we ran naked into each other.

"Cohesion! I want cohesion in this platoon! Do you understand me?" The drill instructor wanted cohesion. I wanted to be out of the line of naked men. To be back in Albany with normal people, doing normal things.

"Who is that pervert with the erection?" The drill instructor demanded.

"Jones Sir!" Again Jones gets dimed out. But the troublesome thing is he had an erection which presumably violates the "don't tell" part of "don't ask, don't tell." And as I'm turning over this policy dilemma in my mind, the man in front of me trips, butt naked over the man in front of him. It was a pile-up of nudity. I of course tripped and ended up in the butt-fucking position behind the guy. *I gotta get out of here.* We must have looked like twisted gay-porn actors hopped up on meth.

"Asses to elbows!" *This guy can't be serious.*

"There will be cohesion!" *More cohesion than this? This isn't even cohesion, its homosexual is what it is. It's hazing of the homosexual variety.*

"Westerman! Stop making the fucking steer noise!" Apparently, even the drill instructor thought this was too much, what with the pile-up and all.

"Look at all of the erections now! You bunch of fucking deviants!"

The drill instructor was crazy at this point, yelling random insults. I checked to make sure I didn't have an erection. In fact, I had the polar opposite of the erection. I had never seen my penis so small before. It must have been the stress and fear, but it looked like a pencil erasure. The guy in front of me tripped again, and I would be damned if I was going to mount him again. I timed my leap as he hit the ground. My left heel came down on the side of his head. He screamed in pain. There was no chance that I didn't just give him a concussion. The heel of my foot hit his temple, and I just kept moving, I was running now towards the showers, juking like Barry Sanders, avoiding fallen comrades.

The showers consisted of three posts spaced seven feet apart. Each post had five shower heads that fired out cold water. We had to weave ourselves through like an enormous centipede and let water from all 15 shower heads hit our bodies. Talk about a cluster-fuck. The man behind me kept bumping into me, his penis slapping my ass cheek. *I'm going to walk the fuck out of here! I quit!*

"Where's the soap?" That's what he kept asking out loud in rhythm with his penis hitting me.

"There is no fucking soap! Don't you get it! Now back the fuck off of me!" I yelled at him.

"WHO'S YELLING IN MY SHOWER?" The drill instructor demanded.

"JONES SIR!" I yelled like a ventriloquist, throwing my voice.

We had three minutes to put on our skivvies (Marine for T-shirt and underwear). And our go-fasters (Marine for running sneaker).

"WE'RE GOING TO RUN YOUR DICKS IN THE DIRT." *Good Lord.*

We took off running in the woods. No moon. Pitch darkness. As one might imagine, it was traumatic. The trails were laced with big jutting roots and rocks. Repeatedly slamming my toes into these obstructions, I would yelp and hop, and everyone around me was doing the same thing.

"QUIT YOUR CRYING PUSSIES!" *Totally uncalled for.*

"Listen to my cadence, get in step! A one, two, three, four, hey!" And we would answer with a one, two, three, four, hey! The whole time we were running in step with everyone else.

He would then sing: "I gotta girl at home waiting for me!" And we would repeat it as we did a run/march type of movement.

"She told me that she loves me!" Repeat it back.

"But it turns out she's a nasty whore!" *Oh come on!*

"And Jody is now banging her ass!" *Oh for crying out loud.* I stopped singing. It was too offensive. Most of these guys were far from home and sure enough they had a special girl waiting for them while they were at Marine Corp Base Quantico Virginia, and they didn't need to hear that she was getting ass-banged by a guy named Jody. Jody is a fictitious cocksman that has been the antagonist in military cadences apparently forever. While you're away from home training, Jody is home with your girl.

"Your girl, she takes it in the ass!" *What is with this sicko?* He's singing the cadence at the top of his voice.

"She takes it in the ass like a nasty dog!" I'm done with this. Yup. I'm done. I'm leaving after this nightmare of a run.

Back in the squad-bay now.

"SHOWERS!" *Oh hell no.* We did the shower thing again just like before, except this time some candidates, now pushed to the brink of frustration and exhaustion, started fighting each other; not major fights, more like pushing and shoving, little skirmishes would break out and end just as fast as they started. After all, we were in line shuffling through the water-heads, naked, slipping, and swinging. I noticed that the drill instructors were gone.

The next several weeks were similar to this first night of training. The drill instructors took pride in their jobs, which was to weed out the weak, those who were not built for commanding Marines in combat. This was just the first cut, because the Marines have many levels of review in a young officer's career, and they are exceedingly successful at getting rid of men who would likely do little more than risk the lives of those entrusted to them. But here at OCS, they were determined to get the first dibs. The idea would be to bury a man with various tasks, and as soon as he seemed to get a handle on things, to then heap more shit on his plate. All the while, the drill instructors sit back and observe how you handle the stress. They look for people who become confused, angry, upset, or those who freeze under the pressure.

Jones was gone the next day, so was another guy named Williams (I think), who also pissed his pants that first night. I hung in there. My only real problem was the oppressive heat and sleepwalking. For some reason I started to sleepwalk. I'd go visit other candidates in the dark of night, stand next to their racks, and stare at them. Eventually, I would speak gibberish until they woke up and yelled at me. Sleepwalking will get a man kicked out of the Corps. One night I went over to the weapons rack and was tugging on the lock to my M16A2 Service Rifle. The fire-watch, another candidate who patrols the squad-bay in two hour shifts to make sure there are no fires, came up to me, laughing, and said, "McKenna, what the hell are you doing?" I woke up and in gibberish told him about lockjaw, and what a problem it is in India. He told me to get my ass back in the rack, and if he caught me again trying to free my weapon, he would report me.

"Wake the fuck up! Get your sorry asses out of my Marine Corps racks!" *Goddamn man we just went to sleep! This is crazy.*

"Get on line with your stinking canteens." Before we went to bed, or rather the racks, we had to go into the drill instructors head and fill our canteens. Now we're awake again, standing on the imaginary line, holding out canteens in front of us at a modified position of attention.

"Unsecure the canteens!" *Unsecure the canteens? What does that even mean?* Well it meant unscrew the cap.

"Invert the canteen!" *Drink from the canteen.* We had to chug down all 20 ounces while standing at attention, half asleep and exhausted.

It wasn't easy. But now we could go back to sleep. They only meant to hydrate us, not torture us.

By God, you better drink it all!" *God this is terrible.*

"Extend the canteen!" Arms out straight again. No problem. It's empty and light.

"Holes to the floor!" *What the fuck?* But it wasn't sexual. It meant to turn the opening of the canteen to the floor, as in proving that you drank your water and weren't sandbagging while all the rest of us were chugging warm terrible tasting water from the drill instructors head.

Splashing sounds of water hitting the floor rang out on both ends of the imaginary line.

"Oh hell no! Who didn't drink their filthy water!"

I yelled: "JONES SIR!" People couldn't help but laugh. The drill instructor did not laugh. Jones had washed out weeks ago.

"McNamara didn't drink his water." The drill instructor said quietly. "Janis didn't drink his water. These men cheated you. Tomorrow they would have likely been heat casualties, and you would have had to carry them and their trash on your backs. They jeopardized the mission by being selfish." *Yeah punish those motherfuckers! Let's beat on them. I drank my fucking head water!*

"With the exception of McNamara and Janis, candidates, front lean and rest!"

That's right! Hahaha—what did he say? I was incensed. Why would we have to do push-ups? I drank *my* fucking water. And that was the point. It was a big mind fuck to McNamara and Janis: *we* were punished for *their* sins. They caused this, and they didn't have to do the push-ups. We did push-ups for 25 minutes. I couldn't feel my upper body. McNamara and Janis were mentally deflated. Mission accomplished.

Graduation day finally came. We were in formation for several hours in 95 degree heat. Men were falling down from exhaustion. We were told that the key to surviving the graduation ceremony was to keep our knees slightly bent. If you lock your knees while at the position of attention, the blood doesn't circulate properly, and you pass out. It's madness watching a guy in front of you starting to sway. You know he's going down. It's just a matter of time, and then it happens. Because you're at the position of attention, you're not allowed to move, to assist the guy, to break his fall. So he just collapses and folds and then the corpsmen standing behind the formation walk over and remove the limp body from the parade deck. To treat a heat casualty, they first yank the person's pants down and shove a thermometer (silver bullet) up his ass to check his temperature. At the same time, they dump 50 gallon drums of fetid rain water on the guy to try to bring his core temp down. All the while people are staring, wondering if the guy will die or have brain damage from the heat stroke.

A few days before graduation, the Major who reports to the Colonel (whom we've never heard from or seen since the opening day of torture) came to our barracks.

"Fall-out!" This means that we have to go outside and sit at a modified position of attention for what's being termed a fireside chat. The staff all looks very serious. Something happened. Our Platoon Sergeant was not present. This was the hard scrabble staff sergeant who led us for the last nine and half weeks through test after test. He truly became a mentor to us. We looked up to him.

"Platoon Sergeant stands accused of raping and impregnating his step daughter." *Oh for Christ's sake.* Two candidates started to cry, which I thought was ridiculous.

"He raped her and impregnated her, allegedly." *Okay Major we got that part.*

"Will he be at graduation?" One candidate blubbered, unable to control his tears.

"He raped her and impregnated her. He will not be attending graduation henceforth." *This is surreal.*

"Are there any questions?"

"How do they know it wasn't consensual?"

"It wasn't."

"Where is the Platoon Sergeant now?"

"In the brig."

"Can we write him?"

"No. He's a pervert."

"Is she going to have the baby?"

120

What a bunch of fucking idiots.

So that was it.

Tori continued on with her training. I was on my way to law school. The separation was liberating.

Chapter 11

I showed up to law school in incredible shape and just a bit amped-up from the Quantico experience. My classmates all seemed pretty smart and I immediately made a few good friends. For the first semester I lived with my sister who was having some marital problems because her husband couldn't manage to keep it in his pants. My sister is this incredibly smart, funny person, and it was the perfect balance with the stress of law school and all. We spent many evenings eating hamburger helper and watching old Walton re-runs, even though I was supposed to be reading and briefing cases for the next day's classes. I managed to work pretty hard, but I didn't work in a "smart" fashion.

There is a method to law school, to getting through the first year, and it entails establishing a consistent regiment of reading and note taking, of finding the relevant issue in the cases assigned by the professor. I tended to just read the materials and take a few notes, but to ultimately rely on my memory during class time. Well, trying to do this for four or five core courses, each with their own reading assignments, would require a brain much stronger than mine.

"Where is your outline Andrew?" My friend Lisa asked.

"In my head."

"You're not smart enough to keep it in your head."

"Neither are you Lisa."

"That's why I have outlines, dumbass."

Dealing with the egos of some of the professors was very difficult for me. We had one jackass who really thought he was a ladies' man. At the end of the year, he brought his guitar to class and sang a ridiculous song with lyrics that described some of the cases we had read, and the discussions we had about them. He would name his favorite students in the lyrics. The more cynical ones, like me and Paul, would yell, "Please stop singing, we're not in kindergarten!" and he would just wink and keep singing. Several students walked out in disgust. We later found out that one of his research assistants filed a sexual harassment complaint against him, and then the lawyer he hired had to go after him for the attorney's fee that the professor never paid.

I wasn't the best student in the world, but once I understood a concept, I was pretty good at explaining it to others, and I've never feared public speaking as a result. Also, I have a really deep, resonant voice which can either come out sounding like a demented tree frog, or a Hollywood actor from the old days. When I was on, people really focused on me and what I was saying. It's always been that way. Unfortunately, I've always been paranoid that people are staring at me. When a doctor prescribed me Paxil, it helped in two ways the doctor didn't anticipate. First, Paxil gave me ridiculous erections, and second, I still thought everyone was staring at me, but the Paxil made it so it just didn't bother me.

"Andrew, those are both atypical reactions to this medication," the doctor explained.

"You're saying that they are typical?"

"No they're not."

"But you just said they were typical."

"No, I didn't."

"Yes, you did."

"No, I most certainly didn't"

"Yes, you most certainly did." Then we just stared at each other in silence, until finally the doctor asked if the erections were painful.

"Initially, yes, but then of course, well you know, once the erection is relieved so to speak, then it's not painful, but pleasurable."

With this last salvo, we stared at each other again for a while.

"I'll see you in two weeks Andrew."

I love to drive shrinks crazy.

My core group of friends and I had a lot of fun going out and partying, driving west to Indian reservations and gambling, while the really smart kids were holed up in the library in study groups. One night we were all sitting in my apartment, when Franklin showed up with his bong and some chronic. I was a little paranoid about the pungent odor of the weed, so I opened a couple windows, turned on a fan and turned up the heat. It was the dead of winter in Albany. After several pulls on the bong, we decided that we should hit some bars, and maybe a trip out to the casino. The next morning I rolled in just as the sun was coming up. When I opened the door to my apartment, I saw at least a foot of snow and ice on the floor by the open window. The place was freezing. I looked at the thermometer on the wall which I had cranked-up when I had decided the night before to open windows. I had it set for almost 95 degrees—I remembered telling my friends that we were going to the tropics as I adjusted the thermostat—but now the temperature in the apartment was barely 30 degrees. The curtains were basically flying horizontal from the wind whipping through. *Holy shit*, I thought. *I really need to make some changes.* I looked and noticed that my answering machine was blinking rapidly, and that I had almost 20 or so messages.

Beep.

"Andrew, it's Kent from downstairs. Hey, um, do you have the heat turned up higher than normal," He chuckles. "Ima roastin' down here. Call me, bro."

Mine was the only apartment in the whole house with the thermostat.

Beep.

"Andrew, Kent again, seriously dude, the heat in my apartment is atrocious. Enough with the torture." More chuckles. "Call me."

By the time I got to message 18 or so, the tone had decidedly changed.

Beep.

"Dude, what's your fucking problem? Turn the fucking heat down. I have to bring my dog to the vet because he's having a bad reaction to the fucking heat. Turn the fucking heat down!"

Beep.

"You sick fuck! It is 103 fucking degrees in here. I have a fucking exam in the morning!"

Beep.

"Fuck you! You fucking selfish bastard. When I see you I'm fucking you up! Turn the fucking heat down bitch!"

Beep.

Calmly, but very parched and raspy now, "It's Kent. I'm going to a hotel. I can't take the heat. You have a fucking window open. You're going to break the furnace. You're paying for my hotel."

One big benefit to being a Marine Lieutenant in law school was during summers and semester breaks, I would report to a Marine Base and work as an assistant to experienced Marine attorneys. Immediately, they would get us into the courtroom, or before administrative discharge boards, where we would get to practice and learn advocacy skills. The Marines are the smallest branch of the service, and yet they prosecute more cases than any other branch. Some people say that the Marines are too strict, that they eat their young. Which I guess in some cases is true. Commanding officers make charging decisions, and some of these guys are insane or want people to think that they're insane, and they end up nailing some young guys who just made some bad choices. On the other hand, the Marines just don't fuck around with discipline issues. It's made very clear what type of conduct is expected of a Marine, and if you don't keep your shit in a high state of police, then "get the fuck out of my Corps." That's the explanation that a commanding officer gave me at the top of his lungs at the Officers Club mixer one night.

I was reporting to bases to work during a period when the Marines were not at war. But they were in the midst of a bad hazing scandal. CNN had been showing video of high ranking Marines, enlisted and officers, pummeling newly promoted junior Marines. During these "pinning-on" events, the idea was to drive the pin insignia of the new rank into the Marine's clavicle bone. After all he had earned this new rank and should be rewarded with a good pounding? The video footage was fucking brutal: guys were rendered unconscious, and the guy holding the video recorder, was an officer, a platoon commander, whose job was to protect the young Marines. In typical Marine fashion, from Headquarters Washington, a Marine Corps wide "Stand Down" was issued. I'm still not sure what Stand Down means, but the effect of such an important term was that everyone had to pack into the base theater and listen to experts on hazing discuss how bad it is for organizations, physically, psychologically, and morally. However, the experts had not arrived yet, and so the Colonel asked the Gunny to buy a little time and make some opening remarks about the perils of hazing.

A Gunny is a respected rank, and looked up to by junior enlisted, as being a Marine's Marine through and through. When I walked in late from lunch, the Good Gunny was explaining how to tea-bag someone. He discussed how a Marine is held down by several comrades, and they take turns resting their scrotums on the Marines forehead. He explained that the best time to do this was after rigorous exercise when the scrotum was "moist with sweat and stink." The Gunny then seemed to be unbuckling his trousers for a full demonstration when the commanding officer, the Gunny's boss, jumped to his feet to stop him.

"Thank you Gunny, I'll take it from here!"

"Are you sure sir? Can I get just one more minute? I just want to show—"

"No Gunny, that'll be enough. Thank you for … that."

This was not the type of training that Washington had ordered.

A few days later, I had my promotion from Second Lieutenant to First Lieutenant. I was really excited about it until they decided to combine my promotion ceremony with three office birthdays and two reenlistment ceremonies. The first reenlistment ceremony was a sergeant who was basically signing up for four more years. It's kind of a big deal, but not really. Anyhow, the sergeant's wife was there with a big Kentucky Derby hat and yellow high heels. I looked around for the mint julep but there wasn't one. The sergeant also brought his five children, which sort of explained his need for four more years. Anyhow, as the sergeant was given the oath by the colonel, he started sniffling. I thought it was an allergy attack, until he began blubbering and his voice went really high. He came undone in front of the whole room. Then his wife was crying. His tears were huge and he couldn't catch his breath. Snot was starting to run from his nose. He couldn't get through the oath, and had to repeat certain sections so it was understandable. I sat there with my mouth agape in absolute disbelief. Why are they crying? His youngest child was crying, too. After the oath, the fucking colonel asked him to say a few words. I groaned. So then the long-winded sergeant blubbered for the next 10 minutes and repeatedly said how much he loved his wife, again pouring tears down his face and onto his starched uniform.

By the time they got to my promotion to First Lieutenant, everyone was pretty depressed. I suggested that we do the birthday celebrations first, as a buffer against the blubbering sergeant, but that suggestion was denied. I proudly took the oath to defend the nation against all enemies foreign and domestic. The Colonel removed my butter bars, and replaced them with the shining silver ones. It was a proud moment until he raised both fists up above his head and crashed them down on the silver lieutenant bars. One of the pins penetrated my collar bone, and the other one broke on impact. I almost passed out from the sheer force of the blow, but managed to remain conscious and on my feet.

The Colonel with clenched teeth stared at me crazy like, and just said "Yeah, yeah, that felt good!" This was the guy leading the investigation into the hazing problem in the Corps.

In my last semester of law school back in Albany I received a call from Headquarters Marine Corps.

"Lieutenant McKeena?"

"McKenna, yes."

"Please hold for Major Dunce, sir."

This can't be good. Headquarters never calls me.

"Lieutenant?"

"Yes Sir."

"I have bad news. Henceforth, we are experiencing a backlog of Marine Corps lawyers."

"A backlog, sir?"

"Yes, a backlog of Marine Corps lawyers. As you know, you have to attend The Basic School after graduation. But you must first take a bar exam and be admitted to practice in any state in the Union."

The Union?

"However, by the time you take the July bar exam, the results won't be back in time for you to start The Basic School in the fall."

This doesn't make any sense.

"I know this doesn't make any sense to you Lieutenant, but the needs of the Corps come first. There is no place for selfishness."

What the hell is he talking about?

"Are there any other options sir?"

"The only other option is that you find a state within our Union that allows you to take a bar exam while you're still in law school, this February, the February bar exam."

So, forthwith, I did the research and found that Georgia allows third year law students to sit for the February exam. I went to all of my professors and told them that I needed a month off to prepare. After all, I had to learn the multistate stuff that everyone has to know, but I also had to learn Georgia law. I barely knew New York law after three years of school! I ordered the books and the tapes and went to Marine Corps Base Camp Lejeune where Tori was stationed and studied non-stop for four weeks. I had this tremendous fear that I wouldn't pass the exam, and I cursed myself for not being a better student. Anyhow, I flew into Atlanta on a mission. I ended-up staying with my high school friend Everett and his mother, who was a saint, and a second mother to me when I was in high school. Everett is gay and very emotional. He was going through some tough times at work and with his boyfriend, who he regularly beat on during arguments. He was great guy but he had anger issues. Everett and I always got along like brothers.

"We're going to have a barbeque tonight, have a few drinks and play spades later. We'll be partners," Everett said.

"Everett I have a bar exam in the morning. Tell your mom that I don't mean to be rude, but I really have to study tonight. This is serious stuff."

Everett was not happy about this. He was upset.

Later, at the card table, Everett, drunk as a skunk, started yelling at his mother about his childhood, saying things like, "You didn't even want me to be born! I was still-born!"

"Is it my deal?" I asked.

"No, it's Everett's deal," his mother answered.

"Everett is in no condition to deal," I said.

"Look Andrew, it's Everett's deal and he will deal!"

"Everett is obviously not dealing."

Everett kept ranting about his childhood and not dealing.

I excused myself from the card table. I was a little tipsy from a few beers but nothing too major, however within the next 20 minutes I was really feeling wasted—like someone slipped me a mickey.

"Everett, did you fucking drug me?" I yelled from the bedroom upstairs.

"No!" he yelled back up the stairs.

"I feel like someone drugged me!" I yelled back.

I shut off the light and climbed into bed. The room immediately started to spin, and my skin felt tingly. Every movement of my skin against the sheets sent a wave of endorphins through my body. *Did that motherfucker slip me ecstasy?* I walked into the bathroom and started rifling through the medicine chest. It was packed full. One bottle said to take one before bed. So I ate one. Strolling back to my bed I started to worry that this could cause an overdose, that my heart would stop, or that I would be so disabled in the morning that I couldn't take the damn exam.

"Move over." It was Everett.

"Move over? You move over and get the fuck out of here! What are you doing in here?"

"I need you to hold me." Everett was crying again.

"Everett I am a fucking heterosexual!"

"It's not sexual, well for the most part … come on and hold me Andrew."

"If you don't get the fuck out of this bed Everett, I'll kill you."

"Stop being that way," Everett pleaded, "you always have to act like such a man."

"I am a fucking man Everett! And so are you, so get out of the bed."

Everett sprung to his feet. I could see from the streetlights bleeding in the window that Everett was naked.

"You bastard!"

"I'm a bastard? I'm a bastard? I have a fucking bar exam in the morning. You drugged me and now you're standing here naked calling *me* a bastard?"

With that Everett broke into hysterical crying, almost as bad as the sergeant reenlisting.

He blurted out: "I think I have HIV!" *Oh for God's sake.*

Everett was a nurse in an operating room.

"I got stuck with a sharp, and the guy we were operating on has AIDS."

At this point Everett sat down Indian style on the end of the bed. Someone's sleep meds were starting to kick-in, countering whatever other drug I unknowingly ingested. I could barely keep my eyes open, but for safety reasons, I fought it. My instincts were those of a college virgin at her first frat party.

"Everett, please put some clothes on, I'm not comfortable with this…" I mumbled and slurred.

"I am not consenting to your nakedness…" My voice trailed off. The meds were hitting hard now, and I felt I needed to say these things to get them on the record.

"Hold me Andrew."

"Dude I'm not … I have a bar exam … Jim Crow laws …" I wasn't making sense at this point. Everett crawled forward and lay in front of me. I was involuntarily spooning him. I was paralyzed, but somehow relieved that he wasn't spooning me. He whimpered as I started to drift away.

"God, you won this round God. You owe me God. Please no tax question tomorrow.…" Tax law and my new covenant with the Lord was my last thought as I drifted into the abyss. Tax law was too boring to learn, so when I was studying during the past four weeks, I put that book and tape aside.

Within three hours I was sitting in an Atlanta Convention center with hundreds of other test-takers. My head was throbbing. My thoughts were these intense things that would just come and go, with no focus, no plot, no narrative. The exam seemed impossible; so many damn questions, so many scenarios to decipher, so many potential issues to spot. Each essay seemed harder than the last. The essays were given out one at a time. Finally, we were ready to receive the final essay question of the exam. Over the loudspeaker, the Bar Exam administrator said, "Well ladies and gentlemen, we have come to the final essay question of the Georgia Bar Exam. You will all be relieved to know, it is not a tax law question." The place erupted in applause and sighs of relief. *Okay God, we're even Steven.* And Everett was HIV negative. A good soul that Everett, and a special friend always.

When I received a letter in the mail several months later from the Georgia Board of Bar Examiners I nearly shit my pants. Walking from the mailbox to my front door, reading the return address over and over, considering how thin the envelope was, holding it up to the sun, realizing that in this envelop contained the blueprint to my future.

The opening sentence of the letter read as follows: We are pleased to notify you...." For the next three minutes I jumped for joy, as if I had hit the winning shot in the NBA Championship game at the buzzer. This meant that I could continue to carry out my career plan. Marine lawyer, then Federal Prosecutor, then fame and fortune as a kick-ass exclusive defense attorney handling the biggest cases in the world. That was the plan.

But dark days followed this exhilaration. I came down from the natural high and couldn't seem to get a grasp on who I was or why I was or what my role in this fucking world should be. I hid this depression from friends and family because I was embarrassed for feeling this way. It didn't make sense not to be very happy with the way things were going. It seemed ungrateful or something. I was steadily succeeding, and yet when I returned to Albany for my law school graduation, I was faking it. The feeling was oddly nostalgic—in that I felt this way as a kid. It wasn't the good nostalgic. I was melancholy and it didn't make sense.

After graduation, I went to live and work at the Marine Corps Base in Camp Lejeune, North Carolina. I had the summer to work and unwind before starting the six-month Basic School in Quantico. When I reported for duty, I met again with the Colonel who had tried to break my collar bone.

"Where should we put you McKenna?"

"How about the trial shop sir? I could get a little trial experience."

He hit the roof.

"Goddamn it why do all you fucking newbies expect to go to the trial shop! That billet has to be earned asshole! Now where should we put you McKenna?" he asked again. "Um, God sir, I … I … have no idea. Wherever, I could best serve the needs of the Corps sir?"

He made me a legal assistance officer. A dreaded billet. Legal assistance is manned by Marine lawyers who are able to give legal advice but not allowed to go to civilian courts and represent the "client." Legal assistance is available to Marines and their family members, and also retirees. All day long I would listen to people's problems: bad car loans, divorce battles, bad apartment leases, bankruptcy. You name it, if a Marine could get into deep water, I would have to listen to it. The problem of course was that I didn't know North Carolina Law to save my life, so I would end up doing a tap dance around the actual law pertaining to the problem, and just use general legal terms that any monkey could take out of Black's Law Dictionary. I became an actor; I was not practicing law. Finally I realized that these people, 8 out of 10, didn't need a lawyer anyhow, they needed a fucking therapist!

"I found these in my wife's drawer. They're condos."

"You mean condoms."

"That's what I said."

"Fine. What can I do about it?" I asked.

"Well maybe you could call her and let her know that we're onto her."

"*We're* onto her?"

"Yup."

"Nope."

One day a very attractive young Marine wife came in dressed like an off-duty stripper. She came into my office, reeking of perfume. Because I was so used to talking to deeply depressed, obese Marine wives wearing sweatpants and wondering why their marriages were failing, I was quite intrigued by her. In her one hand was an open box of Cracker Jacks. In her other hand, which she held open to me, was an enormous toenail.

"Well, you see, I knew I had bit down on something hard, and I'm very conscious of my teeth, and well … it was a toenail." Again she held it up. It was an enormous toenail, and I was a little hung-over and not feeling great. I almost threw up.

"That's fucking gross. Excuse my language, but man is that gross."

"Tell me about it," she said.

I wanted to ask her out but was pretty sure that I would get court-martialed if I did, and besides, as pathological as I could be at times, I was determined not to cheat. Just then she touched her breast slightly and smiled, but I wasn't sure that she even realized she had done it.

"So what do you think a case like this is worth?" *A free replacement box of Cracker Jacks.*

"It could be significant, but I'll have to do some legal research first. There are some dead-rat-in-the-deep-fryer cases I should look at that may be of some precedential value. Here is my direct line. You can call me directly if you have any questions. And here is my pager number in case it's after-hours. Remember, there's no such thing as a silly question."

"Wow, you are so sweet."

"Hmm. Don't mention it," I said. "I'll need you to come back in here tomorrow so we can discuss all of this in greater detail. In the meantime, I don't want you to stress about this. You're in good hands here."

After she left, I fantasized henceforth and then I wrote an extortion letter to the makers of Cracker Jacks. It was some of my finest work. I really needed a victory here for this young lady. They responded with an envelope full of coupons and a letter stating that it was a physical impossibility that said toenail came from the manufacturing company. She never ended-up using my direct line or my pager. Case closed. Bullet dodged. Amen.

As the summer winded-down, I started to exercise more to prepare for the perils of The Basic School or TBS as it is known. My peers at the Legal Assistance office who had attended TBS years before would tell me that TBS stands for The Big Suck or Total Bull Shit. That was very encouraging. But I knew that I had to get off some of the extra weight so I ran and ate right and drank light beer. The Captain offered to speak with the Colonel about organizing a send-off party for me.

"No sir. Please not that."

"But we could do it in conjunction with this month's office birthdays."

"Please sir, no. Please no. Thank you, but really, no please."

"You're a strange duck McKenna."

"I know sir, I know."

When I arrived at The Basic School I was a little nervous. I hadn't been fully involved with the hardcore Marine Corps mindset since Officer Candidate School. Legal offices didn't qualify; it was the Marines, just not that gung-ho. The Basic School isn't technically an infantry school. There's a separate school for that called the Infantry Officer's Course, and only Marine Officers that make the cut attend that school. I was told it's insane. Anyhow, I was now a lawyer and The Basic School was nutty enough for me.

The Housing for Basic School Lieutenants was built at Quantico in the old days. I looked up and found a three story military style barracks constructed of cinderblock. Like all Marine Bases, this one appeared immaculate, but the difference was that these were barracks that housed new marine lieutenants busting their asses through six long months of training. This was evident by the smell of sweat and gear and dirt, and of course pine sol, and frustration. I could smell frustration. The barracks contained two-room suites with four bunks in one room, the head in the middle, and a common area room. The floors were worn linoleum. The cinderblock walls were bright white. The lights were fluorescent. Signs of a recently departing graduating Marine Company were evident. Scuff marks, un-emptied trash baskets, old muddy boots left in the corner, and a big "Fuck you, it's your turn sucker!" written with a bold black Scripto on the wall, or as it's known in the Marines, the bulkhead; as a parting message and a welcome sign of what was to come. It seemed very hostile to me. Fuck you, it's your turn sucker. Good Lord.

"What time are the fucking transports picking us up!" I heard one steely looking marine yell.

"I told you they'll be here at 0530. So I need you to get your squad on line at 0330."

"But why do we have to muster two hours before the buses get here!" I asked.

"To ensure that no one is late! It gives us a buffer!"

"But don't you see devil-dog, now the squad leaders will tell their fire-team leaders to muster at 0230, to ensure that no one is late. This buffer system, based on paranoia and fear of looking bad doesn't work. It does not work devil dog! No one gets any sleep this way. That's why everything is such a clusterfuck around here!"

"What a bunch of bullshit!" Everyone sounded so stressed-out.

That was the first full conversation I had when I arrived at The Basic School Marine Corps Base Quantico Virginia. I also observed several people on crutches, several people limping along grimacing in pain, torn and faded uniforms from training wear and tear. Boots worn so thin, the guys were practically barefoot. Black watch caps because it was cold, and these looked worn-out and stretched, too.

The billeting (roommates) was done in alphabetical order, so naturally my two roommates were two other Irish guys. Their names were Meffers and McRudd. For the next six months we were to live closely, train closely, and torment one another whenever possible. Within two days of arriving, Meffers and I were drunk and wrestling in the hallway. Not WWF, mind you, MMA. Choke holds, elbows to the head, arm bars. We bonded immediately. Meffers was from New Jersey. His father was a local magistrate judge. He was Catholic (sort of) and he was a big strong Jersey wiseass. McRudd was from Mississippi, complete with the drawl, and when we drank we made fun of him and accused him of having a lineage of incest.

135

For the first week or so we were in classrooms learning about the basic school curriculum. We also met our instructors and our commanders. Each Platoon was led by a Marine Captain who had already been out in the real Marine Corps doing real Marine Corps things. This put them at a great advantage, because we had no choice but to believe everything they told us. A couple of them were infantry officers and thought they were real hard-asses. One Captain thought he was God. His efforts at trying to look and act tough were herculean. He would walk like he was angry, fists and jaw clenched, with a steely eyed thousand mile stare.

"Look at this asshole. Looks like he's hopped up on amphetamines and just killed his gay lover." I would say things like this to my fellow lieutenants, but some of them were wired just as tight, and they looked at me with disdain.

"You shouldn't say disrespectful things about a senior officer, Lieutenant McKenna." This came from a Naval Academy Graduate, wound very tightly.

"But look how he walks. He looks insane. He looks constipated! You see it too, I know you do."

"He's a combat infantry officer, served in Iraq," the guy replied.

"Desert Storm? Desert Fucking Storm? What was his job, to process surrendering Republican Guard troops? He looks like he hasn't taken a shit since he came back from the big war."

"That's enough lieutenant," he said in a stern monotone voice.

"My name is Andrew. You can call me Andrew. We're the same rank. What's your name? It's Bob or something right?"

"My name is Robert E. Lee the third. I would prefer if you called me Lieutenant Lee."

"I'll call you Bob, and you can call me Andrew."

My Platoon Commander, on the other hand, didn't act like a hardass. I respected his choice to be a normal man. His only hardass thing was not wearing a field jacket, even when it was cold. One day, the transport was late and we were stuck out in some training area. We were all freezing our asses off. And then it started to sleet and then snow sideways as the wind was hitting 30 knots. I was huddled together with Meffers and another guy and we were crying from the pain. I couldn't move my toes or fingers. Meffers was delirious and thought part of his ear had fallen off. He was pawing at it and crying.

"Dude, your ear is still on. I'm looking at it right now!" I tried to assure him.

"But I can't feel it," he cried.

"That's because it's numb, dumbass. It's frostbitten or something."

Anyhow, I look over and there is our Captain in a tee shirt. No watch-cap, no parka, no gloves. The man was blue he was so cold, and yet he maintained perfect military bearing in front of us as an example of what it means to hide the truth of what's really happening. But he was blue and we all could see that he was blue.

"That man is hard," someone commented.

"That man is an idiot," I answered.

"That's enough lieutenant."

I turned around. It was Bob again.

"Bob, what's your fucking problem?"

"You're my problem, lieutenant. You refuse to maintain good order and discipline, you're cynical, and you don't take anything seriously."

"That's considered a strength, Bob. If you tell me 'that's enough' again, I'll beat the shit out of you."

"Sir! Do you want my watch-cap?" I yelled across the field to my Captain. "You must be freezing!"

Humiliated and blue, he answered: "No McKenna. I don't need your watch-cap."

"How about a field jacket? No? But you'll get pneumonia."

"That's enough McKenna, I know what you're doing." The Captain glared at me.

There we go again with the "that's enough" thing.

"Better stop fucking with the Captain," Meffers said through tears. "He looks pissed."

"He looks blue," I corrected.

During our hand-to-hand combat training, I witnessed evil. The instructors were highly trained enlisted guys who loved to sadistically beat on lieutenants under the guise of teaching us. We, as usual, had no idea what we were doing. When they taught us these arm twisting techniques, they made it very realistic. That's one thing I can say about the Marines: when they train, it's for real.

"Ah! Fuck! Let Go! Ah!" The instructor had McRudd's arm, wrist, and hand in a pretzel. "See, see, like this!" The instructor grunted through clenched teeth as he torqued away on McRudd's limb. "You have to twist and pull down! Not pull down and twist. Twist and then pull down!" McRudd looked like he was going to be ill. Just before the instructor released the lock, he twisted and pulled down one more time, extra hard. "Twist and pull down!" McRudd screamed, and then rolled on the ground clutching his hyper-extended, sprained arm. We were directed to another circle of lieutenant's by the instructor, as McRudd lie there recovering.

Two lieutenants were grappling, as we had been taught, but they weren't causing each other enough pain to satisfy the instructor's psychotic needs.

"No! It's like this!" The instructor moved in, grabbed one of the lieutenant's wrists turned it around, and dropped the lieutenant to the deck (ground). The instructor had the lieutenant's hand folded against his wrist, as the instructor drove his boot into the back of the young officer's neck.

"Ah!" came the high pitched scream.

Then we broke back down into pairs to "get it right." The instructors would walk around and observe and demonstrate the right way. Guys would take it easy on each other and then get into trouble. Out of the corner of my eye, I saw the instructor sneaking up on me and my partner. Before he could reach us, I grabbed my partner's wrist and put him in an arm bar, taking him to the deck (ground). I torqued as hard as I could, and he screamed like a girl.

"That's right, that's right, break the fucking thing if you have to." I looked up and nodded at the instructor as if to say, *Hell yes, I got this.*

"OK, recover," the instructor says, which means get up, shake it off.

"Your turn lieutenant." He grabbed for me.

"What?"

"Yup." With that he slapped me, spun me around and executed a rear choke hold until I turned purple.

"Recover."

It took me 10 minutes to physically recover. The fear of dying had never been stronger than that moment when my eyes almost popped from their sockets while this evil person tried to crush my larynx. That night, the three of us just sat in our room in silence and drank beer. The next morning we would go to the rifle range.

Everything so far in training had been this great unknown. Every day was a mystery and it was exciting in that regard. But everyday seemed like it lasted 100 hours. There was so much damn instruction, so much dry practicing, so much time rehearsing tactics. By the time we were actually allowed to "go live" or get real, we were fucking exhausted— mentally and physically.

O Dark Thirty, which means very early in the morning in Marine parlance, we put our ridiculously heavy packs on our backs, got in formation, and force marched three miles uphill to the rifle range. Men were throwing up their energy bars left and right as we plodded through the cold morning air. By the time we made it to the range, we were soaking wet with sweat. It was 35 degrees outside. Within 10 minutes we were freezing as we lay on the ground in the prone position with our unloaded, yet heavily oiled M16A1 Service Rifles. Hour after hour we would "site-in" on an imaginary target and pull the trigger until we heard a click. We were practicing siting-in, and breathing, and trigger control, and range safety. No real shooting. The more senior company, to our left, was firing real rounds down range.

The rifle range instructor couldn't pronounce smooth. He pronounced it "smoof." So as we sat in the bleachers in the dead of winter, he would yell for an hour at a time, always ending each statement with a smoof, as he made a trigger pulling movement in the air. The trigger had to be pulled smoofly. In eight hours of bleacher instruction, with my ass frozen to the bench, I counted more than 380 smoofs. I felt like killing myself. Back in the barracks at night, lieutenants would run around imitating the instructor.

"Hey Smith, that was real smoof! Ha ha ha."

"Yeah, you too, LT, real smoof."

Good grief. I closed the door to our room.

"Could you believe that jackass today? Smoof?" Meffers would say, clearly tired and depressed.

"My ass fell asleep." I said.

"I fell asleep four times lying in the prone position," said McRudd.

"Well, we were lying there going click for three fucking hours. Did you see the size of the shit Greene left in the port-a-potty?" I asked.

"It looked like a piece of firewood. They said he had to go to medical after. He was bleeding," Meffers said. We ate Meals Ready to Eat while at the range. At several million calories apiece, and hardly any fiber, people would become severely backed-up, especially after 14 of them.

"I'm not going to lie, I haven't shit in two days," I confessed. "I'm afraid to."

Water training was conducted in a huge indoor pool. As always, the instructors were highly trained enlisted guys who loved to torment young officers.

"Get in the water!" yelled the lead instructor. He had on Navy Seal swimwear and had cauliflower ears. The man was shredded. We were all standing on the side of the pool in full uniform, gear, and a rubber replacement for our M-16s. It was time to tread water, except there wasn't any room. People started jumping in the deep end. We looked like penguins jumping off a glacier into the ocean. Quickly, the pool filled with bodies of men, weighed down by gear and fear.

"Get in the damn water!" the instructor yelled again. I was among the 20 or so that hadn't yet jumped in. I'm not sure why; I don't mind the water. I looked down and there were tightly packed bodies bobbing and thrashing about.

"Get in the fucking water!" That one was directed at me.

I jumped in and landed on another lieutenant's shoulders, driving him under water. I felt his head between my legs as he tried to surface. Finally, his head popped out.

"You bastard!" he said as he gasped for air.

"Sorry dude. Really sorry."

He was coughing, trying to catch his breath. Then it looked like a shark had attacked him by the way he was being pulled under. I grabbed him by the hair and tried to keep him up, but the downward force was just too much. His hair slipped out of my hand. He went under, and with all of the commotion, and all of the bodies banging against each other, I couldn't see him. Suddenly he shoots to the surface.

"You bastard!" Again with the name calling as he fights for oxygen.

"It wasn't me," I lied, "I was trying to help you!"

Later that day, a rumor was going around that I tried to drown someone from another platoon, that I had kicked the man and pulled his hair, but nothing came of it. This was training, and training never stopped for anything; it just kept going.

Meffers actually did drown. He had to be pulled from the pool. He panicked and tunnel vision kicked in, and he just sank. When we were all back at our room, McRudd and I started in on him.

"You drowned? Jim, you fucking drowned," I said. McRudd was balled up on the floor, laughing.

"I didn't drown. I just became disoriented," he tried to mitigate.

"You sunk like a rock!" McRudd said laughing his ass off. "You had to be resuscitated!"

"Whoa, don't start with your fancy words. You can't even spell resuscitated!" Meffers had scored big with this one. McRudd had failed the grammar test that they administered to us. A monkey could have passed it, just not McRudd.

"Yeah dude, you can't even read!" I added. McRudd wasn't going to let this one go.

"Yeah? I wasn't going to say anything Andrew, but we were surprised you could find the fucking pool in the first place. We were afraid you'd end up in Fredericksburg!"

I had to take the nighttime land navigation test three times before passing it. It was humiliating. I just kept getting off course and would end up lost. I already had anxiety from the Great Air Force Armadillo Attack years before. But damn-- you couldn't see your hand in front of your face out there. Plus, taking off from a known point towards another point that I had plotted on my map using a protractor and compass, to find a box with a number on it seemed stupid. But that was the test. Walking through the dark woods at night pissed me off. On one occasion I got caught up in some old rusty concertina wire that had been left out in the training area. Once you wander into it, it's nearly impossible to get out, and the more you struggle to get out of it, to free yourself, to get the tiny razor blades out of your uniform and boots and gear and skin, the worse it becomes. I was fully trapped by the wire. I couldn't move, and my body was contorted, spread out like Jesus. I bled from the cuts.

I stared up at the sky and thought about dying out there. Anyhow, the way I got out was to start thrashing my body and rolling to one side. It took only 15 minutes but felt like an eternity. The razors had shredded my uniform, my boots, and my skin. The whole time I just gritted my teeth and tore through the razors. This was in no way heroic. I was whimpering like a baby. Exhausted, I got to my feet and tried to get my bearings. Eventually, I got back on track, re-calculated my azimuth, considered my pace count, unfolded the old ass compass and limped off. Well, I missed the objective by about 150 yards. At least that's what the instructor told me when I turned in my card at the end of the test.

"McKenna! Jesus Lieutenant! Did you walk all the way to Fredericksburg? He laughed.

"Seriously sir, how did I do? Did I pass?" I asked.

"No. You failed."

"Fuck."

That happened twice. I failed the fucking thing twice. One more try. If I didn't get it the third time, something terrible would happen, like I'd have to re-do all of the training or I guess, conceivably, I could have been "a washout." Meffers and McRudd were ruthless. Before lights-out, the following exchanges ensued.

"Hey dude, we'll leave the light on for you tonight so you don't get lost if you need to use the bathroom in the middle of the night," Meffers would say.

"Okay, pal, listen: I put a life preserver in the shower for you. Safety first okay?" I told Meffers. McRudd was laughing and reading the back of a bottle of Nyquil or Robitussin or something. We were forever sick at The Basic School.

"What the fuck are you laughing at? Look Jim, he's pretending to read the back of the bottle. Bring that shit over here before you overdose, you illiterate bastard." Jim, never skipping a beat, added: "Illiterate means you can't read you dumb bastard."

After lights out, Meffers would begin the fart assault. The room smelled like he had shit the bed. He'd lay over there laughing and laughing while McRudd just groaned in disgust. Occasionally I would throw a boot at Meffer's head in anger. In the dead of winter we would have the fan in the window literally blowing in snow and sleet. Meffers and I, being from the north, were at home in the cold, but McRudd just shivered. I didn't go the traditional college route and never had college roommates, but I'll be damned if this wasn't way better.

One night we went out to a club and I met a girl named Maria. She was from Colombia. She and I hit it off right away. Maria was doing cocaine throughout the evening, and she was telling me these wild-ass stories from when she used to live in Vegas. She was an escort, but now she was stuck in Podunk, Virginia, because her mother had a brain aneurysm and needed Maria's help. Maria and I danced and grooved and drank and ended up at her mother's apartment in Spotsylvania, Virginia. Her mother was in bed moaning. I think she needed to be bathed or something. Her room smelled of urine. Apparently, Maria wasn't a perfect daughter or caregiver or person. She reminded me of a South American witch, and she had an enormous tongue.

"Punch my pussy," I was going down on her and it smelled like cinnamon toast crunch cereal. I don't even eat breakfast.

"What?"

"Punch my pussy and fuck me."

"Punch your what?"

"Do it goddamn it!" She was masturbating. I was in shock.

"Do what?" I asked. This was crazy time.

"Punch my cunt!" She screamed this and I looked to the door of the bedroom and thought her mom must have heard that.

"Listen I ..." But she was already gonzo.

"Fucking do it!" She was close to an orgasm. I flicked my hand as if I were swatting a fly and made contact with her vagina. This was fucking weird.

"Harder!" she demanded as she rubbed her privates, which weren't private at all. In a fit of pressure, confusion and rage, I sent an uppercut to her vagina as hard as I could. It made a loud rubbery slapping sound. With that she went over the top in orgasm. I just stared down at her. She was in her own world and I was happy for her. As I was leaving I noticed several framed photographs on her dresser. I stopped to look and saw a picture of her with Iron Mike Tyson, and a picture of her with Marvelous Marvin Hagler; all smiles and dressed up, probably from the Vegas days.

Third try. Third try at the nighttime land navigation test. Here we go again. Memories of the Armadillo incident, the barbed wire incident. The night was freezing. Definitely below 32 degrees, which would mean that the water in my filthy canteens would freeze.

"Good luck out there tonight chief," Meffers said as he sipped a beer, feet up, television on.

"Fuck you Jim," I was experiencing anxiety about having to go out again.

"Do you want me to lift the curse I put on you? Because if you do, saying fuck you isn't going to help with that."

"I just don't know what my fucking problem is," I confessed.

"Are you using the compass? You need to use the compass," Tim chimed in.

"You are such a fucking wiseass dude. These compasses suck."

McRudd handed me half a loaf of bread and called me Red Riding Hood.

I stepped off from the starting point with little confidence. My first objective was 1,200 meters on a heading of 34 degrees. I had to cross a rushing stream mid-way which threw me off course by 50 meters or so. When I climbed up the far bank I was soaked to the bone but I was so amped up on coffee and adrenaline that I just pressed on, stopping every 10 meters or so to check my heading on the compass. I found what I believed to be the first objective, found the old ammo can on the post and recorded the number stenciled on the can. Off to my next objective.

I was feeling a little confident now, but not cocky. After getting my new azimuth, recalculating my distance and determining my pace count I suddenly started to second-guess myself. What if the first objective was wrong? What if the box that I found wasn't the right one? Then all the others after it would be wrong. *Be strong, Andrew. Stay focused. Stay positive you fool!*

My effort at the next two or three objectives was squirrely. I forgot my pace-count a few times, daydreamed several times, so when I eventually stumbled upon a box with a number on it, I lacked confidence that I was right. My last "leg," last objective, was in front of me. The cold wind blew as I redid the coordinates and plotted my last objective. A huge wind gust picked the map off the ground and whipped it from my grasping hand, blowing it several feet away. I struggled to my feet and chased the damn thing through the forest. Every time I got close the wind would move the map out of reach. Finally I dove like superman and captured it. I started laughing maniacally like a madman.

With the help of moonlight, I was able to see a pile of razor wire up ahead, directly in my path. Chuckling to myself, I thought, *Oh yeah, oh yeah, you didn't get me this time you sadistic shit.* I walked around the pile, maybe 20 or 30 feet, staring to my right to make sure it wouldn't try to eat me alive again. Suddenly my left foot slipped and I went into a tumbling free-fall down an enormous crevasse. They call them crevasses, but it really seems like a cliff. I hit every rock, every little tree, every goddamn jutting root. Trying to stop my body was futile. With every bump, I felt like I was getting body shots from big bad people. The last thing I heard before passing out was an enormous crunching sound. I had come to rest on a thick stump jutting out from the cliff face or crevasse face or whatever. I opened my eyes. My whole body was wrapped around the stump as I stared into the night. A big fat rain drop landed on my forehead. I couldn't feel my legs or feet or arms or hands. It was a very peaceful moment. Then I wiggled my toes and fingers as I stared up and felt relief that I was alive and not paralyzed.

Are you there, God? It's me, Andrew. Why are you doing this? I don't pretend to understand you or our relationship, but I have to wonder if this is because of my interest in existentialism when I was a freshman. Is it the Camus obsession? Is that what this is about? That was a long time ago God!

I made it to my feet and assessed my situation. The fall had claimed my compass, my map, one of my canteens, and my manhood. I slowly clawed my way up the face, using the same rocks and roots and trees that punished me, as handholds. Deliberately I reached and reached and pulled and pulled until I was at the crest. I took a deep breath and pulled my rocked body over the top. A few feet away lay the razorwire. Ugh. As I stood up I felt an incredible pain in my lower back. Sharp electrical currents shot down my legs and my feet went numb. Grimacing in pain, tears in my eyes, I turned left and just started walking. The only thing I was sure of was the general direction that I was walking would eventually lead me to a road, and from there I would be able to make it back to the barracks. I knew that I had just failed my third try at Night Land Navigation. My body ached beyond belief, but my mind was numb. At this point nothing mattered. I just put one foot in front of the other, and tripped occasionally, and fell occasionally, and got back up and continued to walk.

After about 30 minutes I came into a clearing in the woods and stopped. In front of me about 20 feet was a box on a pole silhouetted by the moon light. I stared, laughing. The chance of this being my last objective was about a million to one. I approached the box, stopping to rest my hand on it. I crouched down and read the number A-17. I reached into my inner coat pocket and pulled-out the sandwich bag that contained my test score card. I patted my other pockets for a pen but none was there. The crevasse had apparently claimed my pen too. A-17 I said aloud.

I get back up, spitting dirt and part of a leaf out of my pie-hole, with three or four bleeding fresh cuts on my legs from the razors.

"A-17, A-17…"

With the test card clutched in my hand, I looked insane, muttering:

"A-17, A-17..."

I stumble out of the woods.

Road.

Humvee idling.

Instructor staring at me.

"Jesus, McKenna, I thought you were dead." I am in a trance-like state now, body still numb, vision slightly distorted. I don't respond other than to hand the instructor the card.

"A-17," I say.

"What?" he says, demandingly. Then: "Ink-stick!" That's Marine-speak for a pen.

"No pen. I mean ink-stick," I say.

I hand the instructor the card. He's inspecting the card, staring intently as he checks his numbers against my numbers, my numbers against his numbers, his numbers against my numbers, his eyes furtively back and forth. I'm sure everything this Infantry Officer does is with furtiveness.

"I don't know quite how to tell you this McKenna."

"A-17," I mumble, barely audibly. If he tells me that I failed I will start crying, and if that doesn't work I will offer him a $500 bribe to pass me.

"Yes, A-17, you passed."

I hold my arms out wide because I want to be hugged. The Marine Captain turns away, gets in his hummer and drives away.

"Bastard!" I turn around expressionless and walk along the road, three miles back to the barracks, A-17 still coursing through my veins.

The next morning, when I wake up, I can't move and my vision is skewed, blurry, and multiplied. I reach up and touch my head and feel a bump. *It's a tumor, I have a tumor.* Instructing my feet to move, nothing happens. *I'm paralyzed. You're not paralyzed and it's not a tumor.* But my back is killing me. *Go to medical. No, you can't go to medical. Why not? What if it's serious? You'll be held back. You won't graduate on time. You'll be put into the company of invalids, Invalid Company, I-Company—broken people trying to heal, trying not to get medically separated from the United States Marine Corps.* What's worse: getting discharged, or getting recycled back to a company that's just starting the Basic School? Having to repeat the training we've already completed? The pool? The wrist locks and chokings? This is the most twisted thing in the world.

"We bought you a night light." Tim is standing over my bed, grinning. "In case you get up in the middle of the night, you know, to use the bathroom? You won't get lost." Tim is known for jumping on me

148

with all of his considerable heft, especially if my arms are pinned under the covers or if I'm in a sleeping bag. Slowly, I move my arms out from under the blanket, into a defensive posture.

"Pain." I shriek, as my back muscles suddenly spasm in unison.

"Where?" Tim says opportunistically. I should have never said the word pain.

"Pain in my ass, you are," I say sounding strained as I try to catch my breath, to deflect, to recover, and it seems to work.

"We'll have to talk about this later," Tim says, "I have to shit."

"Bring your lifejacket." I couldn't resist. Tim drowned in the pool two weeks ago. With that Tim punches me in my thigh full force and runs into the bathroom laughing, shrieking in pleasure. Tim loved to inflict pain.

"Bastard!" I cry in pain. The leg trauma affected my back trauma which radiated in my tumor trauma. My long-term goal, established six months ago, was to convince the base doctors that I need a MRI of my brain. I was convinced that something was wrong with my brain. But now, with my current head injury, I was convinced more than ever that I had brain cancer.

After Tim leaves, I roll out of bed, planting one foot on the floor- - slowly, surely, with deep breaths, until I'm up on my feet. *There you go Marine, nice and easy. Saturday 10 A.M. shower. Motrin.* But this won't work. I end up spending the weekend in bed, resting my back and thinking that my only purpose in life was to complete The Basic School, in spite of the constant pain; pain that would reoccur several times a year for years to come and would unimaginably affect my life.

Marine lawyers go from The Basic School to the Naval Justice School in Newport, Rhode Island. My class there didn't start until May 1997, and because I graduated from TBS in March, I decided that instead of taking leave, I would check into the actual non-training side of Marine Corps Base Quantico, which was my first official post training duty station. Tori, now my wife and also a Marine Officer, was stationed at

Quantico. We had lobbied headquarters hard for me to also get stationed there. The Marines will try to keep couples together and because there are quite a few lawyer slots at Marine Corps Base, Quantico, I didn't have much problem getting that assignment.

Chapter 12

Tori and I had a home built a few miles from the base in a new development. The project had started as I was finishing up my final year of law school in Albany, and was wrapping up while I was in The Basic School. I was essentially living two lives. One I lived when I was physically with Tori: the agreeable appeasing Andrew. And then the life I lived when I was away from Tori: somewhat reckless, happier, and free. Tori was driven by fear to succeed in every way and to attain the things she didn't have as a child, such as stability, financial freedom, property, and a fat savings account. I was driven by immediate gratification, and didn't pay attention to social status and wealth. While she was picking out paint colors and light fixtures for the new house, I was resigning myself to the fact that we had met too young and that we wouldn't grow together as a couple.

Tori was more black and white in her thinking: she had a goal, and was achieving her goal, and for this reason, she never considered the fate of our future together.

Everything was coming together, at least on paper, but something was going wrong in my mind, something was telling me to stop the bus. I think the relationship had stopped growing and that house we had built represented a point of no return. If I didn't look very closely at stopping the relationship right now, at this point of transition from law student to Marine officer to full blown career, I would never really examine it, and might never know what could be. I loved Tori—that much is true. But she wasn't my soul mate.

One significant force moving me in this direction, and this thought process, was that her friend Wendi had just left her husband James. Wendi visited us in Camp Lejeune the previous summer and again earlier in the year. Because Tori had to work, and my schedule was very relaxed, Wendi and I would go to the beach together. We would have these great conversations about life. Totally innocent stuff. She explained the situation with James, about how they had outgrown each other. Wendi was ready to be relationship-free, to get in tune with herself, and to grow without the confines of a romantic relationship. She seemed so free. It got me thinking about the parallels in my relationship with Tori. I had already made the decision to leave Tori, but had not figured out the where and when. This was a really difficult decision, not so much that I doubted my reasoning, but because I didn't want to hurt Tori. I felt like I lacked courage.

Wendi understood this when I told her. She and Tori had grown apart when Tori left for the Marines. Life's funny that way: major geographical and career changes can alter close friendships. Maybe they weren't that close to begin with.

One day at the beach, it started to pour down rain, so I quickly covered Wendi's shoulders with a towel as we ran for cover. We laughed our asses off, and then she stopped laughing and just stared into my eyes.

I am an idiot. At the time I thought I was acting rationally, I believed that my clarity of thought ruled the day, that something divine was happening, and that I was seeing things as they actually were. I believed that Tori would understand and accept that we would have to move in different directions. She deserved better. It's one of my greatest regrets. Not the break-up; that was inevitable, but the way I went about it.

Before I left for Newport, I sat Tori down and told her that I believed our relationship wasn't growing and that we should consider a split. Tori had just been accepted to a master's program in Monterrey, California. So, even though she was technically still stationed at Quantico, her temporary duty station would be Monterrey. I thought this was an ideal time to end everything. She suspected that there was another girl, but she never thought in a million years that it would be Wendi; after all, they were still friends, but not so much anymore. They had gone to high school together, we all went to high school together. I golfed with her husband, the four of us hung out together from time to time over the years. We even went camping, to the beach, vacations of sorts. We laughed together, cried together (well I didn't); we were pretty close.

James and I were never best friends by any means, but I always had a rule that I would never have sex with any of my friends' girlfriends. The only exception was when a friend would give me definitive permission, and that only occurred once. Maybe twice. James and I were not on the sharing kind of level and it's just as well. And to be honest, I wasn't initially attracted to Wendi. It's just that things with Tori had run their natural course, and I was ready for a change. Truth be told, this wasn't a torrent "affair." Wendi is anything but an adulterer—in fact she is fiercely loyal to her friends. She has a dozen great qualities. I had already explained to her that my relationship with Tori was over. It's just existing circumstances brought us together. And predictably, a cloud of guilt hung over us from our inception.

It's an understatement to say the telephone is the root of all evil. In drug rehabs and jail people refer to the phone as the "pain-box." Frankly speaking, a full 60 percent of phone calls leave me feeling angry, anxious, or sad. Or indictable.

I might add that one of the single most destructive options ever invented is call-waiting, and this proved true shortly after I arrived in Newport for the lawyer's course. The base is awesome, as is the entire

Newport area. In my opinion, April was a great time to be there with the beautiful weather, which followed typically harsh New England winters.

I was busy with my career, and again, coasting along mentally. In any event, I was off to Newport to start school, a newly minted attorney. I was in great shape from the Basic School—my back had healed and only flared up occasionally. And most importantly, I was looking forward to 14 weeks in Newport and the challenges of the military's premiere lawyer course. I was identified by instructors as being really good on my feet. During courtroom stuff I stood out as being very persuasive before mock juries. This made me feel very good about myself, even though I was under the microscope for the Tori infidelity. I was competing for the "Best Advocate" award, the school's most prestigious honor. I was busy—very busy, but I always ended up finding time to party at the Officer's Club and off base in Newport. It was April and Newport was starting to jump.

After returning home one night after a good time, in some 50-year-old woman's Mercedes convertible, I called Wendi who was living in New York. I was drunk, which always makes the phone call that much more evil. It becomes the devil's hammer. We were having a good conversation, during which she tells me she has sent me letters describing how she felt. I had received the letters earlier that day and they were sitting on my bureau, unopened. We talked for quite a while. It was probably about 12:30 a.m., just about time for one of my brothers to call from New York as they always did. Sure enough, I hear a click on the line: call waiting. It's got to be Brian with one of his crazy girl conflicts.

"Hold on Wendi, I've got another call." *Click.* "Hello? Tori … hey, what's up? Oh nothing, I'm on the other line with Brian. No, just a couple beers. What? No, I'm not cheating on you. Jesus! We already talked about this Tori. No, of course not. Stop it. Yeah, I can talk. Hold on. Would you relax? Let me click over and get off with Brian. OK, hold on, hold on." *Click.* "Wendi?" Pause. "No, it's Tori." *Oh my fucking God.* Tori says: "I fucking knew it! How could you Andrew? You fucking asshole, you fucking, fuck, fuck, fuck! *Oh my fucking God, this isn't*

153

happening. Fucking fuck, fuck? "You know what Andrew? You're fucked! You are fucked! You are fucked! You are fucked! You are fucked! You are fucked! You are fucked, fucked!" And she hangs up.

The Uniform Code of Military Justice is the law that governs all military personnel. The hot ticket item for military prosecution at the time was adultery. I guess they ran out of homosexuals to persecute—I mean prosecute. Unlike the civilian sector, the Marines court-martial adulterers and Tori was on a fucking rampage. She was not going to let this go. Tori was determined to tell my commanding officer, as well as the commander of the Naval Justice School in Newport, the Secretary of Defense, the Secretary of State, the Ambassador to Vietnam, Pope John Paul II, my first grade teacher and the check-out lady at Giant. I was screwed. My life as I knew it was over. My stomach ached and I passed out.

The next morning I woke up with a serious hangover. I put on my uniform. I walked into the bathroom and looked at my face in the mirror and remembered what had happened the night before on the phone, and threw-up everything in my belly. I'm dry heaving. Nerves, the hangover, and the feeling of an impending court martial and ostracism, not to mention having to deal with Tori and the hurt I caused her, all made me dizzy. This is why alcohol sucks. Bad things happen when I drink, and usually the consequences don't come until the next morning. Wow, this is not good.

As a Marine officer, once you are *targeted* for doing something wrong, whether you did anything wrong or not, you're screwed. Any accusation or suggestion of impropriety by anyone in the Marines can basically tank your career. I knew that I had at least *some* time before it would really hit the fan, but how long? Well, Tori was going through a pretty intense program at school in Monterey and I was all the way across the country in Newport. We were separated by nearly 3,000 miles. Thankfully, this geographic separation alone would surely afford me some time to figure out what to do: discrediting campaign? File for divorce? What? Fuck!

Class that day was painful because of the hangover and that familiar feeling of impending doom. I spent the lunch hour trying to learn a fact pattern from a mock sample case that the instructors had put together. I had to do a closing argument in front of instructors with years of trial experience. It was an interesting time because I was being graded against my classmates, and I loved this nervous feeling that I had, except I don't think I had brushed my teeth that morning. The competition was in a small crowded room and for sure I was blasting people with stink breath. The whole time I'm talking, I'm thinking, *can they smell the alcohol from last night?* My voice normally booms, but I tried to speak without releasing too much air. Despite my turmoil, I'd studied just enough of the facts that I was able to construct an argument for the assignment. I presented my closing in front of eight students and five instructors. Even though I felt like absolute garbage, I came in first place for this portion of the overall competition. This despite believing my life was about to implode, and my breath smelling like a bag of assholes.

Once the hangover started to subside, I came to believe that the issue with Tori might blow over. She would somehow get over it. After all, we hadn't lived together consistently since before Officer Candidate School in 1993. Surely, she would meet someone in California, and all would be well. This was perfectly rational. *But this is not rational thinking.* Besides, what would she tell my commanding officer, that I called her another girl's name? What evidence did she have? It was my word against hers. I left class feeling so much better about everything. Walking into the lobby of the billeting building, I stopped at the front desk and asked for my mail, none. I got on the elevator and took it to the ninth floor where my room was. *I'm going to change out of my uniform and go have dinner, a couple drinks, and relax. I am ready to party, baby. Things are going to be just fine. Tori is in California.* Tori is in my room.

"Holy fucking shit, Tori! You scared the shit out of me! What are you doing here? No, of course I'm glad you're here." *Does she have a knife? I think I see a knife. Is that a knife?* "Welcome."

She's sitting in the corner like a mental patient. The front desk clerk at the hotel where I am staying gave her a key to my room when I was at class, because she was my wife and he didn't know that I was sleeping with her friend, or that she had dropped everything in California in less than a day's time and flew three thousand miles to confront me. I should have briefed the desk clerk about this. Tori was livid, seething. Her eyes looked really small and her chest was rising and falling with every angry breath. I had turned her into an evil person.

"Who do you think you are?"

"Listen Tori, we can approach this problem two ways." You'd think presenting a process to an enraged person is a good way to diffuse them. But it's not.

"Shut the fuck up."

"That's one way," I say.

"You're going to listen to me," she says with her fists clenched. I see the pain in her face, and my heart sinks.

"Your career is over."

"Listen, we can work this—"

"Shut the fuck up." *This is not going well at all.* "You really fucked up this time, Andrew, you really did. You're drinking again!"

"Not really."

"Liar! I knew it was Wendi. I came here to tell you that your life is over."

"Well that just sucks, Tori. This whole experience just does not represent who we are, as people. Have a seat right now and let's parse-out this entire situation right down to brass tacks. Come on, soup to nuts, sit-down!"

With that Tori, calmly left, my room. This is not good. My powers of persuasion, which heretofore were strong, were no match for her rage, her need for vengeance. I knew this would get harder before it would get easier. I sat on my bed rubbing my eyes and forehead. The hangover symptoms were back. I needed to drink something to calm my nerves. I could go get a six pack. The Officer's Club idea was clearly out; I couldn't afford her showing up. I'll just go get some beer, come back to my room and regroup. I grab my keys and immediately notice that my mail is gone, including unopened letters from Wendi. Tori took my mail! This could be the evidence she needs. I need to get those back. First I need a beer. Actually, I need a valium.

Back in my room. I slam a beer, then another beer, and then another beer. Nerves. OK, what to do. Ring, ring.

"Wendi, it's Andrew. She has the letters you sent."

"Oh, no!" she says.

"I know, I know. I didn't read them yet. What's in the letters? Anything bad?" I'm in a state of panic now.

"Well I wrote about stuff," she says.

"What stuff?"

"About what we did. Is this bad?"

"Oh my God, you're not serious! I'm in deep shit, very, very deep shit. There is no shit deeper. This is oceans of deep shit."

"I don't get it Andrew, I really don't," she says.

"Because it's adultery. You slept here with me and then wrote about it, and I'm married, and she found out, and she's catatonic. It's like she's been bitten by a rabid animal, and she wants me to be dead immediately. And it's a crime!"

"A crime? Like court-martial or whatever it's called?" she asks.

"Yes, just like that. They ran out of homosexuals to prosecute! I have to get the letters back. OK, I'll call you back. Listen, whatever you do, don't say anything to anyone about anything." That's advice my older brother's boss gave him years ago.

"Try to relax Andrew. I'm worried about you," she says, clearly stressed and confused.

"I can't relax, please don't tell me to fucking relax."

Ring, ring.

"Tori, it's Andrew. We need to talk."

"Fuck you. I'm telling the Marines everything!" Tori is still fuming.

"I understand … that's fine, do what you have to do, but at least let's meet and figure out who's going to pay what bills and stuff." Tori was a Nazi-soldier when it came to finances.

"No shit Sherlock, you're not going to screw up my credit!"

"I know, I know. I'll come over there. Fifteen minutes. Have you eaten?"

"Fuck off." Tori wasn't going to budge. *This is crazy.* Click.

Tori is staying in guest officer's billeting in an adjacent building. Before I leave, I slam another beer. I grab my daily planner which contains everything important in my life, including my diary where I write important and unimportant personal observations. I'm not leaving anything lying around anymore; can't take that chance. I arrive at her room and enter. The mood sucks. No surprise there. Tori is sitting in the corner again. She knows my mission: to get the letters.

"Tori, you stole my mail which is a federal offense." *That is so weak Andrew.*

"That is so weak Andrew."

"Weak or not, it's a crime and I want my mail back or I'll see to it you are prosecuted."

"OK, Andrew, how's this sound: Go fuck yourself!"

"There are two ways to do this. Why screw everything up for everyone? Let's just get past this, please. This is all just screwed up. I need those letters Tori and I need them now."

"Get out."

"What?"

"Get out!"

"Fine, fucking relax! I'm going." I walk out the door and down the hall. Oh shit. I left my planner in Tori's room. I am so fucking stupid. Notes about what I have told other people about my relationship with Wendi, so I don't forget my "version" are in my planner. Don't ask why but, I was creating an alibi timeline earlier that day. It makes no sense. It's stupid, but now Tori has this additional evidence, and I am screwed.

Turn around and go back and get the damn thing, moron. Knock, knock, "Tori, I need my planner."

"Fuck you." Then the unthinkable happens. Tori has the door just barely open, bracing her body against it. I force it open.

"Give me my planner." I see it on the bed and grab it. She screams. Without even thinking, I cover her mouth with my hand. This is assault. The scream is muffled. A horrible feeling hits me. The reality of what I have done hits me. How did it get this far? The whole event only lasted a few seconds in slow motion. I left, planner in hand, and returned to my room.

They were at my door. Tori or someone in the building had called the base police and within minutes, they were at my door. Because there was an accusation of assault or disturbance, I was taken into custody and booked at the base police station. They suggested I not make any statements. The leader of our class, a Marine major named Jeffrey came to the station to pick me up. Tori already talked to him about the Wendi thing, about me coming to her room, and about everything else that I have ever done wrong. He wasn't happy with me and the entire situation. I told him my side of the story, but none of it matters in the Marine Corps. Plus, my side was the bad side. Just for once, I'd like to be on the good side of the story. Just being involved in something unseemly, as an officer, was taboo. Any blemish would result in destruction of my career. Tori and I were put under "stay away" orders, which meant no contact whatsoever. This was fine by me, but I knew that any hope of this blowing over was now gone. What was worse was how bad I felt for Tori. She never asked for any of this.

The next morning, I received a call from my boss at Quantico. Lieutenant Colonel Anita Fink, probably one of the best Marines and leaders I've ever known, was the second highest judge advocate at the base. She was a fair-minded, grounded, smart, career officer. The first thing she said was for me to stay out of any more trouble, that she had heard that I was doing really well in school, and that I had to focus on that and graduate. She wanted me to make it back to Quantico where I would start my first official tour of duty. The next thing she said was not to discuss any of the details with her because she didn't want to have to be a witness if later I was court-martialed. I didn't expect her to say that. My heart just sank. It was Friday and I decided to go home to Albany for the weekend, to get away from Newport and the chaos.

When I arrived at my mom's house, my mother said that Tori had called and left her number in California. Phew, I'm safe for a few days. I decided to call her and find out what she intended to do. As soon as we get on the phone, she started right in. Questions like, "When did the affair begin? Did you sleep together?" I knew she knew the answer to this one, because she had read the letters from Wendi and it was pretty well outlined. Then I heard a clicking noise, and then the sound of plastic hitting plastic. She's recording this! But this realization came too late. I thought if I were honest with Tori about the how everything went down, that this would accelerate her healing process. Honesty is the worst policy at times like these. I had given her more evidence of adultery—my voice on tape. Ironically she was using a Dictaphone I was given as a class-gift when I graduated law school. Not sure, really, if that's ironic. Now what was I going to do?

On Monday I was ordered to Quantico to meet with Colonel Fink about what was happening. I never thought it would come to this. The following day I drove from Newport to Quantico and the trip felt like it took forever. On Wednesday, I reported to Colonel Fink. As I was walking down the hall towards her office, I saw Tori coming out of the Colonel's office. Somehow, Tori had gotten to her first, which is never good. I felt like I had an uphill battle on my hands. The evidence was going to be the key factor. No matter how much the Colonel liked me, if the evidence was there, she would not be able to ignore it. Tori had told too many people and any perception of a cover-up by the Colonel would affect her reputation and possibly her career. She just wouldn't do it anyway because she had way too much integrity for something like this. *Knock.* "Come in."

"Ah, the other Lieutenant McKenna."

"Yes ma'am. Lieutenant McKenna reporting as ordered." I stood before her desk at the position of attention.

"At ease, Andrew. Have a seat. You've had better days. I just met with Tori."

"I know I saw her in the hallway ma'am." I'm trying to get a read on the Colonel's feelings toward me, her demeanor. How fucked am I based on her conversation with Tori?

"Did you talk?"

"Not really ma'am. She talked, she said I was fucked."

"You're not fucked, relax."

"I'm not fucked ma'am?"

"No, you're not fucked."

"I'm so glad that I'm not fucked ma'am." My breathing returned to normal.

"Frankly, I don't know what's going to happen, as you know, it's not up to me. It's like this Andrew: I think that Tori is overreacting, and she is so angry right now that she can't see straight."

"I know, I feel bad about this. She's having a tough time with the break-up, she thinks that I—"

"The important thing is that you don't talk to anyone, well other than a priest or something, but no one else. She's coming out pretty strong against you, and I suggest you start thinking like a lawyer on this one. If this gets anymore screwed up, I won't be able to support you here. In the words of our Commander-in-Chief, maybe you got a little too close to this Wendi person, but here you're going to be judged on how you handle adversity from this point on."

"I understand ma'am, I know we cannot talk about the particulars, but hypothetically, what if she had some evidence of adultery?"

"Well, she feels that she does, Andrew, and honestly, that could be a problem. I've made arrangements for you to talk to Major Bisci. You can discuss this case with him. He's an excellent attorney." *Wow, this isn't going away. Granted, she's on my side, sort of, but she's telling me to talk to defense counsel?*

I'm sure Tori didn't show her whole hand to the Colonel either, and so what will happen when Tori shows her the letters or the tape recordings? She won't be able to ignore it. There's a very good possibility that I'll be forced to resign my commission and leave the Corps. Worst case scenario, I would be court-martialed. And of course, I always think in terms of worst case scenario. Leavenworth is in my future. I'd never survive prison.

That night, I called Tori at her house and asked if I could come over to get some things. Of course she said no, and again reviewed with me how fucked I was.

"Thanks for that Tori, I had almost forgotten." I think she was drinking wine or something, which Tori never did a lot of. Her voice sounded different in any event, so I pushed the issue of me coming over. Finally she relented.

When I got there, the place was mostly dark. A chill ran up my spine as I carefully entered the house. I thought maybe, just maybe, she would stick a knife in my head because for the past few nights in my dreams, I've been stabbed in my head by people.

"Tori? Hello?"

"I'm in the living room." *Oh God.* I walked towards the living room, noticing all of the blind spots on the way. I felt like a Navy SEAL doing a house search in Southern Beirut. I turned the corner into the living room and there she was sitting in the corner. *What's with her and these corners lately?*

"Are you OK?" I ask sheepishly.

"I'm fine, I have wine. And besides, the doctor gave me something to calm me down."

"Are you supposed to be drinking with it? Can I try one? Well can I at least have a glass of wine?"

162

"It's in the kitchen." *It's a set up.* In the kitchen, I notice a piece of cutlery missing from the block. Chills set in again. About every half second, I turn to make sure she was still safely in the corner. And she was. Whatever the doctor gave her was working.

"What did the doctor give you?"

"You're not getting one asshole, so stop."

"Fair enough." I pour a big-ass glass of wine, close to 10 ounces and take a seat approximately 17 feet away from Tori. If she charges me, I'll have plenty of time to drop kick her.

"I talked to Anita Fink today," I say trying to bait her into a conversation and determine what she revealed to the Colonel.

"We're not talking about it. I'm taking the night off from masterminding your ruin." Smiling now, she asks, "Fair enough?"

"Sure I understand," I say. "How's your mom doing?"

"Shut-the-fuck-up." Tori is wise to my efforts.

"Right, right." We sat in silence for about three minutes. I get a refill. Finally she speaks.

"I have to fly back to California tomorrow and you're not allowed in the house while I'm gone, or ever for that matter." Jesus, another cross-country flight. I learn from Tori that her neighbor, whom I've never met, will keep an eye on things while she's gone. I drink another glass of wine while I again try my hand, unsuccessfully, at damage control. I'm drunk. She's not budging. I pass out in the chair. Tori passes out in the corner.

I wake up before she does, covered in wine, which I think for a second is blood and I scream, but it's only wine that I spilled on myself after passing out. Where would she hide the letters and audiotape evidence that she has amassed against me? My head is killing me from all of the goddamn wine. I think maybe I should kill her before I leave. *That would be so fucking stupid, Andrew. There's forensic evidence everywhere, you have motive, intent, opportunity. You'd fry!* And of course, it's wrong to kill someone which is the reason I wish would come to me first in these situations. Just as I start my search, Tori wakes up and says that I better go. I tell her that we should talk later.

163

"Have a safe trip."

"You too," she says. What's that supposed to mean? Am I taking a trip I don't know about?"

I took the day off to wrap up my affairs. Poor choice of words. Really, nothing was getting wrapped up. If anything, things continued to become more and more unwrapped. Colonel Fink told me that my commanding officer, the person who is in charge of everyone, even Colonel Fink, was asking about me. What kind of officer was I? Was I credible? In other words, was I worth keeping in the Marine Corps? I had to get back into that house and find that evidence or I was fucked. A Xanax would really help right now.

That night, with Tori back in California, I went back to the house, but not before casing the place, looking for the neighborhood watch people. If they were out at all, they stayed well hidden which might be called "cover and concealment" in the Corps.

Like a ninja, I cut through four back yards, was nearly mauled by a beast of a dog in the process, and scrambled up the hill behind the house. I was covered in sweat, scared shitless by that damn dog, my heart racing. *This is ridiculous, how do I get involved in this shit?* From the edge of the yard, I low-crawl to the back door, covered in fresh grass clippings and leaves and dirt. I stand up and climb the four steps and turn the door knob. It opens. *Unlocked?* This is a set-up. *Check the corners first.* The house is completely dark. *I'll be rendered paraplegic any minute now.* I decide to squat down to avoid any potential head blows like any alert Marine would do. *I deserve to be shot.* The anticipation and anxiety, plus my recent steady diet of beer and nachos, causes my body to sweat and my stomach to start bubbling. Oh God, not now. I feel the emergency need to fart now, but I'm in the squatting position and I am reluctant to do this because of the obvious risk. I cannot be caught in this house, dressed like a ninja, covered in grass clippings, sweating, having shit my pants. The Marine Corps would not look kindly upon this. Adultery? Maybe there's some wiggle room. Breaking and entering? Well I'm on the deed after-all.

Officer shitting his pants? No fucking way. Now my stomach is rumbling, my bowels are starting to shift. I stand up like a man, butt cheeks clenched, and waddle to the bathroom.

To say it was urgent couldn't possibly describe my predicament. With a millisecond to spare, I drop my pants, butt over the toilet, and explode. If anyone is in this house right now on stakeout they would either have to be laughing, dry heaving, or vomiting. *Things could not be worse right now.* There was no toilet paper. I had to use one of Tori's decorative hand towels. The toilet wouldn't flush. The water was off.

Down into the basement to turn the water on, which I don't even really know how to do, I noticed a bunch of boxes, four deep, stacked three high. So I start poking around. Then I hit pay-dirt. Buried deep in a box were the letters from Wendi and my handheld Dictaphone. In the recorder was a tape. I hit play and listened to myself explain the situation to Tori, groveling insanely to her. Then I heard myself pretend to cry. Then I heard a series of fuck-yous. And the conversation was over. Rewind. Click. Record. Rewind. Click. Play, and I had effectively erased the tape. It was gone. I wiped my prints from the recorder, which made no sense, and placed it back into the box. I took the letters from the envelopes and started to read one, and considered masturbating, but I didn't. I swear. The letters went into my pocket; I put everything back in its place, and left. When I got back to my room at the base, I decided to take a shower. As I turned the water on, I realized that I had never flushed her toilet. The hand towel!

The following few days were very difficult for me; I can't imagine how bad things were for Tori. As usually happens after I have been especially selfish, guilt set-in. Tori, with the exception of being controlling, never did anything to deserve this. I had hurt her. I could see the pain in her eyes and it made me sad. Without any evidence, other than a shitty hand towel, and given her unsteady appearance, the higher-ups in the Marines decided to let this blow-over, to not bring any charges against me. I was relieved; no doubt about it in one respect, but it didn't do anything for my conscience.

165

Andrew McKenna

When I arrived back in Newport the next day, I decided that I was due a little reward, a treat for my efforts. I mean, I had dodged this big bullet, a fucking .50 caliber bullet! I changed into some casual clothes and headed to the harbor. This particular ocean-side bar was probably my favorite hangout when I wanted to get away from the base, military people, and the military in general. It was where rich people went so I knew I would never see my Marine buddies there. The place was my little refuge, a secret refuge. The bartender was gay and so I immediately had established a strong rapport because for some reason I always have gotten along smashingly with gay men. One time he asked me if I was gay and I said, "No sir, but I have gay friends." And because I needed him on my side (poor guy in a rich-person bar must be tight with the bartender) my central nervous system took over and caused one of my eyelids to close while the other remained open. Some people would say that is a wink— whatever. I'll take another vodka tonic Brad. "Yes sir, sailor." *No, Marine.* "Even better."

A group of beautiful rich people sit near me and I whisper to my bartender that I'm a 3rd year medical student and he winks at me. For the next couple of hours I'm a medical student to these people and the bartender playfully calls me "doc" which makes me strangely nervous, and I want to tell him to stop it because it doesn't sound convincing, and he's overdoing it, but whenever I signal for him to knock it off, he says, "What?" way too loudly.

Anyhow, these folks are the smoothest, most pretentious boobs I have ever associated with. It was fun to listen to Dirk and Winston tell some asshole story from their adventures in far-away lands. I swear I heard the term "on safari." At the end, I'd laugh with everyone else, but then add, under my breath, barely audible: "that's silly" or "what a tool." I think Winston's blonde girlfriend, Jennifer, caught on and she was obviously pretty fed up with her tool boyfriend's escapades and his shameless stories, and his expensive Rolex. I picked up on this the minute I met them and I exploited this weakness to a great extent. Jennifer

166

gradually moved closer until our knees were touching so I did my little secret energy move where I visualize my body's electricity enter from my leg into her leg so that we both feel it, and it's at a maximum voltage. I turn to her and say, "Did you feel that?" and she very quietly said, "Yes." It works if you really concentrate.

Before I knew it, we are touching each other under the table while Winston tells us more ice-climbing stories. I make running commentary undermining him, and Jennifer, who is drinking way too much and too fast, is trying to time her laughter to appropriate times in his stories so he does know she is laughing at him.

After a while I was following Jennifer into the women's bathroom every fifteen minutes to kiss her and touch her breasts. We were all pretty sauced and when Dirk's girlfriend—barely able to walk straight—walked in on us and said, "I want some," in an aggressive jealous sort of way, I kissed and groped her too. They wanted to leave the bathroom separately but I insisted we all go out together which they thought was just the craziest thing they had ever heard.

I announced I was going for a walk outside to get some air. I walked down to the dock, stepped over a security rope where I could get close to some pretty fucking incredible yachts, and Jennifer was making her way down to join me. I wish I could say that I snuck onto a yacht with her and we had a beautiful time, but I can't. I didn't even try. We had sex standing up on the dock against a light post with people as close as 75 feet away. It was getting dark out so I don't think people saw us, but maybe. It lasted about 46 seconds which made me laugh. Jennifer didn't seem to care, although she wasn't laughing like I was.

Walking back I ran into a naval officer who was in my class and we exchanged handshakes and he gives me the "so-you-must-of-trespassed-to-have-sex-with-this-tart-that-is-not-your-estranged-wifey" look. I confirmed with the "everything-you're-thinking-is-true-and-I-trust-my-secret-is-safe-with-you-and-if-you-say-a-word-you'll-have-more-problems-than-just-the-ugly-wife-you-have-on-your-arm-tonight" look. Message sent and received, sir.

The whole encounter seemed so sociopathic though. The public fucking, tricking her idiotic boyfriend, Biff, etc. I remember driving back to the base pretty lit too. It definitely was not the time to get a DWI, but I hadn't planned on an alternative way to get home. I made it through the guard shack and onto the base. Walking from my car to my room, I felt bad about myself and I felt like everyone knew that I got caught cheating on Tori, and that I was immoral. A message from Wendi was on the phone. She wanted me to call her. But the whole thing just seemed so sad. I closed my eyes and tried to fall asleep. But the bed just kept spinning in the opposite direction of my mind.

Chapter 13

After Naval Justice School, I reported to Quantico for official duty. My first job was as a legal assistance officer. On one occasion, we had to do a will for a VIG or "very important general" who was getting ready to retire after 41 years in the Marine Corps. My colleague at the time was Spence, a really nervous guy, but an excellent cerebral-type attorney. He was just really nervous. He and I would get each other laughing all the time, that uncontrollable laughter where tears would run down our faces. And it was always in front of clients, usually while we were executing people's wills. Spence wanted to make a career of the Marines and I didn't. So when the General was coming for his will, I wasn't really sweating it. I mean, it's just another man. "No, Andrew, it's another General, and we need to get this right!" Spence insisted.

I detected hives on his face mixed with perspiration and fear. Spence had a reputation for getting wound up. And he lived up to his reputation while preparing the office for the General's visit. He had the junior enlisted Marines mopping, buffing, polishing, weed whacking, roto-tilling, and planting indigenous flora. The enlisted Marines were fed-up with Spence but no one could say anything to him. For three days, Spence barked orders to people and to himself. He muttered to himself and kept digging at his neck and face insisting that he had a rash, but we all knew it was hives caused by anxiety. When the time came for the General and his wife to come see us, it looked like a team of hostile cats had attacked him. Spence was not well. His eyes were watering excessively; he was perspiring.

This particular General was notorious for ruining the careers of young officers. He would literally pull over cars that were speeding on base and yell at the drivers and their families. He would also go to the Base Exchange (mall) during lunch, approach officers and ask why they were wasting time shopping when they could be reading books from the Commandment's Reading List. Obviously the man was insane. Forty-three months in the Marines will drive a person mad, just imagine what forty three years will do. A call from the General to your commanding officer complaining about you was certain death. Spence knew this. I did not care, and Spence knew this, too. He kept asking me if he I thought it would be OK and I would say:

"It's anyone's guess, Spence."

"I need to make major, asshole!"

"Spence, stop the name calling, it's unprofessional. And besides, the General's people called and said he can't make it until next week.

"Really?"

"No, not really, he'll be here any minute!"

"Fuck you! You never take anything seriously—that's your problem."

A young private was staged at the front door as a look-out. Another was waiting down the street pretending to rake leaves. Suddenly Spence takes off for the head in a sprint. I'm laughing out loud and everyone is staring at me with this "will the General ruin our careers too?" look, and it's this point here that I realize leadership is needed. Assessing the panic among my people, I stop laughing and I yell: "Everyone 'man-up,' he's here! Look busy, God damn it!" I calmly greeted the General and his wife explaining how honored we were, that he would trust us with his will, it being such an important legal undertaking.

"Why wouldn't I trust you?" the General asked.

"Excuse me, sir?" I responded

"Why wouldn't I trust you?"

"Well you would sir, and you are sir, and that makes me nervous, I mean, happy."

"Not nervous, happy?" The General is perplexed.

"Yes sir, very happy and not nervous. Sir, I'd like to give the General and his wife a quick tour of the office, assuming that the General has the time."

"That's a bold assumption, Captain."

"Well the Captain didn't mean to imply—"

"Which Captain?"

"I didn't understand the General's question."

"Can we just get started?" he says, clearly irritated.

"Of course, General. I'll just ask Captain Gripp to join us, he's sort of our Wills expert."

"What's your area of expertise, McKenna?"

I want to say, "Pussy sir, I'm an expert on pussy."

"Well? The General pushes."

"I enjoy tax law, Sir." Why do I default to lies? There's no explanation, and it always turns out poorly.

"Good, because you're going to do our taxes too." See what I mean?

"Of course, the Captain would be honored to do the General's taxes, and the General's wife's taxes. Yes ma'am and sir...."

When Spence walks up to us I am both relieved and mortified. He looked like he was attacked by black hornets in the bathroom.

"Holy—skipper, are you OK? Jesus."

"Fine sir, fine. Just a touch of an allergy."

"Are you sure? I've never seen—"

"No really, I'm fine Sir. Please, thank you."

"He's fine General, he's fine. A little calamine should fix the Captain. Maybe."

"Shall we get started General and ma'am?"

Spence is short of breath and he has lumps on his face and he might not know where he is right now and I'm starting to laugh internally. I learned to laugh internally during church as a child when the priest would read scripture with the word ass (donkey).

"We'll just step into my office here," Spence says.

Spence had already instructed the staff to hold all calls, to not allow any interruptions. You'd think we were performing brain surgery. Things went surprisingly well. Spence and I held it together. I laughed a bit, but was able to hold the laughter until there was an appropriate time or at least a minimally appropriate time.

However, Spence did become very upset when the phone on his desk started to ring. The first time it rang, Spence apologized to the General and his wife and simply refused to answer it. It rang about 20 times and we all pretended not to be distracted by it. Spence asked the General a question about his estate, but the General couldn't hear the complete question because the phone rang just at the wrong second, which of course made me laugh at the wrong time. I prayed not to start laughing. I bit through my lower lip until I could taste a little blood and then I managed to hold my shit together for a few seconds. The phone starts to ring again and this time Spence reaches over and picks up the hand-set without looking and puts it back on the receiver. But, he's not looking and it doesn't set right on the thing and we can hear a woman's voice, I think it was his wife. And she's saying "Hello? "Hello?" and the General and his wife say to Spence, "Feel free to answer that call, Captain." But Spence says, "No, no that's fine," as he tries to hang the receiver up and we can all hear her voice say "I can hear you! What's wrong with you Spence?"

It's too much for me to hold in. I can't, God. God, you're being evil to me God, plain evil as my laugh bursts out of my nostrils and then my mouth and I laugh openly because situations like these make life worth living.

After a few minutes, the phone starts ringing again and everyone freezes. Spence's face is buried in his legal pad and he is ignoring the phone. But I know this can't last. The General and I briefly make eye contact, man to man, our eyes agree that our collective curiosity trumps the rank disparity between us, but that above all else we need to maintain military decorum and good order and discipline. We want to know how Captain Spence Gripp will handle this. He didn't disappoint. He reached down with his left hand without looking, gripped the phone cord and pulled it from the wall, sending a small white chunk of dry-wall flying across the office. He kept his head down and kept writing. The General muttered, "Good lord," under his breath.

Spence had managed to pull the entire outlet loose, leaving a hole and wires dangling. This was sheer madness. Things got even stranger than that. For some reason, it sounded like Spence was speaking a foreign language whenever he asked a question. He was speaking Zulu or something. He delayed the proceedings and at times left everyone speechless and confused.

The good General and his wife eventually got their wills and Spence survived the ordeal and, because he's a great lawyer and Marine officer, he ended up shining in the end. Everything was fine. Everything returned to normal.

"You pulled the cord out of the wall! It was awesome, Spence!"

"That was something, wasn't it?" Spence said very introspectively, still a bit shaken.

"It was unprecedented. You have to tell the grandkids about this one. Put it in your memoir!"

As time went on at Quantico, things became increasingly strange, or at least strange to me because most of my colleagues didn't seem bothered by it. I was starting to become more disenchanted with the Marine Corps and knew I couldn't make a career of it. At one point I worked for a lieutenant colonel lawyer in the Marines who was clinically crazy. He never made full colonel because he was crazy. And he was fat. Many lieutenant colonels who are crazy get promoted to full colonel, but not if they're fat. Insane? Promote. Fat? Don't promote. That's the Marine Corps way. This lieutenant colonel was also a fool. A crazy, fat fool. My colleague, "The Hump," and I would have to endure his one to two-hour rants, while sitting in his office. All he cared about was hunting turkeys—A subject I have no interest in at all. What possible satisfaction could a man get from shooting a fucking turkey? I'm pretty sure turkeys don't even fly. They're so fat that they jump and flap and maybe get 10 feet or so, but then they're walking again. Plus, there's no danger of attack. A turkey is not going to harm you. If it does, you deserve it. In fact you deserve to be in a coma. You'd have to be in a coma not to be able to effectively defend yourself from a turkey attack.

Well the thrill certainly was there for the Lieutenant Colonel. His thrill was evidently comparable to an out of body experience. He explained to me "the turkey grand slam!" I started to laugh because I thought he was joking. It's where you "bag" four turkeys all from different regions of the country.

"Which country, sir?" I ask.

"Our country!" he responds. For the life of me, despite the Lieutenant Colonel's painfully detailed explanation, I cannot remember the names of the four turkeys. I think one was the Okaloosa Turkey from Florida, but don't hold me to this. I was exhausted after he told me about the first two, but there was no escape. I was a mere captain to him, my time wasn't important, and he never paused during the turkey briefing. He was fucking possessed, and obsessed, especially about the one turkey that had managed to elude him every year and keep him from earning the "grand slam" thing. I don't think they call it a title. That would be silly. When I left his office, we were both nearly in tears. He because of the passion, me because I was drained and sad that this fool was a lieutenant colonel in the organization I was trying to dedicate myself to.

"You look sick," a fellow junior officer observed as we passed in the hallway.

"Yeah, I just met with Francis." I stared blankly down and to the left.

"He talked about the grand slam—"

"Of turkeys." He finished my sentence, looking concerned.

"I need to rest," I said.

Chapter 14

I knew that I couldn't remain sane in a job like this, so I started jockeying for the coveted position in the U.S Attorney's Office in Northern Virginia. I spoke with my boss' boss' boss, a full colonel, about making the move.

"Now I think we can do it Andrew, but first (*oh God, please don't make me run the tax center, please no*), I've decided I want you to run the base tax center this year."

The air rushed out of my lungs in the form of an audible "oh God...." He laughed at this. I couldn't take in any air. I needed a paper bag to breath-in, even though I don't know what that does. And then I think I farted, a fear filled one. And then the left side of my body started tingling and getting numb. I was having a coronary episode. My arteries had finally clogged sufficiently for me to drop dead right there in the Colonel's office. This was not the job for me because the base tax center is set-up every year by a competent young judge advocate lawyer who enjoys tedious work and has an appetite for mundane, brutally boring tax law. He or she must love to be held down and shit on by everybody and everyone regardless of rank or social standing. They are servants to people who don't know anything or know everything and if you fuck-up someone's taxes pal, you're fucked.

"The tax center sir? Sounds great, sir."

"Then we'll get you up to the U.S. Attorney's Office."

"Very good, sir. Thank you." Thank you for simultaneously creating an incredible opportunity and reward, and a near cataclysmic opportunity to fail.

The tax center is a place on base where military personnel, their families, and relatives can come to have their taxes done. It's like an H & R Block without the organization and without the fees. Here's where I came in. I was given a modest budget to work with. My first purchase was a coffee maker. I was certain that my drinking massive quantities of coffee would help offset the shame of knowing nothing about taxes, but pretending that I did. My second purchase was "Taxes for Dummies" because I am a dummy.

I had several weeks before I had to "stand-up" the tax center. That's marine parlance for opening or starting, or doing. I used the phrase as many times a day as I could. Saying things like "I am standing-up my knowledge" or "I'm standing up lunch at 1200" or "tomorrow I'm standing-up a day off." I did this until people stopped shaking their heads at me. One morning I got a call from my boss's boss.

"Andrew?"

"Yes ma'am?"

"It's Colonel Parks."

"Yes, sir, I mean ma'am,"

"How's the tax center coming along?"

"Great, it will be stood-up on time ma'am."

"What?"

"We're in good shape ma'am; the standing-up is on schedule."

"Great, Andrew. A lot of people are interested in how you handle this. It's a big deal."

"Well, I love pressure, we all know that!"

"Are you being sarcastic with me captain?"

"No ma'am, why, do people think I don't like pressure?"

"Andrew, I have no idea what we're talking about."

"Yes ma'am."

"Well, the reason I called is to tell you that I'm sending over a newly minted lawyer, to help with things. He'll report to you."

After we hung up I just sat in my chair and stared. *Maybe I should be the big picture strategy guy and we'll make the new guy get into the weeds of the tax center. He could be responsible for the nuts and bolts while I'm busy focusing on the big major decisions like organizational mission statements and goals and master-servant relationships and stuff like that. I'll be a Jack Welch type. Yes, I'll be Jack Welch. I am Jack Welch or is it a Jack Welsh.*

Knock-knock.

"Please enter!"

"Captain McKenna, sir?"

"Speaking!"

Looking around, "I'm Lieutenant Humphries. I thought I heard you talking to someone in here."

"Nope, just me and my dreams," I say, looking intently at the new lieutenant.

"Have a seat LT. I have a book I think you should read. Do you mind if I call you Hump?" I ask.

"Hump, sir? The Captain would prefer to call the Lieutenant Hump?"

"Well, if you don't mind,"

I respond.

"I guess so sir. I seems a bit strange, but yes sir, Hump is fine."

"Good, now that that's out of the way." I hand Hump my copy of *Taxes for Dummies.*

"Hump, bone-up on your tax law. We stand her up in eight days."

As if coming through his nose, he softly said, "Oh no."

Humphreys and I hit it off beautifully. We had identical senses of humor. He knew right away what I was up to, that this was my ticket to the U.S. Attorney's Office, and he also understood that this was just the way the chips fell in the Marines. I helped him, of course, and I was careful to always give him the credit for everything that went right and I took the hits for everything that went wrong. When it came time to stand her up, we had a video conference with every Marine Corps Base Tax Center at every base across the country. Towards the middle of the video conference, the head guy in Washington, D.C., said for everyone to "boot-up" the electronic filing software that "Hump" and I were supposed to install on our computers a long time ago. Hump started bugging out, nervous as hell. He looked at a large pile of unopened mail on the floor in my office.

"Maybe it's in there," I said.

"Great," Hump said, dismayed. I had been busy with a criminal defense case and didn't have the time to open it all. Hump found what he thought might be the software. He tore open the package, jammed disks into the computer and started to speed read the manual. Total ruckus.

Ultimately, we were able to get everything "stood-up" and the Tax Center was an enormous success that year. The number of returns filed exceeded the previous year. We had around 10 full-time employees. Humphreys was given credit for handling the tactical, I had theorized some excellent ideas including standing-up satellite tax prep centers at some outposts, which increased the number of returns we processed, which is the most important thing in the Marines. You have to find ways of getting your numbers up. Productivity, even if it's only evident on paper, is the paramount mission. We were even able to get a few commendation medals for a few junior enlisted Marines who did really great jobs, too. You're taught from day one as a candidate at OCS to

Andrew McKenna

always look out for your enlisted Marines. They do the work and they deserve the recognition typically more than officers do. The enlisted Marines eat first and if there's food left then the officers get to eat. Never the other way around.

My boss's boss called me and I knew the minute I heard his voice that I was about to get the job I had been dreaming about: Special Assistant United States Attorney.

"Andrew?"

"Sir?"

"Good job with the tax center, Marine."

"Thank you, sir. Humphreys really deserves a small fraction of the credit sir."

"Is that right?" the Colonel laughed.

"Actually, a very small fraction sir. I've been meaning to talk to you about him. Did he even go to law school?" Lots of good Colonel laughter, which is second in satisfaction only to baby laughter.

"Well, that's funny stuff. We need you to do an outstanding job in the U.S Attorney's Office, Andrew. The Marines have a great reputation up there. You're the man for the job. I picked you for a reason."

"Thank you sir. I won't let you down."

Getting the position at the U.S. Attorney's Office allowed me to bury the Tori debacle. I could move on from the supervision and culture of the Marines and pursue my long-held career goal of being a federal prosecutor. If I was moving forward, I didn't have to look back and think about my actions. Constant movement away from painful things was good—or so I thought.

178

Chapter 15

I reported to the U.S. Attorney's office in a new suit, pressed white shirt, new tie, shined shoes, in great physical shape, and immediately fell in love with my new boss, Rosie. Rosie was a self-assured, competent attorney who was also a natural leader. She also happened to be a smoking-hot, 40 year-old southern blond. I made a really strong impression. I poured every ounce of brain power I had into learning everything I could about federal criminal prosecution. I read every treatise I could find on the subject. I read literally hundreds of cases in about two weeks, remembering the key points. My mind came alive, because criminal law in comparison to Taxes for Dummies is exciting. This was transformative; I was in my element, I was hitting my stride. I was filling in for Rosie when she was out of the office, and supervising other attorneys. This did so much for my self-esteem.

My job as a Marine at the U.S. Attorney's Office was to prosecute crimes committed by civilians on military bases in the northern Virginia area, including the Pentagon. In this role, I had little to no contact with my military bosses south at Quantico. I was free from the promotion ceremonies, the birthday celebrations, morning physical training, road marches and turkey talk with the crazy lieutenant colonel. Mostly, I had a physical separation from all of the shit that went down with Tori.

Here I was, from a third-tier law school, and Rosie, a supervisor in the top U.S. Attorney's Office in the country, trusted me to be in charge, even for just a few days. I handled a large docket of routine cases and several felony cases. The courtroom stuff was by far my favorite and it's where I belonged. Much more experienced prosecutors were always there to answer my questions and offer advice. I never passed on an opportunity to learn from them. After several months of being in the office, eventually they would ask for my take and my opinion, and I thoughtfully provided my views. I loved the pressure of it all. I was fulfilled. I made some really great contacts within the Justice Department.

The Justice Department hires very talented lawyers from pedigree law schools like Harvard and Yale. I've always felt like I had to prove my intelligence to people. I'm not sure why. Maybe because my siblings were considered smart and I dropped out of high school and left town when I was 18. Either way, I moved naturally in the courtroom and had a really good command of facts and fact patterns. I worked hard to know what I was doing. So even though my colleagues had those tremendous academic credentials, I succeeded in some very key areas of our profession and was looked-up to by many of my peers. In other words, my insecurity was held in check.

Wendi and I agreed that she had to move to northern Virginia. Life in New York didn't make any sense, and moving down with me, and trying to find her niche did. It was a difficult time for her I think because of the guilt, and she didn't have her New York support system in place. Her move from New York to Virginia to be with me was her escape from judgment and ridicule. She had to leave Schenectady. The move to live together was our attempt to vindicate the affair. But wait, it wasn't an affair for her—it was an affair for me.

A year later, my sister moved from New York to Virginia with her two little girls. They were starting a new life too, and set up shop just a few houses away from us. Wendi and Carol became very close – like sisters, and we were all a support system for each other. I think it was Carol's mission to see to it that Wendi and I marry. She loved me, she loved Wendi and was firmly in the camp that felt "it was meant to be." I think she was elected Camp Captain. I believed that marriage was just a piece of paper and something you did for other people, but if it made everyone happy, why not? After several mags of wine and countless dinners with our new support system, I acquiesced, and shifted gears. I was all in. We married on Block Island that summer and twenty minutes before the small ceremony, Wendi was throwing crab apples at my head in anger. What did I do?

So we bought a female Lhasa Apso from a pet store without papers of any sort and "Dalai" became the focus of our attention. Dalai, who is now dead because after we became very attached to her, Wendi got fed-up with Dalai shitting on the dining room table and then on the couch, and insisted that we kill her. They became each other's arch rivals and me being the alpha male, had to take my little Dalai down to the Humane Society to be destroyed. I cried on the drive to the execution. The vet asked if I wanted to hold Dalai while they put her to sleep, but I couldn't do it. The employees looked at me with a mixture of sympathy and resentment. What was so bad about this little nine-pound dog that she had to be put down? She crapped in the house, and Wendi couldn't take it anymore. We got Dalai at the very beginning of our relationship, when things were going well, likely because we really didn't know each other.

As time went on, Dalai's stubborn ways, and personality as a true female Lhasa Apso—complete with wild mood swings—came to mirror the discordance developing in my relationship with Wendi. At the time, I was convinced that Dalai had gone insane, but it occurred to me years later, long after I had Dalai executed, that she wasn't the insane one.

It seems like I ended up in some bizarre time-warp between cheating on Tori, finishing my Marine tour, and joining DOJ. The break-up was almost instantaneous. As soon as I was cleared from trouble with the Marines, and Tori returned to her Marine Corps life, I never really saw or heard from her. When my therapist would ask about it—the guilt, a failed marriage, infidelity to Tori, etc.—my mind would go blank. Before long, Wendi and I began to see a marriage counselor named Ida Lick.

"Well, she made me kill my dog, Ida. She's a little nuts if you know what I mean," Referring to Wendi. Ida interrupts my flow.

181

"Andrew! Focus. You ended a relationship with Tori by cheating on her with Wendi. But you've never once talked about it with me."

"Well obviously I feel terrible!" I said.

"No, that's just it Andrew. It's not obvious at all. Your expression is totally blank, your eyes are distant. I'd think you were hypnotized if I didn't know better."

"What do you want me to say, Ida? I feel horrible about what happened."

"Do you feel it though? Because watching you right now and listening to your voice—look it's just that your demeanor, your body and your face don't match the words that you're using."

Wendi and I never talked about what happened. We initially stewed about it for a couple days immediately following them finding out, but then we never looked back. Whenever my mind would start to go there, I would picture a hurt look on Tori's face—tears—and my mind would look away.

Work was heating up and I couldn't have been happier about it. My case load got bigger and I was steadily improving. The people I was friendliest with were extremely smart—top of their classes at top law schools. Most of them could crank out an excellent motion or brief in a couple of hours. It seemed to take me longer, but my research and writing skills were getting better. I was good on my feet, my personality both in court and around peers, was my strength. For some reason, many people gravitated to me and it felt good. This was in sharp contrast to my marriage and home life. The dark cloud of despair continued to hang over the relationship. Everything seemed so heavy all of the time.

And then everything changed for me. The most amazing rush of happiness and love—my little Derrick was born. The most beautiful little boy the world had even seen. Big brown eyes, a head full of dark brown hair, and a toothless smile from the moment of his birth. The nurse swaddled him, bypassed Wendi and placed his little warm body to me. Warmth and love enveloped us—I would never be the same. Wendi, in a drug induced state, asked "Is he beautiful?" I told her "yes," but I wouldn't let him go. She would have to wait a moment. This was my son.

For the first week at home, I wouldn't look away from him. His eyes locked in on my smile, and I would try to get him to smile or laugh, but he was just too young. But by the second week—and maybe it was just a bit of gas—he looked at me making goofy faces and baby sounds, and cracked a huge smile. I felt something at that moment that I can't describe, but it has never left me.

Derrick was the only shining light, a true bundle of joy, but even with him as a huge part of our lives, something continued to drag me down. Guilt about Tori and James? I don't know, but I knew I couldn't, or at least did not want to picture a lifetime with this feeling.

Chapter 16

I started dabbling in narcotic pain medicine after I left the Marines and for the most part they worked. A few times a year, I would aggravate the injury and the pain would return. Of course I would get another prescription, but I never really went overboard. That's not to say I took them as directed, I just didn't go overboard. Also, things were going pretty well career wise. I was working as a Special Assistant United States Attorney and was establishing a reputation as the go-to-guy when things went wrong. In any event, I was keeping the demon addiction at bay, and was even attending AA meetings as a way to "address" my drinking. It was all working just fine.

When I moved from the U.S Attorney's Office in Alexandria to the Criminal Division in Washington, D.C., my marriage with Wendi continued to unravel. Derrick was happy, which was wonderful, but his birth also marked a change in how Wendi and I were getting along. My new job required that I travel a couple weeks a month, at least. Often I was gone from Monday through Thursday in any given week. I'm sure this was hard on Wendi, because her capacity to deal with life was about as retarded as mine. But she had my mother who had retired in New York and moved two doors down from us, and my sister, who was always ready to lend a hand.

The stress, the travel, the new job, and everything else affected my back pain and I started seeing this old Italian doctor in Arlington. The guy prescribed me virtually anything that I wanted which I thought at the time was wonderful. Lortab, Percocet, Oxycodone, Valium, Ritalin. You name it, I got it—50, sometimes 100 at a time. And this doesn't count the times I would call the good doctor's office and say that I lost them or left them in a hotel in another city; his nurse would call in a replacement prescription right away.

I've always suffered from wanderlust when it comes to jobs. As happy as I was prosecuting, I needed the rush of applying to other places, including the CIA. This rush was a counter-weight to the feelings my unhappy marriage brought. Copious Ritalin helped fuel this natural instinct. I read *Inside the CIA* by Ronald Kessler and low and behold, "spy" sounded like the perfect job for me. I can't for the life of me remember the exact application process but I do remember finding a phone number to call, I think in the classified section of the Washington Post. The person who answered simply said, "Hello?" not "Central Intelligence Agency," not "CIA,"—just "hello," which I thought was intriguing.

I literally went through *eight* hours of interviews with really cool people from "Langley," which is how the CIA is referred to in the D.C. area. I took personality tests, I.Q. tests, and then more tests. At every step of the way, I received a simple non-descript letter in the mail instructing me to report somewhere or to submit additional information like transcripts from school or job performance reviews. I signed releases for medical records, military records—you name it. At night, I would have dreams about recruiting spies from other countries and attending parties at embassies abroad, tricking people into drinking the poisoned champagne, and protecting identities and national security. I was obsessed. I was James Bond. It was very cool. Secrets were my specialty. The next step in the process was meeting with a CIA-employed psychologist. The usual letter had come and instructed me to report to some sign-less building in Virginia. I was prepared to fool him into thinking I was normal and stable and that I would make a great spy. It was a Tuesday, I'm sure about that. And I'm also sure it was approaching 118 degrees that day and my light summer-weight Brooks Brothers wool suit felt unnatural on my skin—like saran wrapped asbestos and pink house insulation. I was in a wool suit on my way to trick a psychologist.

Naked. I wanted to be naked walking down the street. *If everyone agreed not to stare at each other, we could all be naked today.* Anyhow, I couldn't find parking and had to walk five blocks to the building. At this point, I was so Goddamn wet and angry and frustrated—I hate heat. I was muttering to myself like some kind of madman. If I were naked, and cool, and not wearing insulation, I wouldn't have been muttering swear words, I would have been happily greeting strangers, passersby, on the city streets. "Good day to you madam." "Nice shoes!" "Love those shoes." But no, I was sloshing down the street literally trying to will my sweaty underwear from creeping any higher up my ass. I also tried to slow my already strained breathing in an effort to lower my core temperature. It didn't work.

I entered the lobby of the building and was greeted with a wonderful whoosh of air-conditioned air, and I breathed an audible sigh of relief, openly praising God. Fourth floor, here we go, I thought. Stepping off the elevator, turning right now, third door down on the left. Sign says, "Please enter and have a seat; someone will be with you shortly." Open the door and whoosh: I am greeted with warm air. No, *hot air.* It was hot air. I thought, "This can't be right." The rest of the building was like a meat locker, what the hell was wrong with this room? The place was Spartan. A few chairs, a coffee table with no periodicals, and not a human being in sight. *Have a seat; someone will be with you shortly.*

Why is it so fucking hot in here? I sat down. *Shoot, I should have brought a paper or something.* I stare at my fingernails, taking a bite out of one as I look around, spitting the nail to the left. This sucks. Actually, this wedgie sucks. I have to loosen my tie, but it won't—Goddamn it! Why is it so fucking tight?! Jesus I feel fat. Why is so fucking hot in here? Where the fuck is everyone? Relax. This wedgie, shit man! I tug at my underwear through my pant leg trying to pry it out of my ass-crack but it's matted against my skin. The only way is to unzip my wool pants, un-stick my shirt and t-shirt and completely re-adjust my underwear. What if someone comes in? What time is it anyway? I've been here 45 minutes. They're late. They're running late. No big deal. It happens. Relax. Someone will be with you shortly.

This goddamn wedgie! Fuck it, just do it quickly. Pants down, shirt untucked, underwear extracted and adjusted, shirt re-tucked, pants up, zipped fly, belt buckled. That was quick. So much better. It's so fucking hot. *Just sit down and relax. Someone will be with you shortly. My nose itches—on the inside. Just pick it. Ugh! Just pick it, everyone else does. Pick and flick. What fucking time is it? I can't sit still. This is bullshit. Come on! Take it easy, you freak. Smile. Force yourself to smile, I heard it releases endorphins. That's it, wider now. Close your eyes, keep smiling, tilt your head back. Any endorphins? No? Try again. How about now? Nope. Tilt your head back, wider smile. Now? Nope. Fuck it. God this is just incredible. Rocking back and forth now, biting nails, spitting to the left. Come on! Where the fuck is everyone?* "Hello?" I say out loud. *Shut up you crazy fool.* Holding head in hands now. *Please come get me. I'll pay you! I'm ready to trick the psychologist now. Why is it so fucking hot in here?* Droplets of sweat run down my back tickling my skin. This is fucking torture.

Is that a fucking camera? Jesus, is that a camera? A small black ball is attached to the ceiling. Rubbing temple shading eyes from the camera. Oh God. This is so stupid. Nervous laughter now, can't stop laughing because it's absurd. *Stop it, stop laughing. Andrew! Stop laughing! God, please, God, not right now. This isn't funny. Stop laughing. You're in a room by yourself laughing.* Irish laugh. Irish laugh. Irish laugh.

And then this enormous creature of a man is standing in the corridor watching me as I look up. I'm still laughing. He is very serious, very stoic, very strange. "Are you ready?" He is the tallest person I have ever seen in person. I regain my composure and say yes, choking back laughter.

I follow the huge being down a hall, into a stairwell, down a flight of stairs and then, God strike me dead if I'm lying, up a flight of stairs, back into a hallway that looks just like the one we left two minutes ago, and then into an elevator where he—with his back to me—inserts a card key, cautiously looks over his shoulder at me. I smile, he pushes a series of buttons and then we go down. I start counting: one Mississippi, two Mississippi, etc., trying to ascertain how many floors we are going down in case he asks me later. I am very observant. I also count doors, lefts, rights, emergency exit signs, and lights. As I follow him, my eyes dart all over the place. I'm recording data, like we walk for about 15 or 20 minutes. I am sweating again and smiling, and my eyes are darting and I realize all of this, and I think I am going to laugh because I must look like a fucking madman.

His strides cover a full five feet, so for every two steps he's covering 10 feet. He's power-walking through the halls of somewhere and I don't agree that we should be in a hurry because he left me in a waiting room for so long and I'm trying to remember that sign I always see in secretaries cubicles that goes something like: "An emergency on your part doesn't result in a something, something on my part." But, that doesn't make sense and I just passed a clock that had a placard that read Tokyo, but I didn't catch the actual time which could count against me later during the Q&A period that I know will take place soon. But for now, we are climbing more stairs and I'm soaking wet and I just said something stupid again about this being "some walk we're taking." Which again, doesn't get a response. I press my first two fingers to the pulse in my neck and look at my watch and realize I might die if we keep this up—I'm no longer in Marine Corps shape—I'm in civilian "fat person-who-wears-it-well-shape."

187

We stop at what happens to be an office door. I'm panting and let out a "Phew!" We enter and that old familiar cool AC breeze engulfs me and I am happy and nice once again. We left the waiting room, I estimate 50 minutes ago; that's 50 minutes of cardio and I'm thinking it's time I start working out again. Not in a suit and tie and Allan Edmonds though.

"Have a seat. I'll be with you in a minute, can I get you something?" *How about a Gatorade and Power bar?*

"No, I'm fine. Well, perhaps some water? Thank you."

"So Mr. McKenna, you want to work for the CIA?"

"Yes." The word hangs in the air awkwardly and then I add: "That's right, yes, yes." *Stop saying stupid things you moron. You're blowing this.* "Do you have any paper towels?" *Did I just say that out loud?*

"It's just—I'm sweating, I mean perspiring ... and—"

"I don't have any paper towels Mr. McKenna." And then he just stares, so I pick up the stare and we both stare and I'll be damned if I'm the one to lose a staring contest, and neither is he. *I'm* not looking away. And finally, I answer: "OK, no problem. I sweat." *Did I just say that? Oh God.* And he responds by making a strange face and staring, so I chuckle and stare and hold back the absurd laughter that is now bubbling from my toes, up my legs, through my pelvis, and I'm about to explode as I sit there soaking fucking wet and utterly exhausted and I'm hoping he doesn't ask me what time it is in Tokyo.

As I'm walking back to my car completely drained, I review some of the questions he asked me. The one I focus on the most is "Andrew, what's wrong with you?" And then I focus on my answer, which was, "Nothing." And then I think about our third staring contest which I am pretty sure I won. And once again, I am sweating as I reach my car and my underwear feels like a hard taco shell crushed between my cheeks, and as it so happens, I never hear from the CIA again.

I'm sitting at a courtroom table, drifting off. *Please, please, guilty.* I'm sending the jury a telepathic message to find the defendant guilty. I can't lose this case. *I should have stressed the fact that no one saw anyone else enter or leave the building, only the defendant. I should have stressed that more during my closing argument. I have that party tonight. It would be so much more enjoyable if I win this case. Maybe I shouldn't have called him at all. His testimony was confusing to me, and I spent hours with him preparing. No, I had to call him as a witness—why is this jury taking so long? That's a bad sign for us. No, maybe it's a good sign. Yeah, maybe. That clock hasn't moved. I have to pick up the dry cleaning, and pack—don't leave that until the last minute. Must talk to Benita and get that flight changed. Chicago then Miami. I have to hit Chicago first. Retirement party. This planner is shot. Need a new planner. That's funny. It's trashed, but it's good enough to note that I need a new one. No, that's not funny really. This jury is going to be the death of me. Damn, I'm supposed to meet Ruby for lunch! Why isn't that in my planner? Because you're not organized. Yes, I am. No, you're not. You'll be alright. Yeah.*

"Ruby! Hey! The jury's had the case for almost two hours."

"You are the most impatient person I know Andrew!" Ruby was a colleague in a different section of DOJ. She had more confidence in me than anyone I knew—and a true friend.

"I know, shit. Listen rain check on lunch, OK?"

"OK kiddo. Relax with this. You did everything you could with this case. It was weak to begin with."

"Maybe I should have put on another witness. His cousin made conflicting statements. I could have jammed him up on that. Of course I would have had the *Bruton* problem."

Andrew! Stop already, call me after the verdict." Ruby was laughing at me.

"You're a good friend. I'll call you later." *I did everything I could, even Ruby said so. I have to win this.*

Soon I'd have to go to Phoenix to meet with a guy in Witness Security (WITSEC) about another case. The guy was a real piece of work—a Colombian who seemed to know everyone and their brother. He also loved the attention he got from law enforcement, so talking to us wasn't a problem.

189

He was an important witness for sure. In exchange for all of his assistance, the government had moved his family out of Colombia to the U.S., gave them a different last name, jobs, and a place to live. The guy would dump so much information on us—names, locations, money amounts, drug amounts, smuggling routes, etc.—it took three agents and myself furiously taking notes and checking his story during our debriefings with him.

"Get this cab!" yells one of my co-counsels. Tensions are running high and we're late for court. We're in downtown Washington D.C., it's a fall day in 2001, just after 9-11—and I can't imagine all of the important things happening in this city right now. Security forces were on high alert. Wendi was still in bed, shades down, incommunicado, cocooning. She wouldn't answer the phone or the door, even for family and friends who lived a block away. She couldn't eat or shower. On top of that she would enter into crying jags. And despite everyone else during this time wanting to band together after the horrific attacks, Wendi went in the other direction. She was alone in her depression.

Today I finally put "my witness" on the stand: a rogue DEA agent who has had conflicts with absolutely everyone involved in the case. Why me?

"Andrew. The reason I called you in here—well it's good news actually."

"This can't be good news," I half joke with my boss, "no one starts good news this way."

"I need you to handle Agent Robertson. No one likes him. Your personality fits here."

"Is that a compliment?" I ask.

"It sounds like one, doesn't it?" Tom says.

"Not really, but that's okay."

The seasoned agent had "taken a confession" from the defendant. Quite literally taken it. Well, that's what his lawyer claimed. It was on a rickety DEA plane from Colombia to Miami; an extrajudicial seizure of the man, no extradition required here. The agents call it, jokingly, "Habeas Grabis," which makes me laugh every time I hear it. Their sources in Colombia said that the defendant was eating dinner with his family in some little town outside of Bogota. And they went and grabbed him, hence, "Habeas Grabis." No arrest warrant, no local Colombian Police— just DEA agents grabbing him and taking him away. Then, on the plane, while shackled and uncomfortable and having to go to the bathroom, and tired and hungry, he makes some vague statements to Agent Robertson, basically agreeing that he knew some people who worked in narcotics trafficking. The exact details of what he actually said were fuzzy to everyone else on the flight, but when it came time to write the report, Agent Robertson "clearly" remembered everything that the guy said. It was suspicious. And this is why my colleagues don't like him. Plus, he comes across too cocky on the witness stand, which for a cop before a typically skeptical D.C. jury, could mean acquittal for the defendant.

I decide that if I believe the agent is lying or can show that he is lying, then I'll tell my boss. This is serious, though, because if I make an accusation against the guy, an internal investigation will ensue, perhaps ending his career. Then it comes to taking away his ability to feed his family, not to mention throw a huge wrench in the prosecution. No one wants to have to stand up in court and tell the federal judge that the "confession" is no good, that the defendant's rights were violated.

The spotlight was now on me. I felt like my colleagues and boss had handed me a hot potato. Fuck that, more like a grenade. It was some test, and I started by reading dozens of reports relating to the investigation. I was looking for any inconsistency between what the agents thought they knew or thought were facts, with what the defendant said on the plane that night. A good solid inconsistency might set this guy free. Ironically, a *minor* inconsistency would lend credibility to the agent's claims because then it wouldn't be so neat.

I also spoke casually to everyone else on the flight that night. I didn't want it to look like I was conducting an investigation. But these guys were agents, not idiots. Employing my best Columbo-style (taught by my boss Tom), I pretended like I was coming late to the game, trying to play catch-up, trying to get locked-in; all of the ridiculous terms these government hacks use to try and explain what they can't in plain language. And it worked. Sometimes agents circle-the-wagons when prosecutors ask too many questions, but these guys didn't.

To my enormous moral relief, I found no major inconsistencies. I concluded that the agent was not a great defender of civil liberties, that he was not sympathetic to the legally challenged, but also that he was telling the truth about what the defendant had told him. I reported my findings to my boss, and he sort of smiled, a hidden sort of smile, and he simply said, "That's good." Treading carefully, I outlined for the defense attorney the inconsistencies, although I don't think I was legally obligated to do so. Cases exist that say the prosecution must turn over evidence tending to show a defendant's innocence or evidence favorable to an accused. That's "Brady" material. Also, the government must turn over evidence tending to call into question the veracity of a government witness; that's "Giglio" material, and so to be on the safe-side, I outlined what I thought might come close in this case.

Chapter 17

"Andrew, I need your help on this one. I need you on the team."
Of course you do—just say the magic words.
"No one can do this the way I believe you can."
Of course, no one can—that's why you hired me. I'm a genius. Well ... I'm God.

No, actually, you're not God. You are slightly above average. On a really good day. Maybe. Probably not.

We're all given assignments that make us feel good at some point in our lives. When I'm asked to do things that I believe are tailored to my skill set, I get overly excited. I start to believe that I am important, and if I don't pull myself out of that way of thinking, I'll start to believe I am a deity, a Messiah, the most important person in the world. This is very wrong and very bad. The lows tend to be equal distance from the center, too. And therein lies the pain.

If I'm not careful, if I don't pull out of this line of thinking, I will crash. Crash hard, to the point that the ole' internal dialogue turns into emotional suicide, where I can't do anything right and where I am responsible, solely responsible for everything that goes wrong. This is a very dark place to be.

The confident part works well to a point. Walking into court it worked especially well because I really was fearless. And to give myself some credit, I was also well prepared. Some people freeze-up when they have to go to court. One colleague—a very bright Yale-trained lawyer would get so nervous he would sweat through his suit. Sometimes I would have to pry the case file out of his slippery hands and handle the matter, usually a "plea" of some sort. With no knowledge of his case, I would have to make a fast assessment, make some cursory judgments and act quickly. That was my forte. What is not my forte is getting to sleep at night when the voices in my head spell out, with incredible clarity, how high my shit-pile was becoming. Everything from how I missed something at work, to the thought of Halle Berry drowning in a river when it was my job to keep all of the actors away from the river. It's midnight and I just can't shut it off.

I used to snort Ritalin with mixed results. I had to go back to Houston soon. Things were starting to get backed-up with the wiretap; I was developing a mean case of procrastination. Ritalin helped with that. It helped me get caught up. Or so I thought. The side effect that I found

193

most disturbing, other than the unexplained erections, was dry mouth or cotton mouth or, more appropriately, cat-liter-absorption-syndrome-mouth. Never chew or snort several times the recommended dosage before going to court or talking to your boss or giving someone directions to the E.R., or anything requiring clear and competent communication and thinking, because when your tongue betrays you, sticks to the roof and sides of your mouth? It's an absolute show stopper with terrifying results of professional carnage.

So sitting in my office at DOJ with six crushed Ritalin pills laid out in two big lines on my desk, and rolled up travel voucher, I proceeded to "get my head right" before tending to a stack of overdue paperwork that was getting higher and later by the hour. I proceeded to vacuum the first pile as silently as possible. Just as I raised up, with residue particles falling from my nostril, there was a knock at my door. Nearly shitting my pants, I tried to cover the other line. Ritalin stings when you snort it, so naturally your eyes water.

"Come-in!" I say as the door swings open.

"Andrew?" It's Laurie, my colleague who is awesome.

"Hey." I look up, still holding the rolled-up travel voucher.

"Everything OK?" she asked. The rush just kicked in, which causes an involuntary smile on my mug. My heart beat starts to crank up.

"Of course," I say, still smiling, eyes watering profusely, nostrils burning.

"Then, why are you," she pauses, "are you crying? There are tears coming down your cheeks, Andrew."

Bewildered. Staring at Laurie, searching for an explanation, I point to the phone and say, "I had bad news. A death … in the family."

I am so jacked at this point. My eyes are wide. My blood pressure must be 280/120; tears are rolling down, and I can't undo the smile. It is engraved on my face, in stone. Laurie gave me the look of disbelief.

"I am so sorry to hear that Andrew." The Ritalin has hit hard in my brain. My tongue is amped and ready to unleash.

"Not as sorry as I am!" I blurt out at such an incredible rate of speed—like a speed talker, like an auctioneer on Ritalin. It comes out sounding like one word only.

"That's not what I meant to say. Of course you're sorry, Laurie, and so am I, but we can't feel the pain that those closest to her must feel, old frail gramma, but it doesn't mean that you aren't sorry because I know you are because you said it and I believe you and I believe that I believe that when you say I believe you that you believe me! The last two words come out as a shout. Stunned. Laurie, God love her, was stunned.

Then, instantly, the saliva disappeared and I couldn't swallow and I could feel white pus balls appear at the corners of my smiling mouth. My brain sent messages to my mouth to talk some more, but I resisted long enough for Laurie to speak.

"I was going to ask ... if you could cover for me tomorrow at the FBI academy. I have court, so I can't teach the 4th Amendment class to the cadets. But maybe you're ... not up to it?" Laurie explained, looking towards the phone. Poor Laurie doesn't know what to make of me.

My tongue was stuck to the roof of my mouth. Immediately, Elmer Fudd possessed my body and took over the conversation. I'll never forget this for as long as I live. I was so wired I began to stutter.

"Abadie abadie abadie abadie," I say. Clearly, the makers of Ritalin never imagined their ADHD drug would be used in such a manner.

"Abadie, abadie abadie," I said again because of how it sounded the first time. My mouth wouldn't work right. I became frustrated.

"What?" Laurie asks, clearly troubled but curious, too, at this stage.

Very slowly now, deliberately like a recovering head injury patient, I fight the fat numb tongue in my mouth. I concentrate all my energy and effort and pride. "I ill andle it!" emphasizing each deficient syllable, sounding just like a disabled person. I stared into her eyes, and she into mine, until finally she said:

"Okay, thanks Andrew." She starts to leave with a little nod of her head, but not before saying, because she is such a good person, that she is really sorry to hear about my loss. When I struggle to respond, she simply holds up her hand, bows her head and nods no and closes the door very softly and quietly.

"Phew!" That was close.

I look down and see the pile of Ritalin in my lap. It was so silent in my office. All I could hear was the pounding of my heart. Time to get some work done.

I completed a 12-page motion, including research, in under 32 minutes, according to the government clock on the wall. Hitting print, I walked out to the common area where the printer was housed. My focus was so acute. As I walked, I analyzed sights, sounds, smells—everything—eating up all available data on the way to the printer. Someone, I don't know who, said, Andrew, "I heard you had some bad news I'm..." and as he started to say "sorry;" I answered only, "Not now, thank you." I'm sure I resembled Rainman on dope. As I make it back to my office, I could detect in my hyper-Ritalin state, individual microscopic fibers in the rug, fibers not visible to the naked eye. I bent over and stared because I could see the fibers moving, that's how good I believed my vision was. The fibers were like tall stalks of wheat swaying in the wind at 1/1 millionth of a millimeter. I became mesmerized by the small bugs moving around the stalks of carpet fibers. I was hallucinating.

"Lose something?" someone asks from behind me.

"Huh? Nope." As I turn around, I can feel the touch of fabric brush against my enormous erection. The Ritalin. I look down at the tent-like appearance on my suit pants and without making eye contact with the person who is clearly confused at what she is seeing, I say, "Nope," again, and I turn and walk into my office.

Chapter 18

My balls were killing me. I woke-up on the stairs going down to an English basement apartment in Chicago. I had no idea how I had ended up there—the stairs not Chicago. I knew how I had gotten to Chicago—by plane. When I lifted my head-off of the cement stair my head went numb and blank. All I could remember was drinking in a bar. *It'll come back to me.* The area of the city seemed pretty desolate. And I wasn't familiar with the city to begin with. The sun was just coming up. It was a weekday. I had to be somewhere! Abject panic was creeping in. My balls were absolutely killing me. Had someone kicked me in the balls? I can barely stand-up for Christ's sakes. Did a huge roof tile fall on my balls? Or a cinder-block? This isn't natural. Where *the fuck* am I? Everything started to spin. Then I started throwing up. Massive amounts. In liters, metrics. The heaving was all Scotch, Scotch, and more Scotch, and something with a red sauce, and cigar taste, and broccoli and seafood and more cigar. *Seafood.* My eyes are bulging out from the force of the vomit. I feel like I might start swallowing my tongue. Things become blurry, no more heaving please. I can't hold my eyes open … dizzy … I pass out. My head is back on the stairs going down the steps upside down, and my mind drifts. *I couldn't have eaten a cigar….*

"Hey dude, what the fuck? Are you okay? Theresa, call 911!" Some guy who looked like Quentin Tarantino was standing over me. "No, no, please … no 911. No ambulance!" I couldn't stand up, all the blood had rushed to my head as I lay inverted on the poor bastard's stairs. "I'm OK. I'm OK."

"The fuck you are! You are *not* ok!" He yelled. "You are lying on your back covered in vomit!"

"No sir, no sir! I am okay and please just bear with me for a second, and I'll get to my feet so that I'm not lying down." I wasn't making any sense. But I knew that if he called the police or whoever, that this would not turn out well. My mind couldn't focus, but I had to try and keep this guy calm, so I spoke with a firm tone as if I was in control. "This isn't anything sir. Nothing, this is nothing. We will get through this!"

"What in God's name are you talking about? You're insane. I smell lobster and cigarettes for God's sakes! Theresa! Theresa! Get the hose!"

"Please do not get the hose! Theresa! Forget the hose!" I yelled in the direction of his front door.

"You know my wife dude?"

"No. What? No!" At this point I had rolled over onto my stomach, and in a modified push-up maneuver, was able to get to my knees and then to my feet. "Listen, can I just use your phone? I'll call a cab and get out of your way. I'm sorry, I'm really sorry. I don't know how I ended up here. I ... I don't know where I am."

"Holy shit dude. Come on." He turned and led me into his apartment. Theresa stood in her bathrobe, arms crossed, staring at me.

"Good morning." I said to her with a little nod of my head, trying to be polite. She just stared at me, holding her robe tightly together. I had vomit from my neck to my crotch.

"Can I use your phone? I'll call a cab and get out of your way." The guy was walking from the bathroom to the stoop with a bucket of water. "Can I help you with that? Let me get that." The vomit was mine and I thought that I should be helping. He flashed me a disgusted look and mumbled something under his breath, then pointed at the phone on the kitchen table. I was so hung-over that I could barely focus my eyes on the phone. "Do you have a phonebook?"

It took me ten minutes to find a cab company to call. "Where are you going to sir?" The cab operator asked me. I couldn't remember what hotel I had checked into 18 hours earlier. "It's a hotel, downtown." I answered, trying to remember the name. "Which one sir?"

"Um. The um—"

"Sir, just give me the name of the hotel where you're staying."

"I ...." The guy walked in holding the bucket and was staring at my feet.

"Where's your other shoe? It's not outside." I looked at my feet. I had one shoe on. His wife looked at my feet and said, "Good Lord."

"Where's your other shoe?" The guy was frustrated because I only had on one shoe.

"I don't know," I said as I looked at my sock. "It ... I don't know."

"Sir, there are a lot of *tall* hotels downtown, that isn't enough information." The cab operator was also getting frustrated with me. "I remember the color orange on the awnings." I added, hoping this would help. "Or maybe it was red."

"Listen please, just pick me up and I'll figure it out." I said into the phone. I walked to the front door, turning just before leaving and thanked my hosts. They looked ragged. This was a terrible experience for them.

"My hotel is a very tall building and there are trees in the lobby. A middle-aged woman checked me in—I think she was Korean, but maybe Chinese. The entrance is a typical hotel entrance. Bell-hops stand in front, opening doors and carrying suitcases and stuff. Nice group of guys as far as I can recall." I was a babbling fool.

The cab driver kept looking in his rearview mirror and we would make eye-contact. He looked like he had had a long week on the job. He also looked like he might have fought with his wife not too long ago—that look of despair that things will never get better between them. Or maybe he had to move his bowels. He didn't look content with his life—that much was obvious. We stopped at the Marriot Hotel.

"This looks like it could be it." I stared up at the building as I got out of the cab. "Maybe you should wait, just to make sure."

"Did I check in here yesterday? Or the day before?" I asked the man behind the desk.

"You said McKenna, right?"

"Yup, M-C-K-E-N-N-A."

"David?"

"No, Andrew."

"This isn't it." I told the cab driver. The fare was now up to like $50.

"Are you going to be able to afford this?" the driver asked.

"Of course," I laughed, "why would you ask such a question?"

"Where is your other shoe? You're only wearing one shoe."

I looked down at my feet. "That's a fair question. Yes sir, it is." I started to make-up a story about my missing shoe, but it wasn't coming out right and I was having trouble maintaining eye-contact. I may have used the word mugger, and may have said something about me thwarting an attempted robbery earlier that day or the previous night. I can't remember.

"Truth be told," I finally relented, "I don't know. I don't know what happened to my other shoe." He stared at the front of my body. "The vomit? You're wondering about the vomit." I said before he could ask. "I believe the vomit is mine." I almost started to tell a lie about how I had been poisoned—an assassination attempt—because I worked for the Justice Department, and was involved in something secret that I couldn't discuss with him.

"I drank too much. Pretty sure of alcohol poisoning—self-induced. I don't know what happened to my shoe or the hotel I checked into. I don't know." I almost started to cry.

"How are you going to pay me? Do you have cash?" With this I reached into my pocket and pulled-out a ball of money totaling $63 and some change. "Okay, let's go." He said shaking his head.

I found my hotel after two more tries. My conversations with the desk people were nothing short of humiliating. Me standing there with a sock on, spelling my name like a mental patient, hoping that this was my hotel. Finally, I think it was at the Hilton Garden Inn, that I hit pay-dirt. I was practically in tears when the young man behind the desk, said "Yes, of course Mr. McKenna, you're in Room…. And you've had several calls this morning—just press * 9 on the phone to retrieve your messages." With that I walked across the lobby to the elevators in my tattered, partially shoeless state. I held my head high and pretended to myself that I was walking onto the Tonight Show for a chat with Jay Leno—a practice I started some years ago to get through troubling moments. Once in the elevator however I nearly shit myself in utter panic when I reached into my pants pocket and realized that I didn't have my Government Identification—my credentials from the Department of Justice. This was so fucking serious—especially with the terrorism thing going on.

The first message was from Wendi. "Andrew, I didn't hear from you last night. Hope everything is OK." I had no recollection of when I last spoke with her or what we discussed. The relationship was severely eroding, and I felt dread every time I thought of it. It was now a dark cloud.

"Counselor, hope you made it home alright last night—you just disappeared on us. Call me when you get a chance, it's about our boy." Agent Duke was the one that invited me to a DEA retirement party at a local bar the night before. The room was jam packed with gun-toting federal agents from the DEA, FBI, Customs, you name it. Everyone had a gun except for me, I was sure. This made me a little uncomfortable. Duke had had an argument with his overly flirtatious wife, and called her a cunt while the three of us stood together. His tone was so calm.

"You are a cunt, a real live cunt."

I started to leave the triangle and Duke told me not to move, not to go anywhere.

"I want you to hear this counselor. My wife is a cunt and I want you to hear it."

"Listen Duke, I probably shouldn't—"

"You are a first-rate cunt." Duke wasn't even mad about it. He said it with an even tone. He spoke as if what he was saying was a fact and not an opinion. His wife whose name I think was Gail, but I can't be sure, just stared at him with a look like, Oh, here we go again. I only knew Duke for a few months and thought he was a great guy—funny, sarcastic, good agent and everything, but now this. The "our boy" who he was referring to in his message on my hotel phone was a guy named Pablo, a Colombian, who was in Witness Security. Pablo knew everyone who had ever sold a kilo or more of cocaine, or so it appeared. As I started to debrief Pablo, on several trips out west, it became clear to me that yes, Pablo knew a lot of big players from Colombia to Mexico, but he also just liked to talk with agents and prosecutors. Apparently Pablo had called Duke and told him that he wanted out of WitSec. He was tired of hiding his identity, and living a secret life in a shit-hole suburb. He wanted to get "back in the game" and do undercover work. Duke explained that if Pablo did this, he would instantly be killed. And probably tortured first. The phone rings:

"Pablo wants to leave WitSec," Duke said. I interrupted. "Duke, what size shoes do you wear?"

The next message was from an Olga. I thought it must be a mistake, because I didn't know an Olga. Just as I was about to skip to my next message, I heard Olga say, "So that's that Andrew, call me when you get a chance, and again, I hope there aren't any hard feelings." Oh Christ, I thought. This can't be good. I sat in silence for several minutes trying to think, to remember, but I simply couldn't, and it really hurt to try. I decided that I needed to clean-up, to get my shit together. I stripped naked and walked to the bathroom and started to fill the tub with hot water. I reached into the little refrigerator and pulled out two little bottles of booze, probably scotch, and poured them into a glass. I eased myself into the hot bath and felt the water immediately bring relief to my still aching balls. My first pull from the glass was a difficult one, but the next several were not. I must have dozed a bit. The phone woke me up and after I realized that I was in a bath-tub, in a hotel room, in Chicago, I came to my senses.

"Hello?"

"Mr. McKenna." A deep voice spoke my name.

"What?" I answered nervously. "I mean _yes?_"

"There is a package for you in the lobby. Shall I have someone deliver it to your room?" Jesus, what if it's a head or something, I thought. Why would there be a package for me?

"Sure, yes, thank you."

The bellboy handed me the package. I was standing there wet with a towel around my waist. He gave me a look of anticipation—like he was ready to hold out his hand and receive a tip, but wasn't sure if this was a tip moment. I closed my eyes and moved my head slightly from side to side, to indicate that it wasn't. My body language indicated that I didn't have any money left, and that my life was unmanageable.

The box did not contain an arm or a foot or a bomb. It was my shoe. A note from Olga read "Call me." My head started swirling with guilt and regret. _Andrew, this is terrible man. You're a fucking prosecutor for Christ's sake and you just opened a box with a shoe in it. Your head is throbbing with pain, you get dizzy and light-headed every time you move, and again, you just opened a box with a shoe in it—your shoe._

"Duke, can you keep a secret?" Before I did anything else, I called Duke. Duke was a problem solver, a fix-it man.

I explained to Duke everything that I could remember—I mean the guy was an accomplished investigator. In true Duke form, he said "First things first." I told him that I remember a lot of steam, and a strange smell—in fact my body and clothes smelled earthy and woodsy. "You took a cab obviously, right? You didn't leave the bar last night and take a walk, right?"

"That's right, yes, I took a cab Duke."

"And you had a destination in mind? Then you left and got into the cab."

"Yes, presumably I had a destination in mind Duke."

"Your balls hurt and you have a note from a girl named Olga."

"Yes Duke."

"You woke up on someone's stairs, and until a few minutes ago, you only had one shoe."

"Yes sir."

"Hmm … interesting." After a long pause, Duke in a dejected tone said, "I got nothing man. I suggest that you call Olga."

"Fucking call Olga dude?"

"I don't see any other way."

"Olga! Hey, it's Andrew, from last night." I tried to sound confident and excited.

"Oh my God, I didn't think you would call. Are you alright?" She sounded really concerned.

"Me? Alright? Of course, yes, I'm great. How are you?"

"Jesus Andrew, you don't remember do you?"

"What? I laughed a nervous laugh, "of course I remember." There was an uncomfortable silence. "No Olga, I don't remember. I don't remember anything. Please help me!" I sounded hysterical, very defeated, and a little sad.

"My girlfriend beat you up."

"Who? When? Where were we?" I said through sobs.

"At the bath house."

"At the fucking bath house? I was in a bath house?"

"Yeah, and you were handing out pain pills and drinking Tequila Andrew—you were having a great time."

"You mean my pain medication? For my pain?"

"I guess, yeah. You claimed you could call in an airstrike at any time on a moment's notice. Look, are you okay?"

"Who beat me up?"

"My girlfriend." Olga said calmly. "She thought you were hitting on me and she started to get a little defensive. All of a sudden, out of nowhere, you got really cruel."

"I got cruel?" I couldn't get my mind around this. "Is she your *girlfriend* girlfriend? Like your lover girlfriend?"

"Yeah, she basically told you that, but you didn't want to hear it." Olga explained. "You told her to 'put some more peanut butter on her balls and get a rescue mutt,' then you called her a cock-blocker, and she just went off on you. She's strong. She does deadlifts."

"Deadlifts? Did she deadlift my scrotum because I think my balls might be bleeding inside."

"She got you down on the floor—you didn't seem able to defend yourself—and she kicked you in the balls a couple times."

"A couple?"

"Five times. Five-ish."

Well "there you go" I thought. Beat about the balls by a girl in a bar where I was illegally distributing a controlled substance, and talking about peanut butter, following a retirement party for a DEA agent.

"Olga, this is very important. I can't find my Justice Department credentials. If I lost them and they fall into the wrong hands—well you can imagine—"

"Check inside the shoe Andrew. I put your ID inside your shoe." Olga deadpanned.

"Hi, I'm in from out of town and I'm looking for an AA meeting in the area."

"We'll have someone call you back." Minutes later the phone rings.

"Hello?"

"Andrew, it's Tom." My great boss from Washington, D.C. The pain in my balls immediately came back like someone had hit them with a ballpeen.

"Hey Tom! What's up?

"Andrew, how are things going? I called to let you know there was some intelligence about your guy. See me when you get back, OK?" Tom was a case facilitator.

"Of course, that's great news. And yeah things are going really well, we had the retirement ceremony for Agent Smith—good turnout. I think our agent in the Colombia case may have found two additional witnesses—excellent ones—that actually were long-time employees of the *finca*. He says that they have virtually no baggage. So I'll probably have to go back to Bogota at some point. We finally got the search warrant approved for the Houston matter. The judge seemed pleased that all of the government's ducks were in a row, after what he went through with that jackoff from the local office, and most importantly, the agents were happy." I just ranted to Tom, not allowing him an opportunity to ask any more questions.

"Well sounds like you have things under control, Andrew." Tom said.

"Just trying to keep the trains running on time," I answer.

Chapter 19

"Houston, we have a problem," she said seriously as could be. My eyes opened and I saw her naked upper half, her eyes looking down at wet sheets.

"What?" I respond, barely audible, with my sleepy fat tongue and desert-dry throat. Not sure if I just woke up and it's all a dream.

"The bed is wet," she says.

"Sweat?" I say.

"No," she says as she throws the covers back and walks to the bathroom.

"No tan lines." I mumble to myself as I sit up in bed, brain damaged type hangover.

"Momma's little helpers in my purse," she calls from the bathroom.

I reach for her purse, then the telephone, fumbling with might be a bottle of Xanax.

"Can you bring us a pot of coffee, please? Breakfast? No, we'll have to call you back later for that. Right now we just need coffee, oh and Marlboro cigarettes, do you have those? Thank you."

"We'll order breakfast later, okay?" I holler to her.

"Yeah, whatever, that's fine," she answers.

I pop a 10 mg Lortab into my mouth and break it with my teeth into four pieces. With a big swallow of the Hotel Houstonian's finest Colombian coffee, I've started my day. "This is the best cure for a hangover, other than a drink, drink." She ignored this, turning her attention back to the television.

"I only watch the weather channel; it's the only program that makes sense anymore," she says.

"A Bloody-Mary might be in order; that would make sense," I say. She's not listening to me.

"Why would they build a city that's below sea level?" she asks, staring at the television.

"Do you always watch completely naked?" I have to know.

"Don't the waves just roll into their downtown?" she asks.

"This coffee's good," I say.

"Especially with pain killers." Her words bite into me.

"Especially with a pain killer," I say. Emphasizing the singular form of killer.

We have two more days together in Houston before I go back to Washington and her to New York. So far, we've gone to a restaurant, ridden a Ferris wheel, and hit a club where we drank copiously, and danced to techno, real industrial techno. I can still feel the bass beating through my veins. I think we had sex when we got back to the hotel this morning, but I can't be sure. I believe I urinated all over us while we slept because I was in a drunken opiate coma. It's a long holiday weekend. Last night was our first night. She was never technically my girlfriend, but everybody always thought we should be together because we were both "good looking," but that's high school for you. We hadn't talked in 15 years.

"I've never had a guy wet the bed before," she says, still watching the latest storms develop over the gulf. She's standing in the middle of the room naked.

"Is that awful?" I ask, lighting a cigarette and exhaling. "Because I don't ever remember urinating on a girl, at least not while I was asleep." I'm sitting at the desk, feet up.

"You're a devil," she says, finally looking away from the storm.

"I'm not a devil, I'm Jesus," I retort.

"Well come over here and fuck me, Jesus," as she climbs naked onto the dry half of the bed.

"Jesus can't right now, he's busy; he's having his coffee," I say authoritatively.

"How about when Jesus is done?" she says hopefully.

"Maybe," I say indifferently.

We are in Houston for different reasons. I have a criminal investigation that I am tending to, she has a wedding to attend—I'm her date. Except we missed the ceremony and are now headed to the reception in Galveston. She sprayed me with perfume before we left the hotel room, to "mask the smell of urine," which she only said to bust my balls because I had, after all showered.

"That's fine," I say. "Wait until your prissy little friends find out I pissed all over you and that you liked it."

"You smell like a girl now," she said. "And also my friends know Jesus wouldn't do such a thing."

We arrived late and drunk.

"I want to meet the bride's father!" I declared as we walk through the front doors.

"Don't you go near that poor man, Andrew! I'm sure he's had enough stress this weekend," she says, smiling.

"I want to ask him if he likes the groom or if he's merely tolerating him because I believe it's the latter. Have you seen the groom? Let's go find the groom first, okay? We'll be like investigative journalists and we'll find out together if the groom likes his new father." I was on a mission.

"How about we get a drink first?" she says.

"Well we got about six drinks in us already."

"Sir, it's a pleasure to meet you, you must be so proud." I was now shaking the bride's father's hand and looking across the room at my date. She gives me a look of horror but is clearly enjoying that I did what I said I would do.

209

"Yes, it was some ceremony, don't you think?" he says, a bit confused as to who I might be. "Are you a friend of Cathy's?" he asks. Cathy is his daughter.

"No, but I think Frankie is one hell of a good guy," I say. Frankie was his brand new son-in-law. I still haven't let go of his hand.

"Yes, *Frank*," he says his name with emphasis, as if to correct me, "is a fine man." Just as my date arrives next to me and wraps her arm around mine, I say, "So you like him?" He gives me a puzzled embarrassed look, and repeats, "Yes, Frank is a fine young man."

I released the hand-shake. "Have you confirmed whether the groom likes daddy?" I say in my best sleuth voice as she pulls me away.

"You're fucking nuts!" she says.

"I met daddy!" I yell at the top of my lungs as we run out of the reception hall, "and he likes Frankie, he told me so! Frankie and Daddy sitting in a tree! F-U-C-K-I-N-G! I yell as we pass through the front doors and into the parking lot. "Jesus Andrew!" She can't believe it. People were appalled.

At the restaurant, somewhere in Houston, we're sitting at the bar, a big marble slab of a bar, and the bartender is this really cool dude.

"I don't cheat on my wife," I explain. "This is more complicated than I could probably explain."

"Right, this is complicated, because well, I don't sleep with married men," she adds and pops an olive from my martini into her mouth. "We've known each other since high school."

"Ah, high school sweet hearts." the bartender says with too much flair.

"Are you gay?" she asks him.

"Yes, so what, but don't tell," he says with a wink.

"Anyhow," I say, irritated at being interrupted, "my marriage is over anyway."

"Not technically," she says, now to the bartender: "Technically, he's still married," she clarifies.

"What do you do?" the bartender asks.

"He's a lawyer for the Justice Department!" she explains, taking my last olive.

"Let me get you some more," he says.

"Thank you," I say sarcastically, looking at her.

I reach into my coat pocket and pull out two more 10 milligrams and pop them in. The bartender is off helping someone.

"You're going to have organ failure if you keep that up," she warns.

"It's all about moderation," I say. "Moderation."

"Andrew?"

"Scott!" Walking towards me was a customs agent assigned to my case. A criminal investigator. I quickly make introductions, trying not to slur my words.

"Hey man, can you join us?" I'm hoping that he says no. Please say no.

"No, I'm here with my wife and her parents—celebrating the ole' 50th anniversary. Her parents' that is." he explains. I give him the look that says, "This girl with me is a dear old friend, not my wife, and I'm not a dirt bag who cheats, although we slept together last night (I think) and probably will tonight (I think)." He gives me the nod.

"Well, it's nice to meet you, enjoy your dinner. Andrew, I'll talk to you on Monday," he says.

"Monday sounds great. Have a good night, Scott."

"That was weird," she says.

"Just a little; he's a cool dude," I say.

The bartender returns with fresh drinks. Mine is a dirty martini with extra olives, because she loves olives.

"Why is your marriage ending?" he asks, doing his best sympathetic bartender.

I take a huge sip, and placing the glass down, I say, "She doesn't comprehend my anguish." And I stare into his eyes. "She just doesn't understand me."

"Wow, that's crazy," he says and wipes the bar with a towel.

"I think it's ending because Andrew thinks he's Jesus," she says and stares at the bartender.

"Crazy," he says again, still wiping the bar.

She and I are obviously in our own separate worlds right now. The booze is starting to make me hungry. She's barely able to keep her eyes open from the valium. We shouldn't be where we are. We should be in detox facilities. "How about a plate of oysters?" I say with a grin and satisfaction that I said it without slurring my words. The bartender puts in our order and starts to make more drinks.

Addressing the bartender, I say: "We started seeing each other— me and my current wife—while I was still married to my first wife. It was dishonest, it started dishonest-style." I wink knowing the bartender will pick up on my Texas slang. She's staring at me now, listening.

"I was at the Naval Justice School in Rhode Island when the whole thing unraveled," I say.

"Tori was devastated. So was Wendi's husband." I'm reflecting back and even though I'm intoxicated, it seems very clear.

"Life is just cruel sometimes," she says. "We just do things without planning them. It's just cruel." She's staring down.

"It was horrible," I say." "You knew Tori, she was a great person, never harmed a soul, God I was such a piece of shit."

We just sat there in silence. I thought of little Derrick, 15 months old, and Wendi pregnant with Dylan. What kind of person was I?

My marriage with Wendi was on the rocks and I realized spending time with this old friend in Houston was not a good choice. It was around this time that things started feeling fictional, cartoon-like. My life had become like one of those semi-animated movies where things just happen, where the colors are very vivid, but the conversations are blurry. The conversations become just words, and they no longer matter. They're just words with my boss, with my colleagues, family, friends, with myself.

After we left the restaurant, I think we both needed a pick-me-up. We decided to go back to the amusement park and ride the roller-coaster. It's probably ten o'clock and the place is packed with family and she and I can barely walk straight. All around us life is happening, and we're not part of it. This is no pick-me-up.

Chapter 20

I'm sitting in my doctor's office in Virginia lying about back pain. Sure, I felt *some* pain, especially given all of the flying I was doing with the Justice Department, but the fact was I was overweight. Carrying the extra pounds, say 20 extra pounds, puts extra stress on one's frame. This stress is avoidable. I didn't need pain medicine, at least not narcotic pain medicine. I needed Weight Watchers.

I also didn't need valium. Valium tells you that you have a good marriage. That your spouse is normal, despite signs that say otherwise. If everyone ate valium, there would be no divorce lawyers. Valium makes the city bus rides, which are normally dismal and depressing, OK. To catch the bus to the Pentagon Metro stop, and then the metro train into D.C., some mornings required three valiums. The problem was that on occasion, I would miss the bus. Not miss it like I was late getting to it, but miss it as in not getting off the bus stop bench when the bus pulls up and stops right in front of me. I have a large coffee, it's a beautiful morning and I have a *Washington Post* and a Marlboro.

"I'll catch the next one!" I say as I wave off the driver.

Sometimes I wouldn't get to work until 10:30 a.m., even though it only takes 20 minutes and I left the house at 8:30. One time I stayed on the bus too long and ended up in Maryland and rode the thing all the way back to the starting point. I thought maybe it was at the end of the day, that I had worked all day and was going home, but wondered why it was still light outside. Granted this only occurred on days when I didn't have to be in court or if I had just returned from a trip. One day I fell asleep—

or maybe it was a valium induced coma-like state—on the bench. My neighbor drove by and beeped.

"Andrew, you alright?"

"Yeah, oh hey, yeah, thanks—just a little snooze."

Just a little snooze in my suit and tie, and brief case, and sunglasses, with a large coffee and a newspaper, at the bus stop on a week day.

"Do you need a lift?"

Yeah, I need a lift alright. I need a little "pick-me-up."

"No, no the bus will be along any minute," I say.

"But, it's almost noon. I mean, well I don't think they start running again until—it won't be here for another hour."

"It's noon?" I check my watch. Sure enough, it's noon and I'm really hungry.

"I must have fallen asleep. Thanks though."

"OK." And with a dumb look on his mug, my neighbor drives off.

My dear sister Carol lives just down the street, so I decide to go to her house for lunch. Carol worked for a nonprofit and seemed to have a very flexible schedule, too.

"Sis?" I'm at her door.

"Short day?" she asks, assuming I have already been to the office and back.

"You could say that; I actually never made it in. I fell asleep at the bus stop. Art drove by and woke me up."

"Strange sensation waking-up that way," I add contemplatively, sort of to myself.

Carol starts laughing. I don't think she believed me. That's another issue about my life at this time. My reality—stuff like falling into a valium induced sleep at the bus stop—doesn't seem real to others. It's just not believable. So when I explain the truth, people think I'm joking.

Carol always has a ton of good food at her house. One day I was eating over there and my niece Emily, who was only five years old, told me that her house "wasn't a restaurant." We all laughed so hard. Another time, I said the same thing to her. I said "Emily, this isn't a restaurant." And she dead panned, "I live here, Uncle Andrew."

"Dr. Potsa sir, how are you?"

"Andrew, what can I do for you?"

"Well, I left my medication in Los Angeles."

"Andrew, you have to stop doing this."

"I know, it's crazy."

"What do you need?"

"Well, it's the valium and the Lortab and the Viagra."

"Okay, I'll call it in," he says with reluctance in his voice, "but we can't keep doing this."

"No, I'll be more careful doctor. Thank you."

"Hey, I'm on the road this week," I say to Wendi.

"So, we're going to miss our counseling again?" It's not so much a question as it is a complaint. "And you're staying sober, Andrew?"

"Yes, there's nothing to do in Texas, it's basically all work."

"Be careful," Wendi says, concerned about me as she always was.

"I will," I say. "I think we need a vacation. After this case is over, OK?" Wendi didn't want a vacation as far as I could tell. She wasn't happy and neither was I. But I'm not so sure the unhappiness was the result of our marriage. We were each going through some existential crisis that people who are 30 years old can go through. Was this job really what I wanted? Was Virginia and D.C., and this three-bedroom condo, where I really wanted to live? Was Wendi really "meant" to be my lifelong companion? I think that I consistently concluded no or not really to those questions, and yet here I was. Things didn't fit, like an irregular shirt from Old Navy, no matter how I tugged at it or contorted, it was still an irregular fucking shirt. Despite the tremendous joy Derrick and Dylan

215

brought me on a micro-level, like bath time, and watching them eat jelly on bread, and smelling their hair and cheeks, I also felt fear, because on a macro level, I knew something was wrong. Something about my life felt like a funeral. I couldn't sustain happiness or even just a feeling of "OK." My head was constantly swimming in the negative.

I was working on cases that were a little over my head. Which was good; it was a learning opportunity. Our section was working on international drug trafficking and money laundering cases, and there were treaties and foreign laws and domestic statutes that I had never worked with when I was at the U.S. Attorney's office. One of my cases was a major ecstasy and money laundering case that was barely getting off the ground in Houston. The Houston DEA agents were getting fed up with their prosecutors in the Houston U.S. Attorney's Office. They didn't feel like these guys were working diligently enough, so they went up through their DEA channels and requested help from our office in Washington. When my boss approached me about it, I jumped on it because it meant travel out-of-town. Several countries were involved in the investigation, including Israel, Netherlands, Germany, Spain and several cities in the U.S. Incredible! Bart Doosey, the DEA agent in charge of the investigation, was in his own league as far as smarts and leadership. He was able to get all the agencies, including the FBI, Customs, and Immigration to work together, which is a huge task. These were real-world turf wars.

Our biggest challenge was getting a special type of wiretap approved by the Assistant Attorney General. This special wiretap, known as a "roving wiretap," allowed law enforcement to combat the use of cell phones by drug traffickers, whereas the traditional wiretap authorization, at the time, only worked well with landlines, home or office phones wired into a network. Criminals knew that if they change or drop cell phones every three days or so, the government would have to play catch-up by finding the new phone they were using and then go back to the judge and ask for permission to monitor—or "go up on"—the new phone number.

By the time this happens, the criminals have already dropped that number/phone and gone onto another phone. Under this process, law-enforcement missed conversations and was always one or two steps behind. It's maddening for an agent and prosecutor. The wiretapping statute allowed for a roving wiretap—that is, it allows agents to just go up on the new phone without asking the judge's permission first.

Anyhow, at the time, the Justice Department was only approving maybe 11 every year, so it was significant. It was an uphill battle, though. Main Justice does not like to approve these. We worked every possible angle. I worked overtime on the application, I busted my balls, and finally it was approved at the Justice level. The federal judge in Texas, despite being an octogenarian, had never seen a roving wiretap application, and after some extensive explanation, he approved it. It proved to be the law-enforcement tool that broke the case wide-open. We had the criminals' voices on tape now talking about deliveries, payments, organizational structure, everything. Nothing else plays as well before a jury as a defendant's own voice while conducting business.

Every week I flew from Washington to Houston. The agents and I worked hard and played pretty hard too. The outskirts of Houston are riddled with watering holes. I think they call them beer stands or something. One particular prosecutor in the U.S. Attorney's Office and I would go to happy hour several times a week together and usually end up in a cigar bar around midnight or so. One night we were trying to help a damsel in distress—she and her boyfriend had just fought in the parking lot. I think he kicked her in the side of the head. And now, she was all alone at the bar, with an ice pack. Poor thing. Anyhow, I offered all sorts of protection for her, everything short of calling in an air strike.

I always had a healthy portion of pain medicine and valium at my disposal because Doctor Potsa back in Virginia kept prescribing them. My behavior became more belligerent. I was spending more time high and drunk and less time being an effective lawyer, but so far no one really noticed. That was about to change.

Chapter 21

We held the takedown meeting in an auditorium. Agents, police officers, sheriff's deputies, Texas Rangers, the whole gamut of law enforcement, were brought in to assist. Bart set the tone right away by talking about the gravity of the case. He introduced me to the room as the "Washington Outsider, turned Houston Insider." Dressed in a dark suit and white shirt, I cut quite the contrast with the roomful of cops. They were an impressively wild looking group. Most did extensive undercover work, so they literally looked like the guy you'd go to if you needed 12 pounds of cocaine by 3 o'clock, or a handgun with no number, or a shoulder-fired rocket, or a whole crate of shoulder fired rockets. They had dangerous jobs where the line between right and wrong is often blurred; where the playing field of perceived good and evil meet. I knew a few of these guys, and even though I was just a white collar guy, I had gained some respect when I pulled their wiretap out of the toilet. The operation was scheduled for sun-up the next morning. That night I went out by myself to an out-of-the-way bar. No agents, no prosecutors, just me and a bunch of freaks. I went overboard with drinks, pain medicine, valium and something I've never really cared for so much, and that's cocaine.

The takedown went off without a hitch. Due to his sound principals and exceptional leadership, Bart orchestrated the arrest of dozens of defendants listed on our indictment, the search of businesses and homes and subsequent seizure of drugs, guns, money, and documents that would help prove the conspiracy portion of the charges. By any standard, the operation was a resounding success.

While the agents did their jobs early that morning, I was just climbing out of the taxi at my hotel, high out of my fucking gourd. I managed to get into the shower where the water just poured over me as I leaned against the shower wall trying to get my bearings when the auditory hallucinations began.

"Did you say something?"

"No, I was just talking to myself."

"Did you hear that?"

"No."

I shut off the shower. *"It's the phone, you're phone is ringing, shut off the shower and listen."*

"I still don't hear anything."

"I swear I heard it ringing."

"Did you just hear that?"

"No."

"It's the door; someone is knocking on the door, shut off the shower."

I shut off the shower. *"No, I still don't hear it."*

No one called and no one knocked at the door. The cocaine was the only thing making any noise. I hate cocaine.

After slipping into a clean suit, I ate two Valium in order to chop the top of the cocaine head, and just one Ritalin to help me with my concentration. I jumped in the taxi and headed to the DEA Headquarters to make a lawyerly assessment of the take down. Riding in the taxi, I experienced mild visual hallucinations, seeing people on the side of the street as we passed, but when I'd look again, they wouldn't be there. And every time I turned my head there was this wet swooshing sound inside my brain.

"How much longer can you go on like this Andrew?"

"Not much longer. The drugs are killing me."

"This is so true. After this case, maybe I'll clean-up a bit."

"Promise?"

"No, I can't make any promises, but you already knew that."

The combination of Valium and Ritalin created a tunnel-vision, fog-ridden, echo chamber effect. So much so that after I talked to someone, let's say for instance, a "good morning" to someone at the DEA office, the words would ring in my ears, and then I would instantly erase the idea of having said good morning in the first place.

Sitting in an office chair now watching the scene unfold as the agents poured over what seemed like piles of seized evidence. Guns, drugs, money, jewelry, cash, electronics, you name it. It was being marked and placed in an evidence inventory bag.

"You look like you could use some coffee." Someone places a cup in front of me.

"Yes, I could, thanks, thank you."

I remember staring at the cup for what seemed way too long.

"It's black—that's how you drink it right?" The female voice says.

"Yes, thank you."

Then things went totally blank and black. Then I could see again, the steam rising from the coffee. And then I listened as the agents worked around me. I listened as life went on around me.

I don't remember going back to my hotel later that morning, or how I got there, but I did. I woke-up in the bed a few hours later, covers over me, fully clothed, shoes on, dazed and fucking confused and freezing cold. I called Bart but there was no answer. Nervous, panicked, I got up and rushed over to the U.S. Attorney's Office, a place I hadn't been in days. I had a horrible feeling like I was missing something, but I made it to the office and sat down. *This will be fine.*

"Mr. McKenna, Agent Doosey on line one."

"Andrew, we're missing evidence."

"What? Say again?" I say, not sure what he's talking about.

"Someone took a watch, a Rolex that we seized this morning. It's gone."

"Are you kidding me?" I say. "Whoa, are you sure?"

"It's gone. It disappeared this morning."

And then the question that almost made me throw-up.

"Andrew, have you seen it?"

"What?" I say, pissed that he asked. "No, Bart I haven't seen it."

"Well, I'm asking everyone." He back pedals a bit, clarifying that we have to find it.

"Well I agree," I say. There's a long pause before he says:

"Listen, I have to take this call."

"Okay, but—" And he hangs-up. *This is crazy.*

Rushing to the bathroom to vomit. The virtual pharmacology experiment coursing through my blood is suddenly going poorly.

"Counselor! Congratulations on the take down!" A colleague, who used to be assigned to the case months ago, until he got into a pissing match with Bart, is talking to me.

"Thanks, Kris. I appreciate it. The credit goes to the agents though," I say trying to keep it moving.

"Oh, I don't believe that Andrew, *you* got the roving tap approved, *you* presented the case to the Grand Jury, *and you* kept Bart reigned in."

"Well, Bart kept himself reigned in Kris—he's a super-agent, I don't think anyone can dispute that now," I say, undercutting any additional argument on this point, especially from douche bag Kris.

"As for the other stuff, the system worked," I add.

"Too humble, too humble." Kris says sarcastically, he strolls away, a case file in hand. Asshole.

"Andrew, you have Agent Doosey on line two—it sounds important." The secretary says.

"Bart, what's up?"

"We have a problem," He says. "We're trying to narrow down who may have had access to the watch."

"You still haven't found it?" I say irritably. Evidence missing from a seizure is a huge fucking deal. I thought for sure something would turn up by now, or at the very least, the agents would "determine" that they made a paperwork "error" and nothing was missing after all.

"Jesus, Bart, this is a major fucking problem, we'll fucking polygraph everyone who was there this morning," I say.

"Everyone?" he asks.

"Everyone," I answer.

"Everyone, including me, including you?" he asks. I pause, thinking to myself.

"Everyone," I say. "Andrew, Tom Knight is on line one," the secretary says.

"Bart, I'll call you back."

"Tom, what's up?" I say into the receiver, my mind is scrambling a bit. I could use a big fucking beer. I check my watch—an hour until the workday ends.

"First of all Andrew, congratulations on the takedown," he says.

"Thanks Tom, the credit belongs to—"

"I spoke with the ASAC down there," Tom interrupts me. The ASAC is Bart's boss. "He says there's a problem with the evidence." Tom pauses.

"I know, I was just about to call you Tom. It's insane. They're missing—"

"I know what they're missing. Apparently everyone is a suspect at this point." Another pause.

"Right, well I suggested polygraphs," I say. It comes out awkwardly.

"OK, well listen, I just called to check-in, Andrew. Good job with the takedown. Be careful. And I'll see you when you get back to Washington. Be careful."

Tom was a super-conscientious boss, extremely helpful, hands off, but also very protective of his prosecutors. And he himself had tried about three 300 felony cases, so he was like the master that we could turn to whenever we needed guidance. But I wasn't looking for guidance. Tom had called me. And he had spoken to the ASAC, which wasn't unheard of, but a bit surprising nonetheless. I reached into my bag and pulled out a prescription bottle. I opened it and took out two Valium, popped them into my mouth, maneuvered them under my tongue and let them dissolve, slowly dissolve. I stared at the phone and just thought.

Minutes later—I think it was minutes—a knock on the door.

"Come in please," I say. Bart appears in the doorway. "Bart! Come in, have a seat."

Bart has a bag with him, more of a carrying-case with a strap. Bart never carries a bag with him. He doesn't even use a holster—he just tucks his Glock into his waist-band. He looks solemn, very solemn and cold.

"Andrew, you need to call Washington," he said instantly, very clearly.

"What are you talking about?" I respond.

"Call your boss, it's about the watch." There's a tear in his eye. We had grown pretty fucking close over the past 11 months.

I need a drink now. Now I need something to calm my mind because this is so fucked up. Is Bart crazy? I pulled off a great indictment for him and his agents—a totally career-enhancing case for him. The guy from Washington comes into town, cuts through bureaucratic bullshit between local prosecutors and agents and indicts 35! I'm the guy. Months and months, and he's going to question my integrity? Is he fucking nuts? I'll get his ass fired for this bullshit. I just can't believe this, I need a drink. I reach down next to me into my bag, push a couple of prescription bottles aside, the Valium—my friend—makes a rattling noise. I hear Bart react to it with a sigh. I sit back straight, staring into Bart's eyes.

"I found this earlier today," I'm holding up a shiny new Rolex Oyster Perpetual with Day Date.

A long pause ensued as Bart and I just stared at each other.

"Call your boss, Andrew," Bart says as the blood drains from our faces. We both have tears now and the air was just sucked from the room as we stare into each other's eyes.

But I'm the go-to guy. Bright, handsome, articulate? My old boss used to leave me sort-of-in-charge of things when she was out. Her e-mail to everyone used to say, "I'll be out this week at a seminar, if you have any questions or problems, see Andrew!" I made it to the Justice Department! From a small regional law school! People respected me. People loved Andrew McKenna.

"sensitive to others' predicaments"
"calm under pressure"
"thinks on his feet"
"exceeds all expectations"
"promote immediately"
"outstanding Marine Officer"
"handles more than his peers"
"hardworking"
"smart"
"trustworthy"
"impulse control problems"
"risk-taker"
"narcissist"
"demonic addiction"
"drug addict"
"alcoholic"
"bad-tempered"
"manipulative"
"angry"
"charming"
"thrill-seeker"

Chapter 22

I can hear the waves break on the shore and can feel the warm sunshine on my face. Breathing in the sea air, I am alone. Alone and at peace with myself. No mental traffic, just peace and quiet. Deep breaths, in and out, thoughts come and go, no need to cling to any one thought, just let it go on, like the clouds in the sky.

"Hey Tom, listen, I have some really bad news."

"Andrew, hey—what's up? You're doing a great job down there, it can't be that bad." Tom, after all, is a big fan.

"Well Tom. I stole some evidence seized during the take-down," I calmly explain.

"What?" Tom says after a pause. "You're not serious," he adds, laughing.

"Unfortunately, Tom, I am serious. I was drinking all night and eating valium and Percocet and doing cocaine, and when I went to the agent's office this morning, I took a Rolex watch out of the evidence bag and stuck it in my suit coat. I have a problem Tom, and I need help. Please help me."

Who knows how the rest would have gone. I'm pretty sure I could have salvaged my career as a prosecutor, but who knows. Tom would have gone to bat for me, if I would have agreed to treatment, which I would have. But my mind wasn't operating right. Instead, the conversation with Tom goes like this:

"Tom, it's Andrew."

"Andrew! What's up?" Tom says enthusiastically.

"Tom, you're not going to believe what happened," I say, my voice cracking with emotion. "They think I stole evidence, the watch, they think I stole the fucking watch. I found it in my bag, maybe someone planted it?"

"Who? What? Andrew, what the hell are you talking about?" Tom couldn't believe what I was saying to him.

We agreed that I had to return to Washington, that this had to be dealt with immediately. I drank a fifth of scotch on the Continental Airlines flight back to D.C.

Sitting in Tom's office now.

"Tom, I didn't take the watch," I pleaded. "Tell me you believe me! Tell me you believe me Tom!"

"Andrew, relax. I believe you," Tom says, trying to calm me down.

"It's my career—what will I do?" I say. Sober now, but not wanting to be sober.

"We're working on it with the leadership in Houston to try to sort this out. For now, you're off the case. I spoke with Jodi (our boss) she said to take a few days off, but to call-in at least once a day."

"Oh, and Andrew," he says to me as I'm walking out his office, "the stories out of Houston, from the agents, about the drinking—disappearing for hours at a time. I think you need to take a look at it—a serious look. Call me tomorrow morning."

"Tom, I didn't do it." Words I will regret for the rest of my life because Tom deserved the truth. My mind couldn't get around what was happening, or even worse, I couldn't comprehend what I had done. It wasn't real. The drugs and alcohol made it fictional. My colleagues just couldn't believe it. No one could. But DOJ wasn't going to let it go away.

The Inspector General got involved, launching a several month investigation. They talked to everyone involved in the case. The consensus was that I delivered huge with the indictment, the roving wiretap, the fact that I came in from Main Justice in Washington because the agents in

Houston could no longer communicate with the Houston prosecutors. I was there to salvage this case, to rope in defendants from several countries and states across the U.S. It was big and I had worked it very hard and professionally for months. We got the job done. But my using was off the fucking hook. People knew this too. As the revelations came out and people heard from the agents, I suddenly appeared unstable.

Pacing the floor at home, on the phone with Tom. "You're going to have to hire a lawyer," Tom says. "The IG is recommending prosecution. They say they have enough to convict you. I think you need to do your best to be cooperative with this. Most importantly, I think you need to do what's best for you and your family." Everything turned bright white, and then dark. All of the oxygen left my body and I next woke up on the floor. The phone was laid out beside me. "Tom?"

The U.S. Attorney's office in Louisiana would handle the case from here because other offices had to recuse themselves because either they knew me, or were involved in some way with the case. I called a lawyer in New Orleans named Ron Rakowski, the guy who represented the rapper C-Murder.

"Mr. Rakowski? I'm in trouble," I said, completely numb, having just downed a shot.

"Who is this?" he asks.

"Andrew McKenna," I answer, barely able to say my own name.

"Oh, right, Andrew, DOJ ... no talking on the phone."

A mutual friend had recommended Ron because he is a great attorney, respected by the prosecutors in Louisiana for being ethical and a good trial lawyer.

"When are you coming down?"

"Tuesday," I say.

"See you then. Oh, and Andrew, do me a favor: stop telling people your story."

For a while I was trying to convince people of my innocence. The problem is not that one makes inconsistent statements during these times, in fact, if anything, the statements are too consistent when you're lying.

No, the problem is that the listeners' recollections of what you told them are inconsistent. That's where it breaks down. And investigators start to hear that you told one person one version, and another person a different version. Now they have a target making inconsistent statements and then you're sunk.

"I have to go back in two days, this time to New Orleans," I say to Wendi, who was curled-up in the fetal position staring at the back of the sofa. Derrick is taking a nap with his best friend Buzz Lightyear. My mom, who lives a few doors down, and who's been spending a lot of time with Derrick just called to say how much fun they had earlier in the day. My mom also asked about Wendi. She was concerned that Wendi was depressed. Who wasn't?

Wendi was unresponsive, so I went down into the basement area where our little home office was. I laid out on the futon couch, popped a drug, and just sat there. I felt so sad. The medicine hardly ever worked anymore.

Later on, I had to go out and pick-up something to eat because we had no food at all in the house. I decided on Thai food. If I went a little early, I could sit at the bar and sneak a few drinks while I waited. The booze now was an essential part of my day, a couple drinks were just enough to take the edge off.

When I got home, little Derrick was awake and standing at the front door looking through the glass when I walked up the walk. He gave me his big toothless grin, held out his arms and said, "Ump? Ump?" Which was his way of saying "Pick-me up, dad."

"Want to take Martin for a walk?" I asked Derrick. Martin was our surviving family dog, playmate to Dalai, who I had murdered a few months back. Martin was a very fast runner, so we had to keep him on a leash. His speed in the neighborhood was the stuff of legend. Anyhow, Derrick points to the backpack, which means he would prefer to be a passenger for this walk.

"OK, big boy," I tell him. "Let's get you suited up."

"We'll be back shortly," I say to Wendi. No response. We start all of our walks with a quick stop at grandma's house. Usually a knock on her front window.

"Want to join us?" I ask.

"Of course!" my mom says, clearly happy. Derrick has a big toothless grin when he sees my mom. He's securely in the backpack and he points with his finger as if to say, "Okay, this way, it's time to walk!"

Derrick was still just a little guy when Dylan was born. Derrick liked his little brother and everything; he just wasn't sure why he was there. When we would come home from our walks—where we worked on the alphabet— Derrick would go to see if Dylan was still there.

I spent all of my time with the boys and my sister and her family. They were my refuge and the only thing that brought me happiness anymore. I was so attached to the boys that I would find myself just staring at them, watching their every move. For some reason I was hyper-sensitive to their feelings and emotions, watching their reactions to things, especially that Derrick, because he was older and more perceptive. Sometimes my worry for him was so overwhelming that I couldn't shut it off. I was more of a worried, panicked parent who was able to hide it, because I didn't want the boys to sense the panic and feel less than secure.

"Mom, they think I took the watch."

"Oh, Andrew."

Chapter 23

"We should move to New York. We should move to New York and be closer to both our families, you know, for comfort sake?"

229

"It'll work out, right?" Wendi asks.

"Yeah, it'll work out. Did I tell you Frank Costello called me? He wants to meet." Frank's one of the best criminal defense lawyers in the United States. I tell her in part to assure her that I'll get a lawyer job, and we'll live happily ever after.

"That's great! It will be OK," Wendi says. The prospect of moving back to New York, closer to her parents and brothers, gave her something to hold on to.

"No worries," I added, just to be sure.

Wendi didn't know anything about what had happened with DOJ, but she knew something was up. I didn't feel I could talk to her about this because her mental state was so fragile. But not telling her had more to do with me. I didn't want to reveal that I had fucked up in such a major way. So I lied.

Brian, my brother, flew down from New York to help us pack-up and move. He had just gone through a shaky job situation and we were both quickly proving that we could be there for each other in times of crisis.

"What did they say?" Brian already knows in his mind how the whole thing went down at Justice. He's too fucking smart. I believe he is asking me because he doesn't want me to hold it in. Also, he is probably interested in how I am processing it, to see if I am lying to myself.

"They said to get some help. That I'm a great talent with room to grow, but the addiction would kill me."

"Is that true?" he probes.

"Yes Chief. It's all true," I concede.

"Good, well than you already won half the battle. We'll get through this."

I left Washington, D.C., without saying goodbye to a single friend, colleague, or neighbor. The strangest, most bizarre way to close a chapter in one's life is to just walk off without explanation, without apology. Before leaving, I had locked up employment at one of the top firms in

Albany. My interview had gone really well. I never talked about why I had 'resigned' from DOJ other than to say that Wendi and I wanted to raise the boys closer to family.

Wendi and I bought a nice little house in Delmar, New York—my commute to work was measured now in minutes as opposed to the D.C commute which was measured in train transfers. My brother Brian—recently divorced—moved into our basement. The boys were doing great, Derrick was still a toddler, and Dylan was crossing over from infant status. Wendi and I continued our marriage counseling with our counselor from Virginia via phone, when we moved to New York. Things looked okay, but they really weren't.

By now, Wendi and I had mutually reached that point in relationships where the parties can't stand each other anymore—where watching your spouse eat makes you sick. Between her depression and my chronic escapism, we were some couple. I was also still toxic from constant drug abuse, and I was a little overweight and sweaty.

"So let me get this right Ms. Smith. You were at the pet store walking down the aisle, when you tripped over a wooden pallet?"

"That's right."

"Uh huh, and I see that you're wearing a full back brace?"

"Yup, I have degenerative disk disease."

"From the fall?"

"No, I've had it for years, and arthritis; they're related."

"I see."

My office was nice though. Wood paneled and nice expensive carpet. The furniture was better than the government crap furniture made by prison inmates. This was good cherry wood. So I would sit in my private practice office and pretend that what I was doing was as good as my old job in Washington. My self-loathing at this point was palpable.

The boys were the only thing that brought me joy, but even the time I spent with them was doubled by my despair and feeling of grief. Depression. The bad feelings were constant now. I had started taking anti-depressants but I don't think they worked. The damn cloud was all around me. The doubt, the frustration, the doom. Being back in New York was a weird feeling, too; in a way it was nice to be back closer to family, but it was also a constant reminder of my recent failures. I can't discount the nuisance my relationship had become. It was over. I think we both felt trapped and instead of rehashing and laying blame, it's enough to say that I felt trapped, and I was unhappy.

One day my back felt tight, and my brain felt even tighter. So I called a local doctor and made an appointment. Unlike my doctor in Virginia, New York doctors are alert to drug-seekers. I had no idea until this particular doctor laughed at me.

"A narcotic? That's funny!" the doctor laughed. "How about some Motrin, ice-packs, and little light stretching Andrew?"

The next doctor I saw suggested acupuncture and what essentially amounted to aroma-therapy.

"But didn't you hear what I said? I fell down a cliff?"

The next doctor recommended, after I talked about my relationship with my Virginia physician, rehab.

"It sounds like you have a physical dependence on opioids."

Good grief.

"It sounds like you are afraid to fucking properly treat pain, doctor!" I countered.

Flipping through my Blue Cross/Blue Shield booklet of providers, I looked for ethnic sounding names. Indians, Pakistanis, Afghanis, thinking that they needed my business more than the WASPS because they had just recently emigrated. More addict-type thinking on my part. Erroneous thinking; erroneous on all counts.

"Dr. Singh, my point is that I worked as a prosecutor, and also in the immigration field, and I respond to you people, your challenges, your hurdles—"

Dr. Singh berated me as a racist, drug seeker and so on. Before I hung-up on him, I told him I hoped his shitty cow went to hell.

"Mr. McKenna, I don't know what you're talking about. At all."

Finally, a young white doctor (usually the worst) gave me Lortab for pain. Seven and a half milligrams. I told him I was allergic to the weaker five milligram ones, almost a fatal mistake on my part. I think he ignored this statement. I took a few and my depression went away. I was more involved with Wendi and the boys, more involved around the house, the back pain that Motrin, an ice-pack, and light stretching would have erased, was gone. Four days later, the pills were gone too because I had eaten them all. When I called the doctor to tell him that the bottle had fallen into the toilet and the pills were ruined and needed to be replaced, he told me to never call him or come to his office again or he'd call the police.

At this point I had actually tried Paxil, Wellbutrin, and Zoloft in varying dosages and nothing seemed to help. I had stopped drinking at this point because it only made me feel worse and Wendi had figured out that I was doing it behind her back when we lived in Virginia. She could smell it on me. As far as the other stuff, like Xanax, Valium, and Ritalin, my supplier, that is my doctor, in Virginia wouldn't write scripts across state lines. I know because I asked him. Oddly, the doctor who told me not to call him had given me Viagra samples and one day, while home alone I thought it would be fun to take one and see what would happen. Let's just say it was one way to kill two and half hours by myself. It definitely helped with my raging depression. I actually experienced the four plus hour erection that the commercial warns about. The damn thing wouldn't go away. I hit it with cold water, hot water, ice cubes, a curling iron. I hung clothes off it, danced around with it, laughed about it, cried about it (well whimpered a bit, maybe), prayed it would go away. Threatened it to go away. Christ, I practically water-boarded the damn thing. Finally, after utilizing it solo one more time, I passed-out from exhaustion. When I woke up it was gone, Marine down. But my depression was back.

I doctor shopped for another few weeks in secret, trying to keep my head above water at work and a smile on my face for family and

233

Andrew McKenna

friends. The only thing that seemed to help us through was the pain medicine, and I was running out of doctors. The sensation of shame was returning.

"Doesn't anyone sell painkillers in this fucking town!?" I yell at my good friend over the phone. It's 6 a.m.

"What's his name gets Percocet around the first of the month from his doctor, but I know for a fact that he's out now, already sold those."

Back to the law office, the lady with the back brace who tripped over dog food is back. I had no recollection of rescheduling another appointment for her, but here she was sitting in front of me in my office.

"So you say that you live with an enormous amount of pain."

"That's for sure," she replies.

"I wish I could recommend a doctor for you, I just don't know of one—I just recently moved back to the area."

"I have a doctor Mr. McKenna, that's not the problem. The problem is that all he does is prescribe medication that makes me loopy and—"

"Loopy?" I interrupt her. She has my full attention. And with that she reaches deep into her enormous tote bag and instead of pulling out the assault rifle that I thought she was going to, she pulled out a freezer bag full of brown prescription bottles.

"Good lord," I say. "May I see the bag please, ma'am?"

"Of course."

"Valium, Hydrocodone, Percocet, OxyContin." I read all of the labels. There are multiple bottles of each and the most important factor here is that they're all full.

"This has certainly put into perspective for me the extent of your injuries, and of course the pain and suffering." Knowing she is familiar with the latter phrasing.

"I am troubled by this," I add. "And of course, I'll need to have my secretary make photocopies of these bottles immediately. I'll be back in a moment. Can I get you a coffee or tea?"

Or a humanitarian medal of some sort?

"Photocopies?" she asks, perplexed. "Of the bottles?"

"Standard procedure ma'am," I answer.

Walking with purpose now towards the firm washroom, with the bag of bottles concealed under my suit coat, it sounds like I'm a sales rep for Tic-Tacs, not a lawyer. I try to glide as I walk instead of step, hoping this would make less sound. I looked ridiculous.

I had never tried an OxyContin but I had heard about it. Apparently it was in a league of its own. While in Washington I'd get e-mails about how this "hillbilly" heroin, as it was called, was literally killing people. But of course, they were injecting it and since I didn't inject drugs, it wouldn't hurt to try one. Or two. How much stronger could an OxyContin be then say Percocet or Lortab? It's all the same family! Sure *The New York Times* recently did an extensive piece on it, but I am an experienced pill artist, after all. I could really use the relief. Things seemed so bleak.

When someone, a colleague, passed me on the way, I raised my voice to drown out the Tic-Tac's noise and addressed him while he was still a good 10-12 feet away, more than a reasonable distance to initiate a greeting. No doubt about it.

Once inside the bathroom I made a bee-line to a stall, closed the door behind me and sat on the hoop. I was sweating, as usual; a typical symptom of opiate dependency. I opened the freezer bag and removed a prescription bottle which read OxyContin forty milligrams, and almost shit my britches out of pure joy—elation really. Next came the bottle of Xanax, then Percocet, then OxyContin again, then what appeared to be birth control, and anti-anxiety medication, Lortab and another OxyContin bottle which I opened with slightly shaking hands. I ate three. Right off the rip!

The bathroom door opened and someone with a pair of $500 Ferragamos, must be a law partner, took the stall next to me. On my lap was the noisy freezer bag. You could have heard a pin drop in the bathroom so I had to keep them still. The only sound was a quiet buzzing from a slightly malfunctioning recessed ceiling light. I froze. I didn't want to risk any noise that would give away what I was doing. I thought that if I just sat there, Ferragamos would finish his business and leave. Then I heard the rustling of a newspaper. Good lord. The OxyContin was starting to go to work, starting in my bowels, the same feeling I get when I go into a bookstore, working its way simultaneously from my gut down my legs—slowly—up my torso into my chest and shoulders into my lips and teeth. My personal injury client wearing a back brace is sitting in my office. I let out an explosion, a grenade into the toilet.

Quiet as a mouse, I place, one by one, the pill bottles back into the freezer bag, timing each movement with my loud cough. I am irrationally trying to disguise my cough because I have a deep voice and I'm afraid that if my cough sounds too deep, Ferragamos will know it's me, Andrew McKenna, stall two.

As I depart the stall, a colleague comes into the bathroom and we meet virtually toe-to-toe. The bag is tucked under my arm under my suit coat and a film of sweat is bubbling on my forehead. I'm essentially a clammy mess. He saw me come out of the stall so I must wash my hands all while keeping the ziplock clamped under my arm.

"Everything okay?" he asks.

"Yeah man, everything's great."

I consider telling him that I have a stomach malady, a severe case of diarrhea because I feel by his question that he suspects that I'm not well. The sweating, the physical contortions associated with keeping the drug bag from falling onto the floor. "Everything" is clearly not "great" but that's what I said, so to come back with "I have a severe case of diarrhea" would make me a psychopath. Only a psychopath would think it was "great" to have a serious case of diarrhea that causes perspiration and contortions. I must have looked like hell because as I

SHEER MADNESS

made eye contact with him in the mirror he stood completely still and stared at me.

"I have a severe case of diarrhea." And with that, I left the bathroom.

"You're back."

"I'm back. Sorry that took so long—there was a line at the copy machine." After listening again to her and confirming the name, address and telephone number of her doctor, I concluded the meeting with: "I'll have to do some research and get back to you ma'am. Obviously this is a serious matter which will require research."

"Well okay. But do you think you'll take the case?"

"Well as I said, it's a little premature at this point, but I think you have a case here. The pet store shouldn't have left the enormous pallet of dog food in the middle of the aisle—it was negligent and it caused you significant injuries as is evident to all who see you in your body cast—I mean your back brace, excuse me."

"Mr. McKenna?"

"Yes?"

"My medication?"

"Of course, sorry, here you go." I hand her the bag.

"Steve, I think the woman might be insane, but she may also be the victim of a tort."

"The woman with the back brace?" He chuckles. "Insane? Why?"

"She seemed a little paranoid—she clutched her bag too, her bag filled with medicine."

"What kind of medicine?" Steve asks.

"I'm not sure."

Three days later I'm on the phone again with my friend. I'm shouting.

"You're telling me that no one has anything!"

"No Drew, it's totally dry out there! Christ! What do you want me to say?"

237

"Say that you know some real fucking drug dealers, bona fide dealers who take some goddamn pride in their trade, their ability to have inventory, not like these goddamn 'corner boys' you work with!"

"Wow, you are fucked up Andrew!"

"I'm going to need you to come back in. I did some research and talked to my boss. I'm a little frustrated with the pet store. The more I think about … man! These people think the rules don't apply to them! You could have been maimed! Or even killed if you had hit your temple just so on the pallet! It's ludicrous! No, no this can't wait until Friday. I need you to come in now. Yes, right now. Okay, then when does he get home? That's fine I'll see you at 2:30. Oh, and make sure you bring the medication and any medical records or timelines you might have. Great, see you then." *Shit.*

The first time I tried Heroin, I already needed it. Leading up to this event, I had been taking 80-milligram Oxycontin pills daily. Chewing and swallowing them. I was up to about five of those a day. And then the supply ended. The guy who had them was nowhere to be found. Dressed in a nice suit and tie, and properly groomed, with polished shoes, I left my house to go to work, got in my car heading to work. I flipped open the cell phone, dialed up my friend—it was about 8 a.m. on a chilly fall morning—and heard the bad news. The air was crisp and it sort of stung the inside of my nose and I breathed in the words I had just heard: "George is gone."

"Gone where?" I asked in a panic.

"Who knows? There's no answer."

"Are you sure?"

"That there's no answer? Of course I'm sure."

"This is fucking crazy." And then I realize that my friend is not panicking. "Why are you so fucking calm?"

And there's silence.

"Well?"

"Because there's nothing we can do," he says.

"Bullshit! Why are you so calm?"

And there's silence again.

"Pretty soon, I'm going to be throwing up sick, hoping I die, you are too! So why no panic?"

A long pause.

"Come over," he says

"What?"

"Just come over."

Driving along, I notice that I'm speeding 15 to 20 miles per hour over the limit. I slow down to five over and drive. *I know, yes I know, I know it's not oxyies, so it can only be the one thing.* I'm speeding again. License suspended—if I get pulled over, I'm done. My tie needs to be loosened, I crack the window, cool air rushes in and feels so, so good; my whole body feels it right down to my feet. Just staring at the beautiful fall colors.

I'm speeding again. I know what it is. My heart races a bit faster and the cool air feels good. Pay the damn toll—40 cents—what a waste of time. When I walk in, he's sitting there, obviously thinking about something. Then he looks at me, but not at me, and says, "I promised myself I wouldn't tell you."

"I know," I say in a way that tells him everything will be OK. I understand that. I already know.

We've been best friends since second grade and here we are 29 years later and he is seconds away from pouring, almost against his will, a little Heroin on an antique round mirror, and I am seconds away from altering my life forever. But, maybe I was already altered forever a long time ago? No.

Heroin looks like light brown powdered sugar, smooth and it smells vaguely perfumey, and it tastes a touch tart. It doesn't necessarily burn your nose like when you get "the drips," as with cocaine. A little Heroin drips into your throat from your nose, nasal passage, but nothing gets numb.

"I never knew you could sniff it," I said. "I thought you injected it—God this feels incredible." My friend had a pained look on his face. He didn't want me to do this. He understood the misery.

Injecting it means you have crossed a certain line. It's saying, "Let's do something where we will lose all control forever. Let's do something that will alter us forever; something beyond that singular point of no return. Let's go to the Wasteland, just to see."

He had already injected and I knew it.

"How do you inject this?" He wouldn't look at me.

When we were 12 or 13 we used to ride his moped all over town with bandanas on our heads; we both looked like Rambo. We were crazy kids. He drove most of the time and would buzz through red lights, yellow lights, hugging sharp lefts and sharp rights, screaming. We would laugh so hard at the near misses and just keep going. We had no restraint of any type. We were crazy kids.

"It's different, you know." He's staring off now.

"No, I don't know, but I want to know and we both know you're going to show me."

Nothing. No response. And now I'm really intrigued and have some real nervous like energy. I light a Marlboro and drag deeply.

"Coffee. We need coffee," I say.

"Yeah."

In high school he and I dated two girls who were really good friends, and so even though he and I hadn't hung-out together for a year or so since middle-school, we were reunited through these two girls. All a bunch of pot head, keg party, leather jacket wearing teenagers. I had already read Jack Kerouac and even though I was only 15 or so and didn't understand it the way I do now, I knew it was something great, something that mattered. I believed I knew what it meant to be "beat" and I romanticized it just like most people do. I remember that no matter where my friend and I went together—school, parties, the park, wherever—that people stared at our contagious energy. People wanted to be with us, hear

240

us, near the energy that was at times raw, at times deviant, rebellious, productive, destructive. We were howling mad.

"It's important not to dull the top of this needle or it's a bitch getting it into the vein. It's a bitch to "hit.""

Me: "To hit?"

And later, when I left for my first shift in the military, we were both a little lost without each other. I always equate it with a twin being separated with his twin. Our connection was that strong. Brother like, really. And here we are, years later, and there's a safe feeling to it because it's him and me, just like old times.

Holy shit ... Holy shit ... Holy...

I know ... I know ...

I never made it to work that day. I drove straight home barely awake. Window down and cool air, a cigarette dangling—a prop really. Music on but I only hear it if I try to hear it. Wow. This is incredible. I am on top of the world. My job is going well. Everything is going well right now. And it's so good when I walk through the front door. The boys rush me and hug me and she's in a good mood and I just blew off the entire day and used Heroin. All is well.

The Oxycontin dealer reemerged with a boatload of pills. He may have been in jail for a while, and so I had gotten used to Heroin. But Oxyies were back now, and my use skyrocketed. "I need to go to the hospital!" I say to him hugging my toilet which is filled with my bile. Wendi is knocking on the bathroom door nearly hysterical with worry. After stealing all of the OxyContins from the client, I had turned to an old friend who introduced me to an OxyContin dealer. There was a reason they called Oxyies hillbilly heroin. The withdrawals were apparently just as bad. I had eaten my last one about 36 hours earlier and woke-up sweating and shaking and after a short time, I was puking up guts. The dealer was gone and in a panic, I called my friend.

"You'll be fine, try to relax Andrew," he answers me. "You'll get through this."

"Andrew! What's going on in there?" It's Wendi and she's pissed, she knows something is up. And I'm terrified because I'm hyperventilating. The vomit comes in contractions where my whole body tenses up during which time I fucking can't breathe, and until my body relaxes, I can't catch my breath or take in air. My eyes are almost completely out of my head, my face is purple with pressure, veins popping out of my neck and Wendi wasn't to come in. I hang-up the phone, manage to reach-up and un-lock the door, contract again and vomit black blobs of bile into the toilet as Wendi walks in and screams. "Oh my God Andrew!"

"Call Brian! I have to go to the hospital."

This can't be from the Oxy, it can't be! Something is seriously wrong with me. Maybe it's cancer or an infection.

I was scared to death because I had never before felt anything so terrible. But it was the OxyContin. I was withdrawing and going south fast.

When Brian and I arrived at the E.R., I could barely catch my breath between the dry heaving. Bile was the only thing coming-up now, but again it was like my body was contracting—this wasn't normal vomiting.

The nurse wanted to know who my doctor was, and my mind was so scrambled from the trauma, I just said "an Indian sounding name." She rolled her eyes because at least half the doctors in Albany have Indian sounding names. She rolls six or seven names off, and I'm just shaking my head wanting to be dead and finally I just nod yes and she said:

"Dawani? Yes? Dr. Dawani?"

"Yes," and then I have another contraction and brown phlegm comes up into the plastic pan. Brian is horrified. I'm horrified.

"Okay. We'll get Doctor Dawani over here." She leaves, yanking the curtain closed behind her.

"Brian," I whisper, "Come closer."

"I'm withdrawing from opiates, no one can know," I say as I start to heave black globs so thick it clogs my throat and I can't breathe.

"You're turning blue! Andrew! Nurse!"

She comes in and looks into my mouth, sweeping out a blob of black stuff.

"OK, just relax, it's OK. Dr. Dawani is coming." With that she says to Brian, "We can't give him anything until we figure out what's going on." She leaves quickly. The E.R. is busier than expected.

"Brian you have to tell this doctor it's opiates, no one else can know. I will lose my job. Wendi will leave me, please. Only tell the doctor, maybe." Tears are pouring out of my eyes now.

Brian was conflicted, not an enabler, just on the horns of a very real, very emotionally-charged dilemma. Dawani shows up, a big man with a friendly face. He had spent seven years as an ER doctor in the Bronx as he later explained to me, and knew the minute he saw me what was going on. I look at Brian with desperate eyes as if to say, "Please make this stop."

"I won't tell Wendi what's happening, but when this is over, you will get help. Understand?" Brian is not happy about this. I've put him in a shitty position. He looks like he wants to punch me in the face, and I can't blame him.

Brian pulled Dawani aside and explained that I was a lawyer fresh from Washington, D.C., working at a top firm in Albany, that I had "accidently" got hooked on medication and that the firm, no matter what the cause, would not look on this favorably. I would lose my job and my family. Dawani does a quick examination.

"Nurse, give Mr. McKenna twenty ml morphine." And he ordered a series of tests, EKG and other stuff that I was too fucked-up to understand. My skin was gray and clay-like. I was only half-alive.

The morphine, which I had never had in my life, seeped into my body from the IV. "Float like a feather ... in a beautiful world," played in the background, or maybe just in my mind—a Radiohead song. My stomach slowly relaxed a little at a time. The bright lights on the ceiling of my E.R., cubicle swayed just a touch and I heard voices around me and I drifted. The pain was over.

"I'm going to admit you for a few days, alright?" Dawani says quietly to me. It's just him and me. Brian had gone out to call Wendi.

"I don't know how this happened." I'm gripping his arm tightly. "I'm not a bad person, Doctor; one minute I was fine and then I was sick. The OxyContin really screwed me up. I don't know." And that was the truth. I didn't know what it could do. Lesser opiates like Percocet and Lortab put me in a bad mood and made me a little edgy when I'd run out in the past, but that was it—nothing really at all. Not 1/1000th of what the OxyContin did.

Dawani admitted me for a little over a week, running tests and bringing in specialists. He was my primary doctor so he controlled the flow of information. Dawani gradually weaned me off the opiates by slowly reducing the dose of morphine over the next nine days. By day nine, they had finally done an endoscopy and noticed a minor peptic ulcer. This became the official diagnosis for me. The insurance company, through a nurse rep, wanted my ass discharged.

"Have you considered a rehab Mr. McKenna?" the fat bureaucrat asked.

"For an ulcer?"

"Well isn't there something else going on here?"

"Who the hell are you?" I'm lying in bed staring at the ceiling when this insurance rep snuck in and started strong-arming me.

"You've been administered a fair bit of opiates here recently," she says, in a very accusatory tone.

"Well, I'm not a doctor, lady. I didn't prescribe my own meds. Come to think of it, you're not a doctor either!"

"It's obvious you have a problem Mr. McKenna, and BC/BS isn't—"

"Isn't what? Going to pay their part? Instead they're sending you in to harass a guy while he lives in a hospital bed? I'm going to sue your fat fucking ass!"

Now I'm sitting up in bed shouting at this fool, pointing, spit shooting out of my mouth.

"Who's your boss motherfucker? Give me his fucking name, motherfucker! Who the fuck do you think you are?"

The woman looked alarmed. It was like she'd never seen a madman before. She started slowly backing up, towards the door as I made my way towards the edge of the bed. My intention was to attack her, to strangle her insurance ass. "I pay my monthly premium you fucking bastard!" A nurse runs in and screams at the site of me. I caught my reflection in the mirror. My face was contorted with rage. The IV had come out of my arm and blood dripped from the hole. Another nurse ran in, a hot one with big breasts and nice hair, and told the terrified bureaucrat to leave immediately. She just stared at me in disbelief, like she was in shock.

"We were just talking, and then, and then, he just snapped," she said as she hurried out of the room, as if broken from a trance.

"Andrew, it's alright Andrew, take a deep breath, she's gone, please sit back down and try to calm down. Deep breaths, that's it. OK now, everything is OK. That's it. Let me clean up this IV. I don't know how she got in here."

"Nurse?"

"What honey?"

"My stomach is killing me." I grip my belly in pain.

Chapter 24

The bags are actually wax paper folds about the size of a standard postage stamp. They are folded three times and secured with a small piece of scotch tape. You break the tape seal and unfold the bag. On one end is an opening. The Heroin is in the far opposite end. You tear off the excess bag so that the Heroin is easier to pour. Needles are sold at drug stores for about a dollar each. All you need is a valid ID, no questions asked. You just have to endure the dirty looks from the pharmacy techs. The syringe comes with a little cap on the end. This is where you pour the Heroin from the bag; it fills the bottom third of the little cap. Next, you use the syringe to draw-up a few drops of water and then squirt the water into the cap. You then stir the Heroin and water mixture until combined. Next you take a BB sized piece of cotton and roll it into a ball between your fingers, moisten it a little with your saliva. You then place the miniature cotton ball onto the end of the needle tip. Carefully place the cotton covered tip of the needle into the Heroin and water mixture being careful not to puncture the bottom of the cap because this will dull the needle and make it more difficult to insert into your vein. With the stopper of the syringe between your fingers, slowly draw back. The suction draws the Heroin through the cotton piece, which acts as a filter for the impurities in the Heroin water mixture, getting excess air out of the chamber.

As you draw back on the stopper, the Heroin enters the syringe chamber. Sometimes you lose suction and have to repeat the drawing process until all the Heroin is drawn into the syringe. Next, remove the cotton ball from the end of the syringe. Place the needle carefully on a flat service, being careful not to damage the end of the sharp needle. Roll up your shirt sleeve and chose something to use as a tourniquet, preferably a belt or a piece of rubber tubing or your neck tie. Tie the tourniquet above the area of vein that you will use as an injection point. The crux of the arm where the forearm and the bicep meet is a good spot. The veins there seem bigger and closer to the skin's surface. After you tie the tourniquet tightly around your arm, pump and clench your fist until the target vein bulges from your arm. With your other hand, pick-up the loaded syringe and place the tip of the needle at a horizontal angle and press it into the vein. Once it is in, draw back ever so slightly on the plunger of the syringe until the blood is drawn from the vein and appears in the chamber of the syringe. When the blood enters the chamber you know you have "hit" the vein properly. Slowly depress the plunger into chamber of the syringe, squeezing the Heroin mixture into your vein. Be sure to get rid all of it in. Remove the needle from your arm and set aside. Release the tourniquet.

The Heroin now travels up your arm, into your shoulder area, up your neck and finally into the neurotransmitters of your brain, releasing endorphins and serotonin throughout your body, starting at the top of your head, then engulfing your face with numbness. Traveling down your neck and into your shoulders, a feeling of numbness overtakes your chest, your torso, your waist, your legs and feet all the way to the tips of your toes. Pure-unadulterated-bliss. A floating sensation takes over your entire body. Your respiratory system depresses, and you float. All worries or anxiety about anything, ever, in the past, present, or future vanish. Rent, car payment, food bills, insurance, love, hate, work, utilities, good health, bad health, past friends, present friends, stress-free living, stress-filled living, deadlines, cell phones, war, terrorism, celebrity divorces, celebrity marriages, dying, living, breathing. None of it matters because you are floating down a river and everything is good. In fact, nothing matters. Depending on the quality of the Heroin, you will remain high somewhere between one and 12 hours. Don't plan on taking part in any activities. Just find a comfortable chair and float. Seize that most beautiful opportunity to not think, to forget. You won't have a desire to have sex because sex doesn't compare. You won't want to eat for a little while because it, too, doesn't compare, and there is no guarantee, again depending on the quality of the Heroin, that you will be able to hold a utensil anyway. You might feel like answering a ringing phone, but chances are you won't be able to participate in a coherent conversation. Just float. Take it easy. Relax. Everything will be alright. Everything *is* just fine. All of these activities, other than sex, including work, driving and living will become possible in a few weeks or months after you have built a tolerance to the drug. That is not to say that you will perform these activities well; you almost certainly will not, but you might be able to fake it for a while.

After hours of not feeling, not worrying, not caring, you will slowly emerge from the stupor. As life begins to bleed back in, one of your first thoughts will be, "How will I manage to do this again soon?" This is the point where King Heroin gets you. This is the time when your wheels will start turning. This is the moment when life, as you once knew it, forever changes. Never again, without Heroin, will you feel as good or as happy or as content. You are gone. Replacing you is an agonizing void, satisfied only by Heroin. You are now powerless. Recreation has now turned into survival. You find that addiction to Heroin it is not merely uncomfortable, it is, as a matter of absolute truth, not survivable. You will try to find joy in regular things, but nothing will be as good or good enough. You will try to pretend that life without Heroin is manageable, or even just OK. It will never be. Now begins the greatest undertaking of your life. You have just purchased a ticket to hell and the train is slowly, methodically, leaving the station.

Chapter 25

I left Wendi, Derrick, and Dylan for a 28 day inpatient drug treatment program in December at a facility in western New York. As I said goodbye to Derrick, in his little three year old voice, he said, "Why are you crying?" As much as I tried to hide this fact, all I could say was, as I choked-up, "Daddy's a little sad Derrick, I love you."

Aside from business trips, this was the first extended period of time I had spent away from Wendi, Derrick and Dylan. It was hard to tell whether the move back to New York helped Wendi's depression or not. But moving ensured that ready reinforcements to help care for Derrick and Dylan in my absence were now in place. Wendi's parents, while always skeptical of me, were just a phone call away. So eliminating that worry from my mind allowed me to focus a little better on the task at hand.

A very diverse group of patients from all walks of life came together with a common purpose—to address their demons. It was also the first time that I tried to take a serious look at who I was. I had essentially been let go from my position at a good law firm in Albany, my marriage was all but over, I was addicted to opiates, and I was about to lose Derrick and Dylan. My relationship with Wendi sucked. In fact, it was literally sucking the life out of me. She had her own problems, her own demons, unrelated to substance abuse, and our lives together were miserable. Rehab was the right choice.

My first therapy group consisted of seven of the strangest people I'd ever seen. The counselor who led the group, I think his name was Tim, had been sober for 20 years and he took his recovery, and ours, deadly serious. The first patient to introduce himself was Sanchez. He told us that he suffered from "suicidal depression," that he was abandoned as a child and that this was his thirteenth rehab.

"Welcome, Sanchez, welcome."

The next guy was Tommy, and Tommy felt comfortable telling us during our first group together that when he was a boy, the neighborhood kids had dragged him into a large dog house and raped him.

"I think it's important you know that about me." *Anally penetrated in a doghouse? Jesus.*

"Anyone else like to introduce themselves?"

Next up is Catherine.

"I don't belong here." *I was just thinking the same thing. In a doghouse?* "I know you probably hear that all the time, but in my case, it's true. I don't belong here."

"Then why are you here? What brought you here?" Tim asked.

"I got drunk, I blacked out, and I woke up 250 miles away from home. In clothes that weren't mine."

Next up was Roger. "Whenever I smoke methamphetamine, I end up having sex with young men."

"Well are you gay?" someone asks, cross-talking, which is allowed in this group. Roger lowers his head in a meek voice and replies, "No."

Why am I here? Maybe they put me in the wrong group. I don't think I'm supposed to be in this group. I start to daydream about my boys and what they're doing right now. I make a mental note to check my neighborhood for registered sex offenders. Roger might be a sex offender. He's definitely offensive. Two other people introduce themselves, but I don't really listen. One is an accountant, I think, who is addicted to Xanax, and the other is a pimp, or maybe it's the other way around. It doesn't matter. I'm hungry.

We file into the cafeteria. The food looks surprisingly fresh as I take my tray to an empty table. I would like to be alone and eat but I know it's only a matter of time. Methosexual Roger sits down across from me. I knew this was coming.

"Can I join you?"

"Huh? Yeah, sure, that's fine, Rog."

"I noticed you zoned out towards the end of group, not to be nosey."

"Yeah," I pause. "I was thinking about my wife and children."

"Do you have pictures?"

"No." *Out of the question.* Out of the corner of my eye, I see Catherine sitting alone. Oddly I am drawn to her. Not for sexual reasons, I just want to know whose clothes she ended up in. I was astonished at the level of security at the facility. There were cameras everywhere. Nothing like adding a good dose of paranoia to early recovery. The facility was co-ed, and rehab romances were strictly prohibited, hence the surveillance. If you were caught in relations with another patient, it meant certain discharge. Nonetheless, it was common. After all, when a bunch of addicts are cooped-up with no drugs or alcohol, they will find something, or someone, to make them feel good. That's just the way addicts are. I think everyone is like this. It's just human. Addicts might be a little too human.

Groups went along pretty well. I listened to some pretty shocking shit, though, especially from my new favorite patient, Rachel. Rachel would make up crazy stories in group and everyone believed her except me and she knew I didn't because she would say, "Hey Andrew, what did you think about that one?" And I would say, "Not enough sex." So the next day she would jazz it up a little more. And she would later say, "Well?" and I would say, "Getting closer," or, "That's a little better." And she would pretend to be disappointed, bite her lip, and stomp her foot and walk away like a child that was just told no. The first time she did this I knew I had to fuck her. Whenever she asked what was missing, I would always say blow jobs, more blow jobs, and she would lose herself and start laughing before going right back into character. God it was fun. Sometimes she would pretend to flirt with another guy, the whole time looking at me with a coy smile. I would give her a dirty look and we would both laugh and look away.

We started eating most of our meals together. Potatoes au gratin was served with nearly every meal and I would make stupid jokes about how I couldn't get enough of them, and shovel them into my mouth. It was just being silly, but man, it felt good just having fun. Sometimes Rachel would get really depressed and I'd offer to get her a plate of au gratin potatoes and sometimes it would work, at least for a second or two, to bring her out of her funk. We were all pretty drained, with the drugs and alcohol leaving our systems. The mental dependence on feeling artificially good was the killer. Trying to find happiness in anything seemed impossible. The saving grace was these little moments, private moments really, with people like Rachel. And others. The rehab staff would plan these activities, designed to have you reach back into your earlier life, your pre-drug life, to a time when you had fun, unassisted fun. We played musical chairs in an enormous room with 80 people. That was fun. Don't get me wrong, part of the fun was watching all of these newly clean and sober people with short nerves, running around, not wanting to be the boob who couldn't get a seat when the music stopped. It was weird because I was always embarrassed to have fun like this as a kid, to just let my hair down and go wild, uninhibited, as kids should. I remember being invited to a birthday party, maybe I was 10, and there was going to be dancing. I didn't want to go. I was paralyzed with anxiety. Why? So I guess it's no surprise that I felt really uncomfortable doing the rehab musical chairs.

Fuck, my brain was playing its own version of musical chairs! I weighed 241 pounds at the time, and so I intentionally thrashed and hip-checked people who tried to get the chair I was going for. Oddly, at one point, I bumped this guy who had just arrived at the rehab, maybe a day or two earlier. His face was absolutely mangled. He had fallen out of a third story window, by accident. Threatening suicide during a two hour drunken stand-off with paramedics, he fell asleep on the window sill and ultimately fell and landed on his head. Well I didn't know any of this. I mean, I was just trying to get to a goddamn seat, after all. Well, would you believe that when I "bumped" him, his skinny self flew, I mean he flew several feet, maybe eight or nine feet, probably only three or four feet. Regardless of the distance, he hit his head and it looked like he was having a seizure. The music stopped. I sat in my seat that was almost his, looked over at him. He was completely laid out, shaking, making a "wada, wada, wada" sound. I was horrified, quickly looking around at everyone staring with their mouths open.

My eyes met Rachel's (she found her seat apparently), she had a look of shock and surprise and she said, "Oh my God!" Then everyone quickly gathered around Dan. Did I mention his name was Dan? The staff was on the job. Now I've never seen a seizure before, and I thought he was dying, and Rachel, who was holding onto my arm watching Dan, still in disbelief, kept saying, "You killed him," under her breath, so only I could hear it. She was fascinated, absolutely intrigued and she was saying it to bust my chops, and I just stood there and tried not to laugh. It wasn't funny at all, but Rachel's twisted sense of humor was. "He's not dead, is he?" I mumbled.

Dan, of course, lived. They instituted a moratorium on musical chairs, threatening to impose three-legged races instead, until we started talking about an all-out rehab revolt.

Crazy things started to happen. This one guy named Jed and I became pretty good friends. We had identical senses of humor and he had a hard-cover book of Charles Bukowski's poetry. He had also written his own poetry which was intensely good. Groups turned into fun, except during certain times when things got really serious. Some patients were beginning to dig pretty deep into their pasts, and their secrets. By the third week, we had all been in group together for dozens of hours. I grew pretty close to some of these wacky bastards. One day Jed tells me that he is checking-out early. He had grown close to this girl in rehab. Can't remember her name. I think it was Tammy.

"I'm leaving, Andrew."

"No, you're not."

"I am, and I'm taking Tammy."

"Against her will?" I ask jokingly.

"Yes, against her will."

"Jed, don't be a fool, you have one week to go."

"They told us that if they see us together, they're throwing us out."

"You have a week to go! What does she have? Ten days? Eleven?"

"Something like that. It doesn't matter, Andrew. I've never met anyone like her before."

"Are you hearing yourself? What about Adam?" His five year old son. "You said they wouldn't let you near him unless you finished treatment. What are you thinking man?"

"I don't want to lose her."

"Lose *her*?"

Tammy was a whore by all accounts, including her own. And yes, I'm supposed to be compassionate towards everyone, especially when

253

they have addiction issues. But this girl, for whatever reasons, was bad news and Jed was not thinking clearly.

"I can't support this decision. I can't!" I plead.

"Think of your son," I continue. "Think ... what happens when she leaves you? She will leave your ass. Just as soon as she finds someone with cash in his pocket."

"Don't talk about her like that!"

"Oh my God. You're gone. It's too late."

"Yeah, fine. It's too late. I thought that out of everyone, I could at least count on your support."

"Well you can't. Not when you're thinking with your dick! What about cocaine? How soon before you do coke on this plan?"

"I'm done with cocaine," he said.

"Forty-eight hours. You're high within 48 hours."

The thing about Jed leaving was that it tapped into my fear reservoir big time. After all, he was so committed to not using, to staying in treatment, to being with his son again, and to not returning to the insanity of active addiction. And then he does this total 180 over a girl. Has he lost his fool mind? I'm here doing this. We've suffered together through this whole process! He can't leave. He was playing out what scared me the most, and that is, how delicate sobriety, especially early sobriety, can be. For a guy as sincerely dedicated to getting better as Jed was, to throw it all away just like that, means I could too. No stability or predictability. It didn't exist. Jed was like a rehab star. And now that star was on a certain crash-course. The next morning he and Tammy were gone. Never to be heard from again. Not by me anyhow.

So Dan lived, as I said. Rachel was very happy that I thought that Dan wouldn't make it. Wendi came for a visit that weekend. We met with my counselor—an Irish lady with really red hair. I can't remember her name, but I remember her sincerity—this wasn't just a job for her, she cared about me. I explained in the meeting that I didn't know if staying together was what I wanted. Wendi basically stated the same position.

What I did know was that I could have used a little transition time, no matter what was decided. It was my first shot at rehab. So far I had lost two good jobs due to these fucking opiate drugs that I couldn't seem to say no to. Perhaps things would end up over between me and Wendi, but I learned in rehab not to make any major life decisions within the first year of getting sober. The year wasn't written in stone, but it was in place for the addict and his family to ease into the changes and challenges that early sobriety bring. It would take time to work out why the addict used in the first place, and time for the addict to come out of the stupor and think clearly.

A therapist told Wendi the same thing; that this was a disease, and it would take patience and time, and work, for a family to thrive, but that it could be done if the parties were dedicated. No matter what, I wasn't ready to jeopardize being a full-time father by rushing a break-up with Wendi. What was the hurry? We weren't having knockdown drag out fights; the boys were so young, and oblivious.

Chapter 26

On January 9th I came home after successful completion of rehab. I was hopeful about my recovery and had a plan in place for staying sober, a plan put together by me and my counselor. On January 13th—my 34th birthday—I came home from outpatient group therapy, and the house was dark. Derrick and Dylan were gone. That's it, just gone. I would never live under the same roof with my sons again. A scribbled note from Wendi said something about it not being safe. I screamed at the top of my lungs, "No!" For the life of me, all I could do to hold it together was sleep; deep, scary sleep where I dream that I have lost my boys.

For months, I am not allowed to see them. Wendi's hysterics have now taken over the world. Hers and mine. Nothing I say or do can persuade her or her parents to let me see Derrick and Dylan. Nothing at all. We spend weeks waiting for a family court date. I cry constantly wondering what Derrick must be thinking. I can't eat because I end up throwing it up. Walking only a few steps at a time I have to stop because I'm tired and too sad to walk further. My eyes were bloodshot and watery all day long, and when I would go into a store to get cigarettes or whatever, people would look at me with concern and pity. When we made eye contact, and I saw the looks on their faces, I would just stare down at the floor. I couldn't go on, I thought. I wanted to kill myself but thought that the boys would someday blame themselves, or that the minute after I killed myself, the phone would ring, and it would be Wendi offering to let me see them. Those two possibilities were the only thing keeping me from putting a gun in my mouth.

I started to go to Narcotics Anonymous meetings. After about a week of this I found a sponsor who's job it was to guide me through the meetings and the 12 steps of recovery. I was just going through the motions—I couldn't think straight—but I was able to stay clean and sober. As much as I wanted to dull the pain with substances, I needed to do the right thing in case the call came for a drug test as a condition for seeing the boys. I spend time with my sponsor who likes to eat breakfast at a depressing diner in a fucked-up section of Albany, where most people don't shower or have the ability to pay for their meals. He says that it keeps it "green" for him. Well, I said one day, "It keeps it disturbing for me, does that count for anything?"

Next he tells me that he thinks I would benefit from attending meetings several counties away. But he doesn't want me to drive myself, you see; he wants me to take public transportation, also known as a bus. He wants me to take a bus. He says this will show humility on my part which is good for my recovery. But I have a car and buses make me self-conscious for some reason.

"You're fired," I said.

"What do you mean?"

"You're fired from being my sponsor."

"Just like that?"

"Yes, just like that."

It was equal parts the bus thing and the fact that he had intentionally not gotten laid in nine years. He was quite proud of this fact, too. He thought being celibate helped him stay in touch with himself, and I'm sure it did. But I don't want a sponsor who hasn't gotten any in several years, and is proud of it.

I had lost my marriage, two children, a sponsor, two jobs, and basically everything else good in my life. I couldn't hold-on anymore.

"Doctor? Thanks for taking my call."

"No problem, Andrew. What can I do for you?"

"Well, I strained by back again, lifting a piano."

Interrupting, he says, "Andrew, did you ever go to the physical therapist I referred you to?"

Lying now, I say, "Yes doctor, and it helped, man that was a lifesaver. But now I'm in a bit of a bind. I have to be in court—a big trial coming up next week, and well I'm in pain doctor."

"I see, well I could prescribe you something that'll help, but you don't want to be dopy."

To myself: "Yes I do doctor, you see, I don't really have court. In fact, I lost that job a while ago, and I just fired my sponsor because he was trying to teach me humility, and I thought firing him was a better choice than killing him, and I want to be dopy because it beats worrying that my children will hate me and not love me. Dopy is better. God damn it."

He says: "I could give you Naproxen. It's non-narcotic." *Here we go.*

"I've tried that before—and unfortunately, it doesn't work. In fact, I think I'm allergic—it makes my heart speed up."

"It makes your heart speed up?" he asks.

"Yes, that's right. Does that sound right?"

"Well, I don't know. I ..." he says.

"The Lortab works well, as much as I hate to take that stuff, I had a trial in D.C. and I had to take Lortab because of my back problem and well, it worked, and it didn't affect my performance, because I was so careful. Very careful."

"Okay, come by in a little while and pick up the prescription."

"And Andrew?" he continues.

"Yes Doc?"

"Good luck with your trial."

And so I ate a few of those and drank a few of these, and low and behold, the pain subsided. I sat and stared at the little playground set in the backyard that Derrick and Dylan would never again play on. I lit a cigarette. From time to time a tear would roll down my cheek as I pictured the boys playing on the slide, or me pulling them around the yard on a big plastic tarp. The phone rang a few times—it was my ex-sponsor—I didn't answer it. I just sat and stared.

The next morning I woke up in the same lawn chair, and there was the plastic playground. *My God, something's gotta give.* I called Wendi's parents house and asked to speak with Wendi. Her mother told me that Wendi didn't want to talk to me. I asked how the boys were doing and she said, "Fine." No details.

Completely relaxed, heart beating slowly, deep breaths of cool air, cool air at the back of my throat, my throat open, no tears running down my face, no pain in my heart, completely relaxed. In control, heroic, euphoric, driving south on a grey day, sweaty stolen money, somehow they will know that I love them, that I didn't leave them, that they weren't bad and that I live for seeing them, again and again, smiling, thinking, appreciating life on its terms. This will all work out. Somehow they will know.

As I handed the note to the teller, the old me came back. Confident, important, goal oriented, take charge, leadership. I'll call the shots here, folks. My fear of my current life, my feeling of absolute nothingness went away, came back, went away again and I occupied the space on the ground where my feet stood, where my body stood, sturdy, stoic, simply in control. I'm back.

The teller listened. I was being heard, loud and clear. The response was a response that I wanted, that I intended to evoke. This wasn't family court; my wishes this time were acknowledged. I'll call the shots here. In court, my case, my judge, my witness:

Gosh, he does a fine job moving that docket along. Good job, counselor with a nod and a smile the old famous, notorious, judge appreciates that I didn't tie up his morning with too many speeding tickets and drunk-driving trials. He has motions to decide, lunches to attend, new upholstery for his chambers to consider. McKenna will handle it, he always does, the judge tells my boss. A pleasure to have Andrew in my court.

Alive again, I don't want to go back to my cage. My mind doesn't want to hurt anymore because of the nothingness—the fear that owns me about Derrick and Dylan, my boys that I love so much. I'm right here guys. I'm right here. I'm so sorry. You can hate me, but please don't forget me. I didn't think this could happen. I want you back.

Family court.

"What about sleepovers?" I ask the judge.

"Not yet, that's at least a year away. Let's see how the visits go," he answers.

"Why?"

"Because we're not there yet."

"But I'm clean and sober! I pass all my tests! I'm not a threat to my boys!"

"We're not there yet." The judge won't relent. He won't give me an inch.

"She won't let me call them on the phone!"

"She doesn't want you to."

"But why is it up to her?" I plead.

"You're the judge!" I add.

"I'm not going to require her to do something she doesn't want to. Anything else folks?"

"What! The hearing's over? I'm doing all the right things and I'm not getting any time with the boys."

"Well then, if there's nothing else, we're adjourned." She is winning. *This is unbelievable.*

She's smirking. No one sees this but me. No one is looking at her so they don't see her smirking. They only look at me as I try to hide my look of crisis. I'm shaking in frustration and I don't want them to see me coming undone. The tears of anger and pain well in my eyes and through it I see her smirk.

I'm on my shrink's front porch looking haggard. His car is in the driveway but no one is answering the fucking door. Finally the door opens. "I'm dying doctor. I'm dead inside. I can't feel my blood moving or my heart beating." Suddenly my body folds down onto his floor. The grief forbids me from holding myself up like a man.

When I came to, I'm in a living room chair in a large circle of empty chairs—the site of tonight's group therapy? I'm alone. I sit for a minute listening to my heart thump along. Every third or fourth breath is a heave, like after a hard childish cry. My body is soaked with sweat. The doctor had lifted me into a chair assuring me that I will get through this. I tell him I won't, crying hysterically. That I can't get the bad thoughts out of my mind. That the boys are gone from my life. That I have nothing to live for.

As I pull away from the curb, feeling the coolness of the seat pressing against my wet back, I see the good doctor on his porch calling to me with the front door open behind him. I accelerate away thinking how hard this all is. The doctor is a good man and I feel bad for him because he can't help me and I see his despair in his face and shoulders.

Chapter 27

A time of darkness, despair, disillusion-so black only as the inferno of the human mind can be-symbolic death, and numb shock-then the painful agony of slow rebirth and psychic regeneration. —Sylvia Plath

"Do you feel like you might harm yourself?"

"I don't know."

"You don't know? Okay, well why don't you tell me what's going on. Andrew, I think it's best if you were admitted to our psychiatric floor. Until we can feel better that you're going to be alright."

My boys. They'll think they were bad. That I left them because they did something bad. When I get to my room, I can barely keep my eyes open. Two large orderlies walk me to my bed in the far corner. I climb onto the bed and lie on my back. Through my eye slits, I see one orderly walk away and I see the other one start to go. I say, "Please don't leave me, please don't walk away." He turns towards me, places his hand on my forehead like a mom would do and he just leaves it there and it feels cool and he says a little prayer that went something like:

Lord take the sadness from this nice young man, Andrew
Somehow he ended up here and he needs your help. So Lord,
Raise Andrew up to the mountain top with you and love

Andrew McKenna

Him and take the sadness from him. Restore him, Lord. Amen.

My "dream" was the worst that I had ever had. I wasn't asleep though, it was a hallucination, a vision. Everyone in my family, every blood relation, was dead except for me. I walked through a rainy forest naked and freezing cold and all I could hear was this loud laughter as I made my way barefoot. I came through a thick row of pines, exiting on the edge of a cliff several feet high. Below was black water, a lake or river. I stepped off the cliff because I couldn't bear the laughter, and I fell and fell and fell and then woke up alone in Room B of the psychiatric floor and I could hear a patient down the hall laughing a maniacal laugh and I couldn't tell if it was a boy or a girl.

The next day I placed a call to a family member. I was upset and really needed to hear a familiar voice. After the call, I laid there and my mind went blank for a while. Later that night I tried to call once again but, the recording stated that at the customer's request, calls from this number will be blocked.

I was put on a floor with people who talked to themselves, argued with themselves, yelled at themselves. Or maybe they were arguing with voices in their heads, as I have, and occasionally still do. Maybe they couldn't shut it off either. I remember my first meeting with my treatment team. Albany Med is a teaching institution and so there were students and a supervisory doctor sitting around a conference table when I stepped through the door and took a seat at the head of the table. The room was hospital sanitary. The smell was hospital, and the faces were hospital. I told them that I miss my children. That Wendi had taken them away from me six months ago and that I was sad. I told them that I couldn't understand the intensity of the pain. I explained that I was a really good father to the boys and that I loved them more than anything. I explained that four days after my release from a 28 day rehab, January 13th, my birthday, I had come home after a group session to find that the house was dark and a note from Wendi said that she was leaving with the kids. I also explained that Wendi would not let me see them, that she was acting evil, that my family court case wasn't going well, and that my lawyer was making too many concessions and that I had fired her ass because she sucked, she was ineffective, she was selling me down the river!

For the first one 120 hours on the ward, I slept a total of four hours. I couldn't stop the thoughts from coming in, I was shot-- completely stressed, exhausted. I would walk the halls at night, pacing up and down, up and down, waiting, hoping that I would get tired. And I was tired, but my brain didn't know it. A dozen times a night I would return to my bed and close my eyes and within seconds my body would sit up, and my feet would be on the floor, and I would start walking again. I couldn't wait for the morning to come so that I could complain to the doctor that I couldn't sleep and that I needed something at night to help me sleep. The standard response was that no one ever died from lack of sleep. I told her, the doctor, that her words were too simple. I told her that I was suffering needlessly. Everything looked different, the lighting, the faces, my eyes were sore as hell, nothing looked normal, my voice sounded weird. I was so God damned tired.

One patient fell in love with me. She was probably 40 but looked 70, and she was missing her teeth. When she was a kid, her father kicked and killed her dog in front of her and then she jumped into the shallow part of a lake and hit her head on a rock and according to her, she died. Things got a little sketchy from there because she would break into song. Usually something spiritual. She couldn't sing worth a damn, but sometimes she would want to demonstrate "her range," beginning with this little number: "JEEEEEEEssssssUSSSSS!" and the orderlies would come running thinking something was wrong.

Another patient was insane and the poor guy couldn't seem to keep his hands out of his pants. He also loved to shake people's hands. Hell no, I thought. I would have to pretend that I didn't see him extend his hand to me, and walk away. But he persisted. Finally I told him that I can't shake hands with him unless he washes them for at least five minutes with soap. He started washing his hands, between 25 and 100 times a day to the point that they were raw. His parents became concerned when they visited and he wouldn't come out of the bathroom because he was busy washing his hands again. My only other friend insisted on "taking his meals" on top of the piano. So the orderly would say, "OK," and place the meal on the table: "There you go Beethoven."

When I woke up, I was lying on my side in bed, staring straight ahead. I observed four feet away a man staring at me.

"I thought you were dead," he said, looking at me intently.

"You just scared the shit out of me." I was so thirsty, my voice was weak and raspy.

"I'm James, your new cellie." James came in late Friday night because he was hearing voices.

"Cellie?" My mind was just starting to work again.

"Roommate."

"What day is it?" I ask, totally confused, disoriented. I look around the room.

"Sunday."

"Sunday?" This is crazy. I put my head back down.

"James, I'm Andrew. Why are you sitting so close to me?" I was barely coherent.

"It's almost time for lunch." With that James stood-up, all 6'5" of him and walked to the bathroom, closing the door behind him.

Immediately Derrick and Dylan came to my mind and then a half panic attack. Had I missed a call to them? No, Wendi wasn't allowing calls, not from the Mental Hospital. She did come to visit me a few days earlier which really surprised me because I thought it was a really sensitive thing for her to do. I mean granted we were in love at one point, had two beautiful children together, I was obviously in total crisis. And then she took out the U.S. Treasury, tax refund check which required my signature, and then she left. A tremendous feeling of despair returned within minutes of me regaining consciousness. My body was so stiff from the slumber; it felt like I'd been in a car accident. They had me on 50 milligrams of this and 20 milligrams of that, but no matter what I took, it seemed that I was always one fucking thought from tears.

As part of my mental wellness program, the shrink wanted me to take part in as many activities as possible. The activities coordinator (probably not her title) was an incredibly attractive 25-ish girl with a rocking body who wanted me to make collages.

"Hey Andrew!" It's her.

I'm still laying on my side, staring at the chair that James was sitting in on the verge of crying.

"Hey sleepy-head."

My dad used to call me sleepy-head when I was a little guy, and that's the thought, however, inexplicable, that starts my seemingly unlimited tear capacity. I'm staring at her ample, perfect breasts. It's unmistakable. She must notice.

"We're doing papier mache today."

"Papier mache today," I repeat out loud, softly. Then to myself papier mache today, staring still at her beautiful figure. They have me so jacked on meds that an erection is out of the question, and I say this to myself as I stare, an erection is out of the question, an erection is out of the question.

"Yup, papier mache today, and I want you to come."

"I really would love for you to come, Andrew." She stared into my eyes.

My wet eyes move from her breasts to her eyes which appear sultry and for a short second I thought maybe, just maybe, an erection was not out of the question.

"What did she want?" James asks coming out of the bathroom wiping his hands with a paper towel.

"Papier mache today."

"Fuck that! I got a visit: ole daddy needs to catch a rip."

The part about catching a rip caught my attention because that's also what I called getting high, and I hadn't been high since coming to the nuthouse. In fact, I had only been low, extremely low. And I was tired of being low.

265

"A rip," I mumble.

"Yes, a rip. James here is going to catch a mother fucking rip and Andrew is welcome to come along for the rip," he says. He sounds like Richard Pryor (the early years) and when he says it, all wide eyed, the whole bit, he looks crazy. He's back in the chair and has again picked up the stare.

"While I was in there taking a shit, and you was out talking to that white girl, it occurred to me that I need to catch a rip." We're now staring at each other and I'm trying not to blink but my eyes sting when I don't blink, but he's not blinking and I'm certain he knows that we somehow ended up in the midst of a staring contest. There's no way I can win this. I'm not well. I was just crying.

"I know you get high! She's bringing my H right here this afternoon."

If I get high, in order to combat this low, then I am fucked. Why can't I just be with the boys? I need them and they need me. Why can't Wendi see what she is doing? *But she gave you more than one chance to clean up, Andrew. Outside looking in, you're wrong.* I strung together months and months of not using, AA meetings, etc. How would anyone know if I caught a rip with James here? I'm so tired of feeling this way.

Since James mentioned it, my heart rate has jumped and my mind is racing. Now I'm sitting on the edge of the bed, gripping the edge of the mattress staring at the floor. My mind is banging back and forth between the idea of continued suffering and short-term relief. I can't seem to focus or problem-solve or weigh choices or anything.

"So what's it going to be big dog? Are you with me?"

"James, I don't know man. My life is so fucked up right now. It's just—"

"Oh come on, dawg. We're not talking about a week-long run, we're talking about a little bump afternoon vacation. A vacation from this cruel world."

James talked like a street poet. Very dramatic. Very intense and serious.

"Look, don't make me party by myself man, that's a buzz kill!"

I think he wanted another staring contest. I didn't have the energy.

"It's just a little buzz," I said.

"Just a little buzz," James watched as I turned it over.

"I feel so shitty in this place. I didn't sleep for something like five days when I got here." The psychiatrist was adamant that I would not receive anything to help me sleep. She cruelly said, "No one has died from lack of sleep." I said, "Watch me bitch!" With that, James laughed.

"If you think these people care about how you feel, you're delusional!" James was as clear and certain about this as anything. I didn't believe this, but I was mad that the psychiatrist didn't give me something to help me sleep.

If I could get out of here in a few days or maybe a week, and right into a rehab, maybe Wendi and the judge would let me be with the boys. Getting high, just today, wouldn't affect that plan at all, really.

"You deserve a vacation, man! Now are you with me or what?"

What if Derrick and Dylan think that I don't love them or that they did something wrong, I mean, I was there with them and then I was gone.

James and I stared at each other. His eyes wide open, I mean really wide! My eyes, as usual, seemed to dry out almost immediately. I wanted to blink. It got so it felt that if I didn't blink, they would bleed for Christ sake. How is he able to do this? We stared and stared and then his stare turned to a confused scowl, like he was losing control of something, some superior force was dominating the game and then it happened: his heavy, pained lids flapped-down like curtain shutters.

"No," I said.

"What?" he asked, defeated.

"I said, no. Papier mache today."

I saw a bunch of people get restrained for acting up. They were moved quickly from the area and I wouldn't see them again until the evening. When I asked about them, the nurse would say, in a cheerful voice, without looking at me, that they were resting, and I thought how nice it would be to rest.

After Wendi's visit, so I could sign over the check to her, I came undone. I started screaming at the staff and other patients, saying that they were insane. It was a Wednesday. And that's the last thing I remember. I woke up on Friday and then my wits came back. My first thought when I woke up was that I have to get the hell out of here. My next thought was that I have to fight for Derrick and Dylan, that I need a rehab, and then I fell back to sleep until Sunday.

Following the mental ward stay, I attended another 28-day inpatient rehab. After rehab I moved in with an old friend for a few weeks. Things there were really difficult for me because even though I had several weeks of clean time, my mind wasn't firing right. My friend lived in a small one-bedroom apartment. It didn't take long for us to argue about money and space and dishes. I also managed to break his toilet—I have no idea how—and I don't know how to fix toilets. Over the course of several days, he had to replace a part or two, and it was right after my bowel movements. He was livid.

"Dude, I didn't break the fucking toilet!"

"Andrew! I can still smell the shit you just took. There are only the two of us living here! You broke it!" He was incensed. Neither of us had any money, and now we weren't just two poor people living together, but we were two poor people without a working toilet.

"Where are you going?" he asked, wrench in hand, working on the bowl.

"To the backyard." I had a large spoon in my hand.

"You're going to shit in the backyard in broad daylight?" He was really coming unwound.

"What would you have me do Charlie? Hold it in until you're done replacing the flushing mechanism?"

"You wouldn't know a flushing mechanism if I shoved it down your throat!"

Wendi allowed me to meet with the boys at a McDonalds every few weeks, but this just drove me further towards total insanity. My brother Peter invited me to move into his house with his wife and children. This would provide me with a stable living environment both as I got better, and as I lobbied Wendi and family court for visits. Wendi approved of this living situation.

His wife's two older children were in college, and their two younger ones were just starting elementary school. They lived in an old farmhouse, which they were renovating, and I helped out painting and doing other little projects. My decision to move in was seen as a good, sober decision. Peter is well-versed in recovery, and was able to give me a lot of good guidance and he also went to meetings with me. He was very attuned to potential pitfalls for me. It didn't go unnoticed when I would come home late, or not hit a meeting daily. This sent up red flags that I was slipping in my recovery efforts. Peter also knew that recovery says not to get involved in a romantic relationship for the first year of sobriety. And so even though they threw me a life-jacket, and I will be forever grateful to them, my living there caused anxiety for Peter and me, and stressed our relationship, which had always been like best friends. Now the relationship was becoming more paternal, and thus more complicated.

I was a mess, but they could tell I was trying. Over time, Wendi agreed to let me have visits with the boys, so long as Peter would agree to supervise them. He and his wife opened their home for these visits and were very supportive. For me the visits were bitter sweet. Being with the boys made me so happy, so happy that I spent our time together fighting back tears. But then I would have to say goodbye, I would fall apart and into a deep depression for the next several days.

Eventually, I found my way into a 12-step program. I was going to meetings regularly and really getting something out of them. I still wasn't seeing my boys consistently because anytime that I might say the wrong thing to Wendi, she would cut off contact, and suggest that I was using

269

again. Nevertheless, I managed to keep my head just above water and I wasn't using drugs. In fact, I hadn't used Heroin in several months. I found a person to sponsor me in AA named Steve Z. And before you knew it, I was spending Sundays with Steve, an incredible man with a great sense of humor. He used to call his ex-wife the dragon lady—often when she was standing right next to us at an AA meeting.

My first meeting with Steve was at his daughter's house where he lived. I was still in early recovery so my emotions were still pretty fucking raw. Steve was about 58 or so and successfully sober. We would sit side by side in wing chairs, fireplace behind us, smoking cigarettes and drinking coffee. Steve was one of those gentle souls, but with an edge. Over time, I came to trust and respect Steve. I could tell him anything and he would understand. It was pretty amazing. Steve understood several things about me. He knew that I was kind of lost but that I was making a good comeback, slowly. He knew that I needed his friendship and that I would take his advice. He knew that over time, I had come to so look forward to our meetings, always Sunday. It was the time where I told another person, a guy, my hopes, my fears, my joys and sorrows. Sometimes we would get laughing so hard about stuff. Other times, it was a bit lower key because Steve didn't feel well. He had a bad heart and diabetes.

Steve lived in a partitioned section of his daughter's restored farmhouse, way out in the country, and during the winter months I remember it would be getting dark outside early, but after a hectic week, I would drive out to see him. The country air was so crisp and fresh, I couldn't wait to get to his place. He always had the coffee brewing just as we began our time together that would go from 7 p.m. to about 8:30. I would update him on family stuff, and he would usually smile and nod and I could tell he was listening but there was something more. He understood me. Steve knew what I was feeling and I swear that at times, he felt what I felt. I've never had this experience except with one girl, and that's Dawn. She and I breathe the same air so to speak. So when I'm telling Steve that I miss Derrick's smile or Dylan's voice and I get a little choked-up, I can see his eyes get moist like mine. When I complain about Wendi not cooperating, he understands—he explains that her anger is directly proportionate to the pain she inflicts on me, and that the worst is not over. Steve encourages patience. He knows I have none, probably just as he didn't in his early stage of recovery. Patience will be a great challenge for me in early sobriety.

Steve became my close friend. When I told him that I was having problems with Dawn's ex and that I wasn't sure how it would turn out, Steve would say that I had to distance myself from his drama. That I had to focus on my own stuff.

"I want to kill him Steve."

"Don't do that," Steve says with an understanding smile.

"I probably won't, but if I thought I could get away with it ..."

"Come on, you're not even capable of such a thing." He's still smiling.

I just stared blankly and then his smiling face turned blank when he realized that anything was possible at this point.

Dylan asked me on the phone if he I could come over for a sleep over. I broke down in tears; I had to cover the receiver. "I told him that I wish I could and that I loved him so much. He said OK in a really disappointed two year old voice.

"I can't do this Steve. It feels like my heart is going to stop from sadness. Sometimes it's like I can't even take a breath. It's like I felt when I checked myself in. I try to change my thoughts about it, but I can't."

"What about the supervised visits with Peter and Suzanne?" he asks.

"They seem so artificial and temporary. The entire time we're together, I can't take my eyes off of them. I must hug and kiss them every three minutes! They love the time together because it's a huge play fest. They're such great kids."

"So that's all really positive stuff, can we build on that?" Steve asks.

271

"But then it's time for them to go home, and to say goodbye and that Derrick hugs me around the neck so hard and he changes from the incredibly fun-loving care free little boy to a boy who doesn't want to leave his dad and he gets a little quiet, and if we still have a few minutes before we have to get them in the car, he'll doze off in my arms. It's so beautiful Steve and then I have to wake him up and tell him it's time to go."

"The other day as we're going out the door, I noticed one of Dylan's little T-shirts laying on the floor in the other room, and instead of grabbing it and putting it in his back pack, I left it there so that I could come back to the house and part of him would still be there," I continue. "That night I put it over my pillow and slept. How can I go on?"

I could tell Steve anything and he would listen patiently. Sometimes he would share one of his experiences and tell me how he handled it and the result. Steve didn't give me advice though. To him, I believe, he thought that was too presumptuous. But what he could do was share his story or part of his story. What a guy. Our sessions would end with a short prayer and then a hand shake. He'd walk me to the door, turn-on the outside light and watch as I made it to my car. As soon as my car started up, he would give a final wave, go inside, and the light would go off. Each time I would sit for a minute while the car warmed up and think how lucky I was to have Steve in my life. And I needed him. After a particularly sketchy few days where I really wanted to use but miraculously managed not to, I decided to call Steve sort of out of the blue. He immediately could tell I had been struggling.

"Meet me for coffee," he said.

Steve grabbed both of my hands and held on firmly. He'd never done this before. He looked tired. Sitting across from each other in a Stewart's Shop we used to go to, Steve broke down some serious stuff for me. He said, "Andrew, what I want you to think about is living, not just existing, but living. Right now you're merely existing, and a lot of people when they get a little sober time under their belt, get stuck in the existing mode and never progress to living. Why? Because of fear."

"You see, us addicts are fearful people," he says. "For some reason, and the reason is not that important in my view, for some reason we're afraid to step out there and live. Things that come naturally for normal people—going to the grocery store, having dinner with an acquaintance, going to a family barbecue or a graduation—scare us. It's a big deal. We don't feel comfortable in our own skin. We're afraid of being found out. Our secret is our secret. To live requires that we tell the secrets, that we tell on ourselves at every opportunity. As soon as what you portray on the outside doesn't match how you're feeling on the inside, you're keeping a secret and telling a lie. If we can catch this early on and take immediate corrective action, say by telling someone, or to stop pretending we're something we're not, to be authentic, then we stand a chance at living. Until then, we're just existing, and it's a tortured existence, and who wouldn't seek a chemical escape from a tortured existence."

"We are who we are, not who we pretend to be. Let it go, let yourself go, let people in on who you really are. This takes practice and it isn't easy, but patience Andrew, and you'll get there."

Steve looked like he was finishing up a long journey at that moment. It was just different from other times. There was urgency in Steve's demeanor and of course he was right. Here I was in early sobriety and his job was to help me make sense of this quagmire I ended up in. Steve knew that anyone who really wanted to be sober or clean could do it if they had help. It wasn't something that could be done on one's own, many perhaps would disagree and say that it was just a matter of willpower. "Just don't drink ... just don't use ..." Steve knew better. He'd lived long enough and lived around enough drunks in and out of recovery to know that getting sober and staying sober required a no-holds barred cooperative effort by other people trying to get and stay sober themselves.

Steve also understood that for a sober person like himself to remain sober, he had to help people like me and that's why every Sunday night, Steve would take two hours out of his life and give it to me even

273

though at times his diabetes would be raging or he wouldn't be feeling great.

Steve required that I call him every day to say hello. We didn't have to talk for long, but I had to call him. Again, this wasn't for him, it was for me. Early sobriety fucking sucks and if you can have something to hang on to, like a daily phone call, something regular where you can talk to someone who has been there, it helps. One weekend, a Friday and Saturday, I was having a really tough time. I remember being very sad and really restless. By the time Sunday came, I had slipped and used again. It helped ease my sense of loss that I felt. I needed Derrick and Dylan, I needed them in my life and they weren't there and I believed that every minute that went by without them, that the loving relationships we had were slowly diminishing. It doesn't make sense that I would get high again. But then again nothing made sense. I called Steve and cancelled. Too low to sit there with him. Too embarrassed to tell him I used-maybe later, maybe tomorrow. Too afraid he would say that sponsoring me was too much for him.

I did not hear back that day or night. On Monday, while sitting at a dead-end job running a scale, a truck scale of all things, I picked up the phone to call Steve to tell him that I used, that the pain was too great, and that I was sorry. Would he still be my sponsor? I would try harder. I got the answering machine, of course, which was a relief because my courage to come clean to Steve was fading with every minute.

"Hey Steve, it's Andrew, just wanted to leave a quick message," then I heard the rattle of the phone being picked up.

"Andrew?"

"Yes."

"Hey, it's Debbie," Steve's daughter.

"Oh, hey Deb. I wasn't sure if Steve got my message." She paused for what seemed like a minute.

"Andrew. I don't how to say this—my dad passed away last night."

"I'm sorry," she says.

"Oh my God...."

Chapter 28

When I saw her for the first time, we weren't *supposed* to be together. But we *had* to be together. Anyone who knows what this means knows bliss, knows what it is to want, without reservation, and knows what it is to smile on the inside, no matter what, at least a little bit every day.

One fall day, I sat and told Dawn, whom I did not yet know, where I had just been. About my break-up with Wendi, about my boys Derrick and Dylan, about how my head was still sort of spinning from everything. And she just listened quietly. Dawn was going through a break-up of a long-term relationship and we just sat and talked. Her eyes are so pretty, and also telling—it wasn't until later that I'd find out that she herself had been through some difficult times in her life—and I knew she could relate.

And then I did something I couldn't believe. I started to tell her the story of how I left the Justice Department, because I *had* to leave. "Because after a huge raid on the targets of our investigation in Houston, I stole a piece of evidence that we had seized. A Rolex watch." I explained in plain truth how when I was hung-over, still intoxicated really with a belly full of valium, I reached into the evidence bag and just took that watch out and stuck it in my suit coat pocket. And I told Dawn that Wendi and I moved up to New York after that. I wanted to put my cards on the table with Dawn. I knew more than anything I've ever known that she and I would spend the rest of our lives together. As I told her my story, I felt a tremendous warmth come over me. A comfortable warmth. With every sentence, I revealed more of myself. It felt so good. And I have never done this, ever, with anyone, not even on a smaller scale, not even in therapy. I needed her to know who I was, what had happened, where I was right then and there. A disclaimer, I guess, but also an openness that was new.

A few days passed. When I next saw her, I felt my stomach flip, but I kept my cool.

"Hey Dawn."

"Hey Andrew."

"Everything going OK?"

"Yeah, you know."

And that was it, I kept it moving. Short and sweet. But I watched her. I watched her walk. I watched her talk to my sister-in-law, I watched her take care of her children. Dawn's youngest, Casey, was about 18 months old, and she was a cute little chubby monkey. She was always on her mom's hip. One day, at my brothers where I was still living temporarily, it was my job to entertain little Casey. I decided that the best thing to do was to walk outside and touch the leaves on the tree. This is how I could always calm down my Derrick and Dylan. It had been weeks since I held one of my little guys and it was nice to do something a dad would do. I would hold Casey in one arm and put out my hand to touch a leaf with my other hand. When my hand got close, I would yank it back and say, 'no, no, no!' That little child started laughing this deep laugh. Oh my God, it was so beautiful. Casey stuck out her chubby little arm, and then pulled it back. And we both started laughing. From that point on, Casey would always come to me when I saw her. It was always good to see that child.

So this new relationship was born with Dawn. Nothing complicated except that both of our lives were extremely complicated at that point. We would typically see each other in the evenings, after the dust of our days had settled.

But of course, anything that appears this good comes at a price. And this was no different. Because I had just finished up my time in the mental ward followed by drug rehab for 28 days, my mind seemed pretty clear, or you might say clean. And so was the case. When Dawn and I started seeing each other, we were sort of discreet about it. She was coming off a 10 year relationship with a man with the last name Richards. This union produced three children ranging in age from two to five. We kept it discreet because Richards was putting the extension on Peter and Suzanne's house, and we were concerned that maybe Peter and Suzanne would be nervous that Richards would react badly to the news. And knowing that often times my behavior was unpredictable, they feared the entire operation could catch fire pretty quickly. Of course my approach was to be open and honest about the whole thing – after all, I had just come from rehab where they teach that the truth will set you free, not kill you, and that you're only as sick as your secrets.

Peter and Suzanne weren't really happy when I explained to them that Dawn and I were together. Peter used phrases like "are you fucking crazy?" and "no fucking way, not if you plan on living here." Peter was at his wit's end. He's a problem-solver, and I proved to be a "problem" that he couldn't solve. He had done everything in his power to help me. Even after I had used his credit card to fund a cocaine-fueled backgammon tournament with a stripper I had met in rehab, he still stuck by me.

At the same time I was dealing with Richards, who agreed to do my brakes for me. Free of charge. "Just let me know if there is anything I can do," I said while standing over him as he crouched down under my car. I had this enormous wrench in my hand, which had nothing to do with the brake job. I was fidgeting, which as a child, would have brought a fierce scolding from my father. I thought about how it would feel if I smacked the guy— Richards, not my father—with the wrench.

"So listen, man. You and I are OK with everything, right?" I asked. We had never talked about it really. I mean, Dawn and I had barely started seeing each other. Maybe a week earlier. Hell, Dawn was the one who asked him to do my brakes for me. The guy grew up on a farm for Christ's sake, I didn't know how to do breaks!

"The caliper's shot," he said.

"Oh it is?" I answer. *What the fuck is a caliper? It sounds important. It sounds like it holds something together. It sounds integral.*

"But if I can bend this piece of steel," he said, struggling. "Hand me that hammer," he says, not looking, just reaching behind towards me. I pick up the big-ass hammer and a vision of me smacking him again goes through my mind.

"If I can just bend this motherfucker..." *Whack! Whack! Whack!* "There, that should do it."

Does he know that I am with his recent ex? That she and I are embarking on a loving, fulfilling relationship? Would he do my brakes for free?

And how did Dawn approach him with all of this? "Listen, you should know that I am seeing Andrew now. You've been asking me, and I've been saying that it was none of your business, but I feel now is the time to tell you that it's Andrew, Peter's brother, Suzanne's brother-in-law, and in the interests of being open and honest, you should also know that he and I have a very physical relationship. I never knew that another human being was capable of making me feel so good, so fulfilled. He has redefined many terms for me, but perhaps the most relevant, the most poignant, would be what I now consider to constitute orgasm." Then, "On another note, his brakes are going, and I would just be heartbroken if he were hurt in a high speed car accident. I don't know if I could go on. So, I need you to do his brakes for him. After all, he's a lawyer, a professional, the real McCoy, and he's used to hiring people to do these sorts of tasks for him. Tomorrow then, OK?"

"This should hold," he said. *Oh my god, I'm a dead man. A sober dead man.*

"So I don't need to order the caliper?"

The judge informed me that I would have to pass three drug tests a week if I expected to spend any time with my boys.

"But I only make $200 a week, and the tests cost $39 each, and I have to make car payments, school loan payments. I'm dealing with everything! Your Honor! Can't this be good enough? Your Honor!"

The judge didn't respond, and often times just spoke over me. I wasn't represented by a lawyer, and I guess he believed what I had to say wasn't important. When you represent yourself, many judges don't view you as their equal, like they might an attorney. And in his eyes I wasn't an attorney anymore. At any rate, I was going in the hole financially at such a pace that I would never get out.

Driving back from Family Court, with a whole new series of requirements on me, I nearly died. Sixty five miles per hour, behind a tractor trailer, maintaining a minimum safe distance of eight car lengths, I saw the truck's brake lights go on ahead of me. I applied my brakes and heard something fall off and clink metallically away. Fucking caliper! Gripping the steering wheel like a roller coaster ride, I screamed like a girl and swerved like a drunk onto the shoulder, down an embankment constituting the highway median, back up the embankment and back into the lane, ahead of the truck that I almost just rear-ended. I shit my pants.

Four hours later I'm at Dawn's house, which doesn't have any heat. The children are in bed and I'm trying to have an upbeat attitude. But I'm freezing. Little does Dawn know, I'm on my last nerve. Wendi and the judge get along great. I'm broke and living in a house with my brother and his wife, and they don't approve of my choices, often side with Wendi, or even worse, "remain neutral." I just need to rest here on her couch for a minute and relax my mind. I drift off. *Knock, knock, knock. Fuck!* Peter is at the door, it's midnight. He's furious. He pushes past Dawn as I wake up. "Outside. Now!" he said, pointing at the front door. Standing outside under the stars on a crisp moonlight night, Peter says, "Did I not make myself clear?"

"What?"

"You need to go in there, say goodbye and get down to the house."

I had officially driven Peter to an emotional cliff-edge. His concern for me, coupled with his need to fix things, had caused him to say and do things that were uncharacteristic for him, and that didn't make sense.

If I don't listen to Peter at this point, I might not have a place to live anymore, and without a stable address to give to the judge, the sporadic, occasional visits with Derrick and Dylan were going to end. As it was they were only every few weekends, depending on Wendi's whim—there was no judicial order in place, the judge left it up to her. Any error on my part would mean a break in communication with Wendi. She held the cards. One time she and I had an argument on the phone. She was being unreasonable I thought, but I had to tread carefully. Any change in my demeanor or tone would justify her "suspicion" that I was doing something wrong. The judge's words rang out in my mind, "Wendi holds all of the cards, Andrew, and she's the credible one here counselor. No one believes a junkie."

"But Wendi, you're being unreasonable! There are times when I can't call exactly at a given time. We have to be flexible."

"Why are you raising your voice to me?" she asked. "Are you trying to bully me?" *Fucking nonsense.* No contact for three weeks was my punishment.

"But they'll think I don't want to see them."

"That's not my problem Andrew. I won't be talked to that way."

One time, when I was feeling exceptionally down, I called her to see how the boys were doing. I would have settled for just hearing their voices in the background. She sensed that I was down, "You don't sound so great Andrew, you must really miss the boys, huh?"

"Yeah, I just don't want them to feel like I left them. That they're bad or something—like I abandoned them."

"Well it's funny you say that because Derrick still walks around the house calling your name, looking for you," she said. This crushed me.

The next day, when I walked into Peter's house, I heard him upstairs on the phone. He was talking to Wendi. "I'm not sure what to say. I don't know if he's using or what, but he's acting funny, making really fucked-up choices. Listen, someone's here. I gotta go. Ok, I'll be around later."

Choosing between my brother's wishes for me and a relationship with Dawn was now on my plate. As Christmas came closer, Peter asked that I leave his house because his stepsons were coming home from college and they needed the space. It makes sense, because things would have been really crowded there, and I'm sure he was thinking: the last thing we need is for Andrew to lose his shit, go on a bender, and steal the Christmas tree. So I had about three weeks to find new digs. Dawn literally lived up the dangerously unimproved dirt road. I don't know how to operate heavy machinery otherwise I would have graded it properly. So I moved in with Dawn in a sort of de facto way — meaning we never discussed it. I just stopped leaving to go somewhere else late at night.

A cool March breeze came through the open window as we lay together, both staring at the ceiling, our bodies pressed together as one. Thinking about our lovemaking, our connection, our ecstasy.

Phoebe, is Dawn's oldest daughter. When Dawn and I first started seeing each other Phoebe was three. A firecracker. This girl was a gymnast in the making too. A fearless little package of limitless energy. And bossy. Bossy like I was at her age. Our relationship had an auspicious beginning.

"You broke my potty," she said. It was the morning following my first official sleepover. I woke up, urgently having to go number two. It felt like I hadn't gone for days, and because Dawn and I just started getting serious, I was on my best behavior, which really just means that I wasn't going to fart around her or go number two during normal business hours. So all the previous night and that morning I was holding it in. You could have bounced a quarter off my bloated belly all the way to the fucking moon. It was traumatic. Arising before anyone else except for the large family dog, Bear, who treated me like an outsider, still loyal to Richards, I snuck quietly into the bathroom. Bear followed because the door didn't latch.

If there's a way to muffle the noise from this activity, it is lost on me—I ripped the loudest fart of my life. It was like *Burrrrrruprupupupupupupupupupup*. Bear is staring at me. I can't stop the fart. *Rupupuprrrgrrrr*. It growled for Christ's sake. The fart. Not Bear.

"You think this is funny, don't you, motherfucker?" I say quietly to Bear. "Yeah, you do, huh? Sitting there all smiling." Uh oh! *Rupruprup* and then the waste product descends, and let me tell you, it was biblical. I got lightheaded from the pressure and release. Pressure and release.

"Goddamn! What the...?" Trying to catch my breath. Unbelievably, no toilet paper was necessary. I stand and stare in the bowl. Bear stands next to me also staring into the bowl.

"Well, Bear, this is never going to go down." Flush once.

"Oh, God. That was so stupid."

The toilet didn't just overflow, it protested. It was angry. Appalled. Thinking quickly, like a Marine, I flung open the window with one hand, reached down in the toilet with the other hand and broke the monster, the dragon, in half with my bare hand. Dry heaving from the foul experience, I flung the specimen out the hole where the bathroom window was supposed to be. I had no choice.

Still, the toilet resisted, as Bear sat and laughed his silent laugh. I washed up the best that I could. When I walked out, little darling Phoebe in her footy pajamas, who probably didn't want me in the house in the first place because I wasn't her father, was standing there staring up at me.

"Hi honey!" I said enthusiastically.

"What are you doing?" she said inquisitively.

"Huh? Oh nothing, just washing my hands."

"It stinks in there," she retorts, holding her nose, emphasizing each word a little louder.

"OK, OK," I concede.

Within a few minutes, everyone is up and moving, which tells me that I should be leaving for work. A big hug for Dawn, who I'm falling in love with more and more every day. And I'm out the door. But not before:

"You broke my potty!" blocking the door with her size 2 Barbie sneaker.

"Shhh. No I didn't, honey," I plead. "Let's talk about it later. Let me close the door honey." Sensing this isn't working with a now indignant three year old, I say, "Bear broke it, I think."

"No he didn't, you did!" Her body is now stopping me from closing the front door behind me, her fists assertively resting against her hips.

"Mommy, Anjew broke my potty!" She couldn't pronounce my name.

"No I didn't!" I say way too angrily, catching myself and smiling. "Of course I didn't."

"Yes you did!" Phoebe screams.

"Listen, I'll call you from work. Have a great day," I say to Dawn with a wink.

As I reach my car, Bear lets out a two-bark: "Ruff, ruff."

"Fuck you too, Bear."

Andrew McKenna

Chapter 29

Winter proved to be exceptionally cold that particular year. Not so much because of an unusual amount of snowfall or anything, but because the heating system in the house was never completed. The place didn't have a bathroom window, just a big hole in the side of the house. The solution, unbeknownst to me, was to bring a Salamander—a small, powerful, diesel-fueled thing—that is supposed to be used to heat outdoor areas like open garages, or football bleachers—into the basement and run it continuously. The fumes from the Salamander engine (imagine running a lawnmower in your living room) at times made me think that we were going to die. So we cracked some windows about an inch for ventilation. It was better than freezing. Could we move out? We had no money – I was trying to rebuild and stay out of the mental hospital, and Dawn was becoming my partner and I wasn't going to quit! I could handle the lightheadedness if she could! Dawn and I were in this together, dammit! So we collected more blankets, bought a cheap space heater, all cuddled around, and somehow found things to laugh about.

One day, around mid-January, Peter called me. I thought maybe he wanted to talk, to reconcile. We hadn't talked since he asked me to leave. I missed him. He and I always had a really tight relationship. We had both expressed more than once that we were best friends. However, things had changed. Richards had relayed some things Peter had said about me to Dawn, and I was angry about it. Where was his sense of loyalty? I couldn't believe that he sided with Richards; I pretended that it didn't happen. Anyhow, he called.

"Andrew," he said.

"Peter. What's up my friend?"

"Not much. How is everything going?" he asked, robotically.

"Busy. We're trying to figure out if Dawn should sell this place as is, or try to get the second half of the loan thing going, and try to have it finished and then sell it or—"

"Listen," he says, cutting me off. "I need the Salamander back. It's mine. I don't know if you knew that. I loaned it to Richards. I have work to do in my garage, and it's cold as hell out there. I realize you guys are heating the house with it. I assume you're still doing that?"

"Yeah, until we can figure something else out, I guess…"

"Alright, well, can I come up and get it now?"

Tough love? Don't really know.

"Yeah Peter. That's fine."

Things were going south, and fast.

Spring always makes me feel happy and hopeful, especially coming off a hellaciously contentious winter of continuous arguments between Dawn and her ex. I tried to stay out of as many conflicts as possible because I believed that these were issues between Dawn and him. I was embroiled in my own post-marital discord. I got so used to hearing bitch, cunt, motherfucker and cocksucker around their disputes that the words eventually had no meaning to me at all.

Her oldest child Josh is one remarkable kid. We would take walks and talk about how sometimes parents argue and say things that they don't mean. We also talked about how the kids were not to blame for this, and how he was a really great kid that I loved spending time with. I also told him he was a great son to his parents.

Trying to get back on my feet financially was next to impossible. My string of fuck-ups at this point was staggering and my only real skills were being a lawyer or writing. So utterly and completely frustrated, I took a job at a recycling plant. I did this instead of proactively seeking readmission to the bar. Everyone said to take my time, focus on my recovery. But that wasn't my life. My life was that I had lost my sweet Derrick and Dylan, lost my job, lost my family, lived in abject poverty and

285

wanted it all to go away, but couldn't construct in my mind how to make it happen. All the while knowing, that a shot of Heroin would give me a break from all of this mess. But I couldn't do it.

Pressure continued to grow. Wendi and I weren't communicating at all and when we did, it usually resulted in a sanction of my not being able to see the boys. As for Dawn and her situation, it couldn't have been worse. Richards and his new wife were not going to buy out Dawn's interest in the half-completed structure we called a house. Between the two of us, we had little or no income. But we were very in love. It was easier to lie in bed and smoke cigarettes and drink coffee and make love than for me to look at the enormous debt I had or to think about how unraveled things had become.

I thought often about killing her ex. I wanted to do it in public, maybe in the supermarket. First, I would corner him, maybe in the cold-cut section, or produce, somewhere cool where I wouldn't sweat too much. My machete, sharp as hell, raised up high, would do the job. Everyone in the community who disliked him would be there cheering me on. "Kill that bastard!" "Chop his fucking head off!" "Hit him with an axe!"

But I thought about how bad his children would feel. Then I thought of how bad prison would feel and then I thought about how I needed to make a sandwich for me and Dawn.

"Hey Matt. It's Andrew."
"What's going on my man? How ya doing?"
"Could I do prison time?"
"What?"
"Well, you did, what? Seven years? Eight years?"
"Yeah. Dude, why are you asking me this?"
"I'm going to write a book about you."
"Dude. Why are you asking me this?"
"Just wondering."

By now, almost all of my days, hours and minutes were dark ones. The supervised visits with Derrick and Dylan, now taking place at my father's house, were emotional double-edged swords. On the one hand we had this wonderful time together, the "explores" in the woods, the snuggling at night as we dozed off. Then there was this constant reminder that it was only temporary, that the next morning around noon, my fatherness would end and they would return to real life without me for another two or three weeks. The constant fear that they would forget me or think that I didn't love them, this fear that went dormant for the time of the visit, would creep back in as we got closer to saying goodbye. After dropping the boys off to Wendi in a pre-agreed upon neutral parking lot, the sadness would overcome my senses to the point it was hard to breathe. Wendi demanded that my father always be with me when I had the visits with the boys. The drop-offs and pick-ups would take place in Siena College parking lot where my father taught. Wendi demanded that I not be in sight during these times. I had to hide behind a tree while the boys were exchanged.

Most times after the visits and the hand-offs, I would drive away about a half mile and just pull over, my face in my hands. By the time I got back to where I was staying, I was practically catatonic, and would fall asleep exhausted. Sleep brought little relief. My dreams were of Derrick, leading our expedition through the woods, looking back at me and saying, "Come on dad, come on guys," with a wave of his hand, and also little Dylan, fearing that he'd be left behind, saying, "Daddy, carry me!"

I'd wake up in a panic that the boys would think I had abandoned them, that they would think they weren't important to me. I couldn't separate this fear from what I understood to be reality. The thoughts were the same. They were one.

The bitter-sweet news that Dawn was pregnant was always on my mind. Dawn was the person I should have had children with in the first place. What the fuck had I been thinking? Dawn doesn't thrive on drama, she's a great mom, she isn't a fucking basket case. But the timing of her being pregnant was impossibly bad. I wasn't exactly on top of my game. Dawn and I talked about it and decided that this baby was made out of our love—not planned—but not a mistake either. We would figure out a way.

My mind was torn between good and evil. I would string together a couple weeks of clean time, but my demons would ultimately win out. The good was my relationship with Dawn and her children. Coming home—even to the half-finished house—was magical to me. Our dinners together, running around the woods with her son, playing in the pond, hunting frogs, this was the good. The evil was my torment over my boys, the constant set-backs in family court, poverty, hopelessness, and depression.

I wish Steve were here.

I feel dead inside. My body is heavy with guilt, my mind full of fear.

"You look nice, Andrew," Dawn said, as I tied my tie.

"Thank you, love. I feel horrible, though. Judge Abramson isn't going to listen to me. I haven't seen the boys in so long. This is just crazy. I just hope that goddamn truck starts. They think I don't love them."

Driving up the highway—north to Saratoga—passing the exits. The grayish-purple winter sky of October in front of me, gas-tank on E, knowing I'll have to pull off and steal some gas. How does it feel to have to steal gas on the way to Family Court? I was a lawyer once.

Back on the highway now, about 4.5 gallons in the tank. I figure they won't send the State Troopers after someone who steals 4.5 gallons. My breathing is shallow as it always is now. I have no energy. I stare at the road in front of me, barely able to hold my body up. I just want to crawl under the covers and sleep. I haven't eaten in two days at least. We have no money and even if we did, I have no appetite. The exit for Family Court is coming up on the right. I see the sign—big and green, New York State Highway sign with reflective white lettering. Hardly any traffic right now on the highway. The sign gets closer and closer. I should have my turn signal on by now, getting ready to get on the exit ramp. I watch the sign approach my field of vision; I'm like a robot, though, not feeling, just numb. I keep driving north. Forget everything. *Just run the fucking car into the pylon. Get it over with for God's sake.*

On the morning of my first bank robbery in Lake George, New York, I was supposed to be in Family Court. As I drove to court, I thought about how fucked-up everything had become with Wendi and the boys. The wheels had come off the bus. I was fully expecting to be dealt yet another blow by the Family Court Judge. Another set-back, even less time allowed with the boys, more restrictions, more ridicule, more frustration. At this stage, I couldn't seem to even think of Derrick and Dylan without crying. I spent my days now either tearing-up or holding back tears. My world was black. I didn't take the exit to Family Court. I continued to drive north.

Dude you didn't take the exit. You're blowing off Family Court. Can you actually do this? Dude, this is crazy, you'll get caught. Everyone gets caught. Can I live with getting caught? Can I live with going to prison?

The internal dialogue continued as I drove into town. Up ahead on the left was a bank. I drove past it, past some shops and restaurants, most closed, a used book store. I love used bookstores.

The house was completely dark when I pulled into the driveway. I put the car in park and sat and stared for a minute. She was gone. The boys were gone.

Now my legs are moving on their own; I am not consciously saying to myself to walk from the car to the bank. Now, I'm standing at an island counter with my pen in hand, writing out a note.

The note on the table said that this decision was about the boy's safety. With that, a soft part of me, an innocence, was peeled away revealing a raw truth, my new truth—I was alone. I called Wendi immediately at her parents' house. She was exceptionally calm. Condescending in tone.

"No, Andrew, you may not see the boys tonight. Not until I know more about what's going on with you."

"Wendi! I'm four days out of rehab! What are you doing?"

"Keeping the boys safe."

"Keeping the boys what? The boys are safe!" I couldn't believe what I was hearing.

"You have access to my urine screens! What more do you want?"

"I want the boys to have a healthy environment."

On the back of a blank deposit slip, the note read: "Give me $100s, $50s, and $20s. No alarms or I shoot. Stay calm."

Next to Wendi's note was Dylan's size 2t t-shirt that he had been wearing that evening when I left to go to group. With it grasped gently in my hand, I brought it to my face and breathed it in. I stared blankly at the note and tears welled up in my eyes. I knew then, at that very moment, that it was over. That the boys would grow-up without me.

Now I'm in line behind two other bank customers. I'm calmly watching the teller—a young man wearing a $20 burgundy shirt and a $10 burgundy tie. I'm wearing a $60 Ralph Lauren shirt, and an $80 Burberry tie. He's going about his business, handing out money and I don't give a fuck about anything anymore.

Walking to my car, not fast, but deliberately, like I have somewhere to be, the moist air engulfs my head and cools it. I take a few deep breaths and hum a tune, quietly. Pulling out, I take a right and drive the speed limit down Main Street.

Some people think the Northeast is ugly in winter time. Everything does tend to get really gray, and of course, the foliage is gone, but if you look carefully at the sky you can see a lot more than just steely cold gray.

It was a warm day towards the end of October 2005, and my dealer wasn't answering his phone. I called his number several hundred times. I camped out in front of his house and drove around looking for his car or any sign of him. A detective looking for a missing kid could not have done a more thorough job than I was doing. They should have Heroin addicts out looking for missing children. Perhaps in exchange for Heroin. I searched the phone book for numbers and addresses of people with his same last name. Albany was dry, meaning Heroin was difficult to find, and my only hope was to find this shit head. Which entailed going to homes of people who had his same last name. Every time I knocked on a door, it seemed an old person, octogenarian old, would answer. They were as confused as I was as I told them that I was trying to find Jeff.

"Who?"

"Jeff. I'm looking for Jeff."

"Who's Jeff?"

Cross that one off the list—on to the next home. Someone's grandma answers this time. I hope it's Jeff's grandma.

"Do you have a grandson named Jeff?"

"What?"

"Do you—I'm looking for Jeff."

"Who?"

"Jeff."

"He doesn't live here," she says.

Bingo. Getting closer, which is good because I need Heroin soon. My eyes are starting to water, the first symptom of withdrawals. "I know ma'am. Can you tell me where I can find him?"

"Who?"

"Jeff! Where is he?"

"I don't know a Jeff, young man," as she closes the door.

Now my eyes are watering, and I'm sweating like a race horse. It looks like I'm crying. I'm no longer making sense. My sentences are choppy, disconnected. Next house, the whole time looking for Jeff's crappy dope dealer car, scanning the streets as I drive to the next address with a phonebook in my lap. Now my body is going through these little convulsions. Nothing too drastic. Kind of like a shudder. Like when you get a chill up your spine. But they're coming back-to-back now, with eyes watering and bad breath.

"Leave or I'm calling the police."

"I'm just trying (shudder) to find (shudder) Jeff."

Door slams. I just robbed a bank a couple hours ago. I should really just get off this guy's porch and drive three hours south to Brooklyn with the money in my pocket and buy some Heroin because this just isn't working out. This isn't fucking working out and I'd never make it to Brooklyn. I'll be throwing up and going into cardiac arrest before I hit Newburgh for Christ's sake. I have to make at least one more pass through Schenectady. This is just painful and painfully stupid and I can barely see because of the incessant eye watering. Ah. A Spanish dude. Roll down window, slow down automobile.

"Tega?" I say, which is slang for dope.

"Que?" Which is "what" in Spanish and which is not the fucking word I want to hear.

Then I shudder as I speak and it comes out "tegagagagaaaaaaah." And even though this guy doesn't know that tega means Heroin because apparently he's not familiar with his slang. He does, he must recognize the withdrawal symptoms I am so readily displaying, and he says "Oh, pull over there."

"Yes!" I exclaim, not caring that I look desperate. He gets in.

"Ok, drive up here," he says in broken English.

"I need a bundle," I say, which is ten bags of Heroin.

"OK, OK. Pull down here," he says, directing me down a narrow side street.

As I steer right, I reach into my coat pocket and discreetly peel off two $100 bills from the roll and hand it to him, the whole time watching the road through my watery vision, trying not to smash into a parked car or hit the curb.

"Pull over right here."

The second I put the car in park, I feel the barrel of his gun on my temple. Derrick and Dylan. Dawn and Casey. Mom and Dad. Brian, Carol. I can't swallow. I can't take in a breath. I can't let out a breath. He reaches his hand inside my coat pocket and takes the roll and then I hear a click-click-metal-on-metal-interrupted. The barrel jumped a little on my temple. The fucking gun just jammed. I swung my right arm in a backward, backhand motion and hit him somewhere either his face or his neck or his chest and I saw a look of terror in his eyes and I was moving like I was fighting off a swarm of killer bees, arms flailing, swatting making a sound like, "Ahhhhhhhhhhhhhhhahhhhhhhhahhhhh!"

He managed to get his door open and bolted out, gun in one hand, money in the other, a few loose bills falling to the ground. Everything got very bright and I took a huge gasp of air like you would if coming to the surface after holding your breath under water for two minutes. Everything got brighter and brighter. I reached down, put the shifter in drive, pressed the gas, turned the wheel. The passenger door slammed shut and I screeched down the street and it felt like he was behind me in the back seat but of course he wasn't. It felt like, when someone is following you, but you won't turn around to check, like a dream.

When I pulled into the convenience store parking lot, it was a purely mechanical action. A $20 bill that had fallen off the roll was sitting on the seat next to me. *He didn't mean to pull the trigger. There is no way that's what he meant to do. It was a mistake. In his eyes I could see that it was a mistake.* The gun jammed. That distinct noise that I knew from the pistol range in Quantico. That "chinging." That clicking noise—so distinct.

"Marlboro box," I said to the clerk.

"Anything else?"

"Power (shudder) ball ticket," I said.

"Are you alright, dude?" he asks.

After a pause, I say, "When's the drawing?" staring at the ticket.

I need to go home now. I've had enough. I want to see Dawn. Every thought is about me, my existence, my shit. I feel this, and I recognize this is all so self-centered, almost getting my brains blown out, what I think was an accident or maybe it wasn't. Maybe the guy was more off the hook than I was. The gun jammed though.

My phone rings and on the caller ID, I see "J" which is short for Jeff.

"Come on," he says.

"Alright," I say, and hang-up.

Jeff just got back from the city where he had a really bad time trying to score. His guy had gotten pretty jammed up and wasn't doing anything. So he had to go outside the comfort zone and deal with some dudes in Alphabet City, Lower Manhattan. He didn't get the deal he had expected and things got pretty heated, he told me.

"Dudes had their guns out the whole time"

"Pointed at you?" I ask.

"No, but it felt like any minute the tide could have come in."

"You mean changed," I corrected the metaphor.

"What?"

"You said that the tide could have come in any minute. I think the correct saying is the 'tide could have changed.'"

"What is wrong with you?" he says.

"What? I'm sorry, it's just—never mind."

"Anyway, I don't think this shit is any good and I'm stuck with a pile of it," he explained, frustrated, eyes very intense like he is thinking way too hard. And then he comes out with, "Are you robbing banks?"

"No. Are you?" I say like a wiseass. "Of course not, are you crazy?" I add.

"Never mind," he says.

Here's the problem: My picture, well a picture of a guy in a suit and a baseball cap pulled down low, who looks and moves like me is all over the news and every time I rob another bank, the news outlets show all of the previous surveillance tapes and it just confirms that it's me. But Jeff has his own problems to deal with and he doesn't make any conclusions either way. I suspect.

"Now I have to move this shit and deal with people's fucking complaining. I need to get a real job," he says.

I use a bag of it and it knocks me on my ass.

"Holy Christ brother."

"Seriously?" he says.

"Serious," my eyes drooping, feeling the intense rush in my shoulders.

"I did a bag down there and it was shit."

"Try again," I say as I fade off down the river.

What happened doesn't happen very often. Whoever cut the Heroin didn't do it right. They didn't mix the cut with the Heroin well enough. This is very dangerous because extremely potent Heroin, if it's not cut, will kill you. Stop your heart. Now Jeff had a dilemma on his hands: Sell it and risk someone dying, not to mention having to deal with buyers who are unlucky and get a bag with no potency. And the crazy thing about Heroin users is that they want the strong bag no matter the potential risks. *Give me the shit that will blow my fucking mind.* That's the mentality anyhow. Some guy found dead with the spike still sticking out of his arm and you know he went out just the way he wanted to go out. If he had it all to do over, he would choose door number three again. It's insidious.

Chapter 30

He started turning blue. I couldn't move. My mind, my brain said to move. It said go slap him in his face, wake him up, throw water on him, save his life. But my body wouldn't move. It was mid-morning, a beautiful spring day, the sun was filtering through the blinds; coffee was brewing. I could hear it bubbling in the background, and I couldn't make my legs move. Opening my eyes now; he's turning blue. That's it. It didn't mean anything to me other than my friend was turning blue. Then my eyes closed on their own, and I drifted and I was in a forest and it was cool and damp and sunny and beautiful and I was happy again. The Heroin was in my system fully and I was warm and it was nice, really nice. Then my eyes closed on their own and he was more blue now and a little yellow, and I thought I saw his chest move a little, and then I thought that he's dying so I tried to move my feet, tried to stand up, but I couldn't move. I tried and then I felt a tickle that ran from my eye down my cheek on the right side and then again on the left side, and I wiggled my toes to try to move and then I tried to say his name but my mouth wouldn't really work right and I don't think he heard me or I wasn't loud enough or something, and he was on the couch and I was in the chair, and I wasn't loud enough, and my mind, my brain said get up, go save him, call the ambulance, but my eyes started to close and I tried to kept them open an I tried to get up, but they closed and I drifted and I cried and I was back in the forest and I was running and crying and trying to find my friend because he was in danger and I was going to save him, only if I could find him, and I was yelling his name but my mouth didn't work right and I was loud enough and my face was soaked but it wasn't sweat, it was tears, and then my eyes opened a little and I saw his eyes open a little, my friend, and my face was soaked and I was scared and yet hopeful because he appeared less blue and I tried to stand up and then these weird voices in my head started going, started asking me questions. *Can you get up? Will you? Do you want to go back to the forest because if you do, just close your eyes or we can close them for you.* No, please let me move, let me save him, he is good, he is good, he is good. He is cold. He is dead.

Chapter 31

"Andrew."

"Dawn. I love you."

"I love you too. Are you alright?"

No. Yes. I'm alright. There's a lot going on right now. Things are kind of crazy. I just want to rest."

Reluctantly, Dawn lies next to me with her head on my chest. My arm is around her and she's staring out of the open window at the sky. She wants to confront me, I can tell. Dawn is not a pushover, she's not an enabler. It's just that I, with my crazy behavior, have presented her with a situation that she doesn't know what to do. She's lost.

I drift off to sleep and I dream that I am in a forest after a snowfall walking effortlessly. I come upon a slow flowing brook. I kneel down and stare at my reflection in the water. Looking back at me is a young boy. It's me and I am probably 11 or 12 years old. I look scared and attentive.

"Tell me something," my reflection says. "Am I normal?"

"Normal?" I say. "No, I'm sorry, Andrew. You're not normal."

297

"Why? Do you know why?"
Because you think too much and it hurts to think," my reflection says back.
"Doesn't everyone think too much?"
"Not like you do."
"I have to go. I won't be gone long."

At this point, I wasn't using so much to get high; it was more just to not feel sick. And this is when the Heroin addict is at his most dangerous.

"Are you using?" Dawn asks. Dawn is incredibly smart. Not gullible at all, but she has never lived with or even known a person addicted to Heroin who is robbing banks every week, and so even though she knows that I'm fucked-up somehow, she is hoping that I'll pull through, and soon. She would tell me daily that the boys weren't going to forget me, or blame me, or feel like they had done something to make me go away. Dawn loves me and wants to be supportive. The stupid thing that's so hard to explain is that she is the only one in the world who I can tell what is happening with me. She tried so hard to reassure me, but it never got through.

"Andrew, please be careful," she says, with utter concern and sadness. When I look at her I feel very sad because she knows I'm not being honest with her, and we both know that this thing is going to play out, for better or worse, on its own.

It's 9:52 a.m. and I'm on my way to rob a bank. My stomach is flipping. Jeff cannot front me, or won't front me, and anyhow, it would only be a small amount, a band-aid on a much larger problem. My habit is at least several hundred dollars per day. I stay away from the house for days because I never want to be around Dawn or the children while I'm high or sick. To do so brings me tremendous guilt. They shouldn't have to see me this way. All of these thoughts flood my mind as I drive. If I don't get something soon, I'm doomed.

Throughout this period, I had no contact with Derrick and Dylan, and for good reason. But prior to all of this, when I was

298

completely clean and sober, going to AA daily, spending time with my sponsor Greg and trying very hard to deal with depression, Wendi still wouldn't let me have any contact with the boys. Does this justify going off the deep end? Absolutely not. Does it even mitigate? Not really. All I can say is that losing the boys and having Wendi being so uncooperative while she held all of the cards was more than I could take. Everyday my soul depleted until I said "nothing matters." Some might say this is weak. To them, I simply say: Fuck you.

I've always loved Vermont, ever since I was a kid, and would visit my grandparents there. My best childhood memories are from Vermont. The Vermont robbery, where the teller was a very innocent soft-spoken girl who was very cooperative and pleasant even though I was robbing her, is the one I will never forget. When I handed her the note and said, "Quickly, no alarms," she started to take the money from her drawer and place it on the counter and she kept saying in a sweet voice, "Like this? Like this?" I thought at the time, as the blood is pumping through my body, needing to get high, "Yes, just like that, just like that." For each robbery, I remember that after I got the money, I would turn and walk out, and that walk from the teller's counter to the door and then to my truck seemed like a dream. A slow motion dream. My legs were moving, I was breathing, I was keeping my head sort of down, trying not to run, trying not to call attention to myself, not looking back, but hyper aware of what was happening. Just like a scary intense dream where everything is so vivid and one's senses are so acute. Scanning the area around me, processing millions of bits of information like the lightening outside, the traffic, the people, the sounds of everyday life, the smell of a fire in a fireplace somewhere close, a car horn. Then when I would reach my truck, I would remove my hat and coat, and put on sunglasses all while shifting into first gear, and then second, and then third. Working the clutch, I listened for sirens, wondering how long I had before I would start dry-heaving from the Heroin withdrawals. Will I puke all over myself and the cab of the truck first? Drive carefully, obey all traffic rules;

stay calm. You'll make it through this. But this has to be the last time, the last bank.

Fuck you Andrew, who are you kidding? This is too easy. What if you get caught Andrew? Then what?

Well, I'll just kill myself or I'll let the cops kill me. They won't take me alive.

Yeah right, like you have that kind of courage.

What? I don't?

No, you absolutely do not. First of all, you could never do that to Dawn and the children. And you're not that selfish.

Yes I am.

You're fucked-up right now, but you're not that selfish.

I need Heroin.

So do I asshole. You got us into this mess.

Looking for the quickest way to my dealer's house, I drive and drive and drive. I can feel the bile bubbling up in my throat. Choking it down, I try to think about something else. I roll down the window. It's snowing now and I'm sure it would look beautiful to me if I wasn't so sick. The cold air blows in my face and hair and in an instant I go from sweating profusely to having an unbearable chill. My body is telling me it needs dope, it needs King Heroin. I drive faster, not thinking I could get pulled over for speeding. My legs are starting to cramp. Roll the window up and the chill subsides for an instant. *Where am I? Shit, was that the exit? No, it must be up here. Hang in there buddy, hang in there. Don't call me buddy, Fucker! Shut up.* Sweating again, I roll down the window. The cramps creep into my lower abdomen and I start to gag, but nothing's coming up because nothing is in my stomach. I taste the sour metallic taste of bile again. I swallow the bile and it makes my jaw bone hurt and my ears sting. I'm burning up now. I roll down the window. Something is crawling up my back, or down, or up and down.

Sweat is pouring off me now, but I'm still freezing, shaking. I think of Derrick and Dylan. They're in school now. I miss seeing them and reading to them and making them laugh. I miss their eyes and their smiles and their smell. I miss the softness of their skin when I put my cheek to theirs and whisper "I love you" and when I tell them that they're such good big boys. Ever since the split she has kept them from me. Even when I was clean and sober and working a recovery program, she still played the "he's a threat" card. She was and continues to exact revenge on me. I hate her. But, today, truth be told, she's justified. I just robbed another bank and I was trying to score some medicine. *Look at yourself, are you a good dad? Are you kidding me? You suck. You're an awful person.*

After a tortuous ride, with bile on the collar of my shirt, I arrive at my dealer's house. Where's his fucking car? I go to the door and knock. No answer. I start to gag, turning my head I throw up bile on his front porch. I knock again. *Please, please, please.* No answer. I'm doubled over now. The pressure behind my eyes from the heaving leaves my eyes bulging, red and wet. I want to cry. I want to die. I want to be better. There are things crawling up my legs now. Electric pulses running up my spine. I'm soaking wet from sweat and freezing cold. I'm dizzy, unsteady on my feet. God, take me now, for Christ's sake, please. *Beep, beep.* I spin around and he is pulling into his spot. My dealer, my savior.

"Dude, you can't park there."

"Too bad, fuck! Hurry, I'm sick."

"I'm messing with you, I'm pretty sick too. Come on," he says.

I hug him and say, "Thank God, thank God." He opens the door.

My skin is tingling as I follow him into the living room.

"How much?"

"A bundle." Hurry!

"Here, here."

The bags of Heroin have a skull and cross bones on them.

"Is it good?"

"Ridiculously good," he says.

Pulling my spike from my pocket, hands trembling, choking back my stomach lining, I manage to load the needle. It takes an eternity. The cotton, the drawing up process. I whip off my belt through the belt loops and it makes a snapping sound. Needle in my mouth like a rose, sleeve up, belt tied around the bicep, pumping my fist, looking for the right vein, a fat one appears, tighten the belt a little more, remove the needle from my mouth with my right hand, steady, steady, insert into the vein, draw back on the stopper, blood appears in the barrel of the syringe, I have "hit," push the stopper slowly, all the way, steady, withdraw the needle from the vein, release the belt, blood slowly trickles down my arm, wait three seconds and then it happens. Sunshine and warmth and comfort engulf me. In my head I hear the ocean, the Heroin forces my eyes closed, and I sigh, and then sigh again, and then smile. The sweating is over, my stomach feels fine, no more things crawling on my skin. I want to live again. At least for right now. No longer am I thinking about the boys or anyone else, or my finances, or my out of control existence. I am floating.

I'll make it another day. One more day is all. Then I'll try to sort it all out. The boys, Dawn, and the kids. The bills, my law license, my family, my life, my future, my past, my present, the whole damn thing tomorrow. Not today because today is not real, not real at all and the only hope is tomorrow. Does this all make sense to you? Because none of it makes sense to me, so I'll try to sort it all out tomorrow. I'll do it then....

Chapter 32

After six months in the Albany County Jail following my arrest, Gene and I put together yet another bail package for Judge Treece. We set up drug treatment, counseling, house arrest monitoring—everything. The judge imposed a list of restrictions on me and let me know, in no uncertain terms, that if I violated his order while out on bail, that he would personally hunt me down himself and lock me back-up. Not really, but that was the import. When I walk through the front door, Dawn touches my shoulders to make sure it was real. We just stood there and held each other so tightly, pulling back every so often to look at each other. It was at that moment I felt something so extraordinary. For an instant, I felt weightless. I knew serenity. And I knew Dawn and I would be together forever.

"Where is my little boy?" I said, tears in my eyes. That little boy was one month old. And beautiful.

"Sleeping, come on." Dawn answered softly.

We crept into his room and little Quinn was wearing his light blue onesie as I reached into his bassinet and softly stroked his silk-soft hair with the back of my fingers. He made a little sighing sound. Dawn was up against me with her head pressed against my chest. She kissed me and tears formed in her beautiful eyes. Life was beginning again.

The End.

Epilogue

"McKenna! Hurry the fuck up. I don't have all morning." The CO was grumpy—probably hung-over. But he couldn't ruin my day. Today I'm leaving prison after 5 years and I have a few friends to say goodbye to. It's his job to escort me to Receiving and Discharge, so I can be on my way.

"Hold on! Give me a few minutes."

I've watched a lot of good people leave prison. The COs always seem surprised when we—inmates, take the time to say goodbye, instead of rushing to get out the door to freedom.

My brother Brian drove down from New York, picked-up my mother in Arlington, and arrived at Federal Correctional Institution Petersburg. Brian, of course, arrived early—he was almost as excited as I was that this day had finally come.

As the gates of the prison cracked open, the CO simply says, "Good luck McKenna. Don't come back."

"I won't." Then I hear probably the sweetest sound ever. Without cuffs or shackles weighing me down, I hear the loud metal clanking prison door close behind me.

As we drove away from the prison, Brian was nervously talking, asking lots of questions. I turned my head to the right and looked over the huge field to the double fence, topped with triple-strand concertina wire. I watched as inmates lifted weights, did push-ups, and jogged around the mammoth yard. I knew what each man was thinking about—his out date. The day he would go home.

One inmate stood at the inner fence and stared out. I reached my hand through the window and waived, not sure if he was looking at me. I didn't recognize him—it was quite a distance. Then he lifted his hand and waived. Maybe it was one of my friends I had made over the years.

The drive to New York would take about 9 hours. After the long drive, I would see Dawn and the children for the first time in years. Everything felt electric, as we made our way towards the next stage of my life.

Andrew McKenna

About the Author

Andrew McKenna lives in upstate New York with his love Dawn and their children. In addition to other personal writing projects, Andrew does legal research and writing for attorneys in the Albany area and Lake Placid. He enjoys spending time with his family, including his two sons from a previous marriage. Andrew is currently working on a second memoir and a novella.

Made in the USA
Middletown, DE
24 February 2017